Evolutionary Social Theory and Political Economy

Evolutionary Social Theory and Political Economy traces the origins, extension, marginalization and revival of evolutionary approaches to social theory from the Enlightenment through the beginning of the 21st century. It demonstrates how changes in understandings of social evolution corresponded to changes in definitions of Political Economy and how both reflected changes in the Philosophy of Science. This book is written for students and researchers alike in all the social sciences. Economists will benefit from understanding how ideas about evolution in Economics corresponded to ideas about evolution in other social sciences, and Social Scientists outside of Economics will benefit from understanding how Economics has related to their discipline.

Clifford S. Poirot Jr. received his PhD in Economics in 1992 from the University of Utah. He has published several articles on Evolutionary Economics. He has taught at several institutions. He is currently teaching courses in both Economics and Political Science at Shawnee State University. He has been at Shawnee State since 1999.

Economics as Social Theory

Series edited by Tony Lawson, University of Cambridge

Social Theory is experiencing something of a revival within economics. Critical analyses of the particular nature of the subject matter of social studies and of the types of method, categories and modes of explanation that can legitimately be endorsed for the scientific study of social objects, are re-emerging. Economists are again addressing such issues as the relationship between agency and structure, between economy and the rest of society, and between the enquirer and the object of enquiry. There is a renewed interest in elaborating basic categories such as causation, competition, culture, discrimination, evolution, money, need, order, organization, power probability, process, rationality, technology, time, truth, uncertainty, value etc.

The objective for this series is to facilitate this revival further. In contemporary economics the label "theory" has been appropriated by a group that confines itself to largely asocial, ahistorical, mathematical "modelling". Economics as Social Theory thus reclaims the "Theory" label, offering a platform for alternative rigorous, but broader and more critical conceptions of theorizing.

49 The Nature of Social Reality
Issues in Social Ontology
Tony Lawson

50 The Evolutionary Origins of Markets
How Evolution, Psychology and Biology Have Shaped the Economy
Rojhat Avsar

51 Evolutionary Social Theory and Political Economy
Philosophy and Applications
Clifford S. Poirot Jr.

For more information about this series, please visit: https://www.routledge.com/Economics-as-Social-Theory/book-series/EAST

Evolutionary Social Theory and Political Economy

Philosophy and Applications

Clifford S. Poirot Jr.

Routledge
Taylor & Francis Group
LONDON AND NEW YORK

Cover image: © Getty Images

First published 2023
by Routledge
4 Park Square, Milton Park, Abingdon, Oxon OX14 4RN

and by Routledge
605 Third Avenue, New York, NY 10158

Routledge is an imprint of the Taylor & Francis Group, an informa business

British Library Cataloguing-in-Publication Data
A catalogue record for this book is available from the British Library

ISBN: 978-0-367-77292-5 (hbk)
ISBN: 978-0-367-77291-8 (pbk)
ISBN: 978-1-003-17067-9 (ebk)

DOI: 10.4324/9781003170679

Typeset in Palatino
by codeMantra

This book is dedicated to all the students who have taken a course in Political Economy with me.

Contents

Introduction

Goal and Purpose of this Study

In contemporary biology the term evolution has a precise meaning: a change in the frequency of alleles in a population over time. Furthermore, evolution is distinguished from embryonic development and major morphological changes are theorized as continuous with the process of variation and selection within a population. This definition, derived from the Neo-Darwinian synthesis, provides both analytical rigor to the study of evolution and a means with which to quantify evolution (see for example Mayr 2001). Some have proposed that Evolutionary Social Theory should also be built on Darwinian or Neo-Darwinian foundations: or in other words, that Evolutionary Social Theory should be envisioned as Generalized Darwinism (Boyd and Richerson 1985, 1992; Carneiro 2003, pp. 179–184). Amongst economists who write on Evolutionary Social Theory, this view is often traced back to the writings of Thorstein Veblen (Hodgson 2010; Jo 2021; Veblen 1919). Evolutionary Social Theory in this sense focuses on the study of how variable and socially hereditable social routines are subject to a process of selection at multiple levels, thus resulting in a change in the frequency of social routines over time leading in some instances to major social transformations.

But prior to the rise of the Neo-Darwinian synthesis, and for most laypeople today, the term evolution is defined more broadly to simply mean change over time. In this less restrictive sense, the term evolution is often associated with major morphological changes such as the evolution of modern humans from our shared common ancestor with modern apes. This looser definition does not necessarily distinguish between evolution and development. In the history of efforts to explain change both within a particular social system and the transformation of one kind of social system into another kind of social system, many Evolutionary Social Theorists have employed the looser definition of the term in the search for general principles that can explain the process of social change. As such, it has often had a global emphasis (Carneiro 2003, pp. 1–3). This looser meaning is broad enough to incorporate the above, narrower definition

DOI: 10.4324/9781003170679-1

of Evolutionary Social Theory as one possible approach, yet also allows for a comparison of the relative merits of differing approaches to the study of social evolution. For the purposes of this study, a theory in the social sciences need not be Darwinian or Neo-Darwinian to be considered evolutionary. Moreover, a theory that significantly predates the use of the term Evolution itself or biological theories of evolution can also be considered evolutionary.

Defined in this way, Evolutionary Social Theory can be distinguished from the use of abstract principles to study how a given social system, or subsystem, functions. This is not to argue, however, that the two approaches are necessarily opposed to each other. In the best of cases, the two approaches complement each other. However, static theories that ignore historical specificity and are based on the application of abstract principles that have seemingly little relation to the actual object being studied, as is often the case in Economics as well as other social sciences, are unlikely to be particularly useful for either the static study of society or as a source of theory on which to base the study of social evolution. Evolutionary Social Theory clearly relies on History as a source of data. But it can be distinguished from atheoretical approaches to the study of history, or the view that human behavior is too variable and complex to be explained in terms of general principles. Evolutionary Social Theory is nomothetic, rather than idiographic. It is the study of the process of social change, both within a given Socio-Cultural System and the transformation of one kind of Socio-Cultural System to another using comparative and historical methods. In this process, it draws on all the social sciences as a source of theory. Evolutionary Social Theory also has a strong relationship to the idea that social order can emerge and change step by step, without conscious design. However, since the study of social evolution also entails the study of conscious, purposive agents, it does not preclude analysis of the role of conscious, purposive design of human institutions. Nor does it preclude the study of rapid, violent social change.

From its inception in the Enlightenment, Evolutionary Social Theory has had a particularly close relationship with Political Economy. But the term Political Economy defies easy definition. Rousseau (1759) had only the inklings of a theory of social evolution and defined Political Economy as an extension or generalization of the problems of the household or estate management to the problems of the management of the State. Adam Smith had a theory of social evolution but his definition of Political Economy was more narrowly focused on the creation and distribution of wealth, structural change, as well as those policies which would augment the production of wealth (Smith 1776). Ricardo defined Political Economy primarily in terms of an abstract deductive analysis of concepts such as value, rent, wages, profits and other similar concepts. Marx (1859) had a similar definition and like Smith maintained a close connection between Political Economy and his theory of social evolution, or Historical Materialism. Others subordinated the concerns of Political Economy to

Evolutionary Social Theory (Durkheim 1894; Steiner 2011). Some contemporary uses of the term Political Economy are nearly identical to the term Evolutionary Social Theory (Wolf 1982). These ways of defining Political Economy are all useful for Evolutionary Social Theory.

But while the term Political Economy is vague, it is clear that the relationship of Evolutionary Social Theory to Political Economy has varied over time and at times in ways that separated Political Economy from Evolutionary Social Theory. Johnathan Stuart Mill (1824) proposed a much narrower definition of Political Economy and advocated a separate method from Evolutionary Social Theory for Political Economy. Yet Mill still recognized the validity of Evolutionary Social Theory as did Alfred Marshall (1890) even if his understanding of social evolution was Spencerian, rather than Darwinian. This separation of Evolutionary Social Theory from Economic Theory was reinforced by Schumpeter (1954) who also, nevertheless, recognized the validity of Evolutionary Social Theory. At some point, the term Political Economy went out of favor, and Political Economy came to be known simply as Economics. Economics, as it is widely practiced and defined today by the mainstream is with a few exceptions limited to the application of formal, mathematical models to the study of economizing behavior under conditions of scarcity. This definition has been the dominant definition in contemporary Economics since at least the 1950s. These approaches to Political Economy and Economics are not particularly useful for Evolutionary Social Theory though the New Institutional Economics makes extensive use of mainstream concepts.

The acceptance of Evolutionary Social Theory in the other social sciences as well has waxed and waned over time. From the time of the Scottish Enlightenment as well as the later French Enlightenment, the predominant approach to Social Theory was evolutionary, in the sense I have defined it above (Meek 1976). Evolutionary Social Theory developed further in the early and mid-19th century and reached its high water mark in the late 19th and early 20th centuries following the publication in 1859 and 1871 of Darwin's *Origins* (1876) and *Descent* (1877). Nevertheless, as I will discuss later in this study, the influence of Darwin on Evolutionary Social Theory was less prominent than is often assumed. In the early and mid-20th century, however, evolutionary approaches in all the social sciences were often pushed to the margins, a process that coincided with the rise of modern Economics and the separation of the social science disciplines from each other. The dominant approaches to the Social Sciences across the disciplines emphasized the use of static methods of analysis (Chilcote 1994; Wolf 1982, pp. 1–23). Yet in the last several decades, there has been a revival of evolutionary approaches in all the social sciences, including Economics along with a revival of earlier and more useful definitions of Political Economy. This revival has also been accompanied by an increased interest in global applications. It has also been accompanied by a re-examination of the philosophical foundations of inquiry in all the sciences.

The goals of this study are to identify those factors that were most strongly associated with the rise, marginalization and revival of Evolutionary Social Theory, how these changes influenced the relationship of Political Economy to Evolutionary Social Theory and to suggest possible directions for research in Evolutionary Social Theory in the future. Because this analysis implicates issues of Ontology and Epistemology as well as developments in the Physical and Natural Sciences, understanding these issues requires an examination of the history of the relationship of Evolutionary Social Theory and Political Economy to each other as well as to developments in the Philosophy of Science. I argue that Evolutionary Social Theory was born in the Enlightenment as a form of empirical inquiry akin to empirical inquiry in the natural sciences, that it has developed best when posited as a form of empirical inquiry akin to empirical inquiry in the natural sciences. Moreover, its relationship to Political Economy is best thought of as symbiotic: Evolutionary Social Theory can inform Political Economy and Political Economy can inform Evolutionary Social Theory. This leaves a place for the use of abstract-deductive analysis of categories such as wages, rents, profits and economic growth that is specific to a given form of social organization and grounded in the actual characteristics of that form of social organization.

The above has ramifications for how we think about possible paths forward for Evolutionary Social Theory. One implication is that analogies between biological and social evolution face specific limits. Consequently, I express significant reservations about Generalized Darwinism and instead emphasize the continuity thesis and cultural emergence (Cordes 2007; Poirot 2007). The path forward I advocate for builds on contributions to Economic Anthropology, Historical Sociology and Global Political Economy. Another implication is with respect to how we think about the concept of open systems and realism in social theory. I express reservations about some aspects of Critical Realism (Bhaskar 1989; Collier 1994; Lawson 2003) and instead draw on Critical Common Sensism, or Neo-Classical Pragmatism (Haack 2006, 2007; Poirot 2008; Webb 2007, 2012). A particular strength of Critical Common Sensism is that it unites ontology and epistemology and provides a theory of empirical inquiry.

Given the broad way I have defined Evolutionary Social Theory, the reader might fairly ask why use the term "evolution" at all when discussing theories of social change? While I share some of the standard reservations about overgeneralizing from biological evolution to social evolution, I am not opposed to all biological analogies in the social sciences. But I emphasize they are just that: analogies. When used with care biological analogies in the social sciences can help to shed significant light on important questions. There is much that social scientists can learn from biology. The opposite is also true. Finally, the term "Evolutionary Social Theory" is less awkward than "the interdisciplinary study of the process of historical change". I can see no reason why we should shrink from the use of the word "evolution" provided we keep the proper caveats in mind.

Scope and Method of this Study

This study analyzes the arc of the development of Evolutionary Social Theory and its relationship to developments in Philosophy of Science and Political Economy from the Enlightenment through the early 21st century. I caution the reader that I do not offer a tight, linear narrative path. Instead, I develop a narrative that recognizes the zig zag and sometimes erratic nature of the path of the development and relation of ideas that takes account of the relevant qualifications, subtleties and exceptions. In developing the analysis of this study, wherever feasible, I have focused on representative works of important contributors, especially of those who in my estimation were or are pivotal in the development of particular lines of inquiry. As such, this study is selective both in terms of choosing the individual authors as well as which texts to emphasize. Unfortunately, I have had to omit multiple important and interesting theorists. In doing so, I have of course sought not to omit contributions that would substantively alter my analysis.

Prior to proceeding further, a few additional preliminary remarks may serve to prevent misunderstandings on the part of the reader. I am generally suspicious of imposing contemporary terms on eras where the categories that people used differed from our own. I am similarly skeptical of telescoping the present into the past. At the same time, the use of clumsy and awkward descriptions serves to distract from the main arguments. By the time of the Enlightenment and subsequently, authors were writing about issues that concern us today in ways that are intelligible to the modern reader. Consequently, I will often use terms that are meaningful to the modern reader to describe their view, even in cases where individual authors did not use those terms. However, in describing their views, it will be necessary in multiple instances to use terms to refer to non-industrial societies that we rightly reject today. While Philosophy and Philosophy of Science are not coterminous, there is a strong enough overlap between the two to justify not splitting that semantic hair. One semantic hair that I will split is that I will use Philosophy, rather than Methodology, when addressing ontological, epistemological and in some instances ethical arguments related to the Physical, Natural and Social Sciences. I will confine my use of the term "Methodology" to specific techniques of inquiry. Both for reasons of space and in order to avoid clumsy circumlocutions, in the places where I address the contributions of Darwin, I will focus on Darwin's role in developing a theory of evolution by natural selection though I readily acknowledge the role of Alfred Russell Wallace whose contributions certainly merit both more research and attention. That said, it was Darwin's contributions that became influential.

Plan of this Study

In addition to this introduction, this study is organized into six chapters. Each chapter addresses developments in successive time periods. In each case, the beginning and end dates are to some degree arbitrary, fuzzy and there is some overlap between time periods. Each chapter follows a similar order. I begin each chapter with a brief overview of important changes in the social order during the period. I then proceed to discuss developments in Philosophy of Science and then illustrate how these developments shaped the relationship between Evolutionary Social Theory and Political Economy in appropriate disciplines. Chapter 1 treats the time period from the beginning of the Enlightenment through the end of the French Revolution. Chapter 2, from the end of the Napoleonic Wars up to and including the publication of Darwin's *Descent of Man*. Chapter 3 addresses further developments through the end of WWI. Chapter 4 analyzes developments from the end of WWI through the early 1970s and Chapter 5 from the 70s up to today. Chapter 6 briefly recapitulates the arguments of the previous chapters. I have provided summaries of each chapter immediately below.

In Chapter 1 I address the rise of Natural Philosophy in the late Renaissance and Enlightenment and its application to the study of human society in the form of Moral Philosophy. Over the course of the 18th century, at least in Britain in France, both Natural and Moral Philosophy came under the sway of Empiricist interpretations of the Newtonian worldview. Though there was some overlap, especially in the writings of Montesquieu, two differing approaches to the study of Moral Philosophy emerged during this period: the abstract, mythological approach of Social Contract Theory and the empirical, grounded approach of Philosophical History. The latter approach can be considered as the genesis of Evolutionary Social Theory. Political Economy during this period was derivative of the more general approach of Evolutionary Social Theory. Evolutionary Social Theory provided a better explanation than Social Contract Theory of the problems of the era and also provided a foundation for the concerns of Political Economy, especially in the writings of Smith and Turgot. In addition, the views of Condorcet pointed to the implications of a scientific worldview for technological progress.

Chapter 2 addresses the development of Evolutionary Theory in both the natural and social sciences, and its relationship to the Philosophy of Science and Political Economy in the early and mid-19th century. I consider authors whose major contributions were developed either prior to, or concurrently with the publication of Darwin's *Origins* and *Descent*, as well as the contributions of Darwin himself. With the partial exception of Hebert Spenser, Empiricism and the closely related Positivism of August Comte were the predominant influences on Evolutionary theory during this period. Evolutionary Social Theory emerged as an integrated approach to the Social Sciences, that incorporated many of the concerns of Political Economy. Yet in spite of its roots in Empiricism and Positivism, Evolutionary Theory in this era was often speculative in nature, which reflected the prevailing influence of Lamarck. Nevertheless, it did provide a concrete explanation of changes in social organization. In some instances, it was apologetic for the social order, and in other cases, it laid the foundations for criticism and reform of the social order. In contrast, Political Economy, as it was understood and practiced by British Political Economists, became increasingly separated from Evolutionary Social Theory both with respect to the scope and method of inquiry. It was in this intellectual milieu that Darwin wrote *The Origin of Species* and *The Descent of Man.* Darwin's contribution, as well as that of Wallace, was to synthesize and refine both the theoretical arguments and empirical evidence for evolution, including arguments and empirical evidence drawn from Evolutionary Social Theory, and to recapitulate those arguments in a theoretically coherent and original concept of and explanation for evolution. The result was a novel theory of biological evolution based on the principles of common descent, gradualism, population thinking, variation and natural selection leading to a branching pattern of speciation. While Darwin's contributions had profound ramifications for all areas of inquiry, Darwin did not propose a new ethics of survival of the fittest. Rather, Darwin provided a naturalistic explanation for Smith's ethics based on sympathy for our fellow human beings. Yet Darwin's contributions went significantly beyond merely biologized Smithism.

In Chapter 3 I discuss the state of Evolutionary Social Theory and its relationship to Political Economy in the immediate Post-Darwin era, or roughly, from 1871 through 1918. I first address the impact of Darwin on Philosophy of Science and contrast the views of Haeckel, the Empirio-Critics and of the American Pragmatists. Darwin's impact was strongest on the latter. However, Darwin had surprisingly little direct impact on Evolutionary Social Theory during this period and with the exception of Thorstein Veblen, the impact of Lamarckian understandings was actually more prevalent. Nevertheless, Pragmatist concerns were often present in the writings of multiple Evolutionary Social Theorists. Evolutionary approaches were prominent in the Sociology of this period as is evidenced in the contributions of William Graham Sumner, Lester Frank Ward, Emile Durkheim and Max Weber. Sociology during this period was envisioned as a general theory that could incorporate the concerns of Political Economy and included both social reformers as well as apologists for the social order. In contrast, due to the influence of Franz Boas, Anthropology began to move away from evolutionary explanations and became increasingly divorced from Political Economy. Political Economy as a discipline was shaped by three different approaches. Following Smith and Ricardo, Marx viewed Political Economy primarily as an abstract theory about the laws of motion of the capitalist mode of production. However, his theory of Political Economy was tied to and dependent on his theory of social evolution, Historical Materialism, which was grounded in inverted Hegelian dialectics. Alfred Marshall continued in the tradition of Mill by emphasizing the separation of Political Economy from the broader approach of Evolutionary Social Theory, while retaining a Spencerian view of social evolution. In contrast, Thorstein

Veblen built on American Pragmatism and applied Darwinian thinking to social evolution. Despite some differences between his views and those of the Sociologists referenced above, Veblen too proposed to subordinate Political Economy to his broader theory of social evolution. Though Veblen incorporated Darwinian analogies into his system, it is a mistake to view Veblen's contributions as "Generalized Darwinism".

Chapter 4 addresses the factors that contributed to the relative marginalization of Evolutionary Social Theory in the 20th and 21st centuries, those factors that enabled it to survive and which contributed to its initial revival. I begin with a discussion of the differences amongst the logical positivists and between the logical positivists and Karl Popper. While noting the shortcomings of Logical Positivism, I argue that though its application to the Social Sciences contributed to the marginalization of Evolutionary approaches, it was not necessarily inconsistent with evolutionary approaches to social theory. In contrast, Popper's approach presented significant obstacles to evolutionary theorizing in the social sciences. However, the more damaging features were grand theory, naïve empiricism, physics envy and overformalization. The strongest inhibiting factor, however, was an overemphasis on the problem of social order and equilibrium which was characteristic of what for lack of a better term I will label technocratic progressivism. The factors that were favorable to the persistence and initial revival of Evolutionary Social Theory were emphasis on grounded empirical inquiry, the need to address social changes, a connection to Political Economy and a critical view of the social order. I address how the above played out in the respective disciplines of Anthropology, Sociology, Economics and Political Science and note in particular how Economics, more than any other discipline, marginalized evolutionary approaches (see Carneiro 2003; Harris 1968; Hodgson 2001; Wolf 1982).

In Chapter 5 I address the resurrection of Evolutionary Social Theory with respect to developments in the Philosophy of Science and Political Economy. I argue that better understanding of the Philosophy of Science helped to enable the revival of Evolutionary Social Theory. I first discuss the contributions and shortcomings of the Neo-Positivist approaches of Kuhn, Lakatos and Laudan. While noting shortcomings in their respective approaches I argue that the net effect was to provide a justification for disciplinary pluralism. I then address the role of two possible alternatives to Neo-Positivism, both of which have a stronger connection to the re-emergence of Evolutionary Social Theory: Critical Realism (Archer 1995; Bhaskar 1989; Lawson 1997, 2003) and Critical Common Sensism as articulated by the Neo-Classical Pragmatist Philosopher Susan Haack (2007, 2009). While noting areas of common concern I argue that because Critical Common Sensism provides a basis for a theory of empirical inquiry it is a more fruitful guide for Evolutionary Social Theory than Critical Realism. I then address the revival of Evolutionary Social Theory in the late 20th century, beginning with the rise and extensive impact of the

Neo-Darwinian Synthesis and its possibilities and pitfalls of its extension to the social sciences. I address three possible approaches: Sociobiology (Pinker 2003; Wilson 1975), Generalized Darwinism (Hodgson 2004, 2010) and its relationship to the Veblenian-Schumpeterian synthesis in Economics (Nelson 2018) and Cultural Evolutionism as it has emerged in Economic Anthropology and influenced Macrosociology and International Political Economy. Though Generalized Darwinism and Cultural Evolutionism have significant points in common, Cultural Evolutionism places greater emphasis on the differences between Cultural and Biological Evolution but is certainly broad enough to incorporate the contributions of Veblen and other Original Institutional Economists. I argue that this third approach provides the most fruitful path forward for the re-unification of Political Economy with Evolutionary Social Theory.

Chapter 6 recapitulates the arguments of the previous sections and defends the conclusion of this study that the future of Evolutionary Social Theory should be as a component of a broader synthesis that builds on the reintegration of the social sciences.

References

Archer, Margaret. 1995. *Realist Social Theory: The Morphogenetic Approach.* Cambridge: Cambridge University Press.

Bhaskar, Roy. 1989. *The Possibility of Naturalism.* Second Edition. Harvester, MO and Wheatsheaf: Hemel, Hempstead.

Boyd, Robert and Peter J. Richerson. 1985. *Culture and the Evolutionary Process.* Chicago, IL: University of Chicago Press.

Boyd, Robert and Peter J. Richerson. 1992. "How Microevolutionary Approaches Gave Rise To History." Pp. 179–209 in *History and Evolution*, edited by Nitecki, Matthew and Doris V. Nitecki, Albany: State University of New York Press.

Carneiro, Robert L. 2003. *Evolutionism in Cultural Anthropology.* Boulder, CO: West View Press.

Chilcote, Ronald H. 1994. *Theories of Comparative Politics: The Search for a Paradigm Reconsidered.* Second Edition. Boulder, CO and Oxford: Westview Press.

Collier, Andrew. 1994. *Critical Realism: An Introduction to Roy Bhaskar's Philosophy.* London and New York: Verso.

Cordes, Christian. 2007. "Turning Evolution into an Evolutionary Science: Veblen, the Selection Metaphor, and Analytical Thinking." *Journal of Economic Issues* XLI (4), pp. 135–154.

Darwin, Charles. 1876. *The Origin of Species by Means of Natural Selection, or the Preservation of Favoured Races in the Struggle for Life.* London: Murray. Sixth Edition. In Whye, ed. http://darwin-online.org.uk/converted/pdf/1876_Origin_F401.pdf

Darwin, Charles. 1877. *The Descent of Man, and Selection in Relation to Sex.* London: John Murray. Second Edition, Revised and Augmented. In Whye, ed. http://darwin-online.org.uk/converted/pdf/1877_Descent_F948.pdf

Durkheim, Emile. [1894] 2014. *The Division of Labor in Society.* Edited and With a New Introduction. Free Press Paperback Edition. New York and London: The Free Press.

Haack, Susan. 2006. "Introduction: Pragmatism, Old and New". Pp. 15–65 in *Pragmatism Old and New: Selected Writings*, edited by Haack, Susan with Robert Lane, (Associate ed.), Amherst, NY: Prometheus Books.

Haack, Susan. 2007. *Defending Science within Reason: Between Scientism and Cynicism*. Amherst, NY: Prometheus Books.

Haack, Susan. 2009. *Evidence and Inquiry: A Pragmatist Reconstruction of Epistemology*. Second Expanded Edition with a new Preface by the Author. Amherst, NY: Prometheus Books.

Harris, Marvin. 1968. *The Rise of Anthropological Theory*. New York: Random House.

Hodgson, Geoffrey. 2001. *How Economics Forgot History. The Problem of Historical Specificity in Social Science*. New York and London: Routledge.

Hodgson, Geoffrey. 2004. *The Evolution of Institutional Economics: Agency, Structure and Darwinism in American Institutionalism*. New York and London: Routledge.

Hodgson, Geoffrey. 2010. *Darwin's Conjecture. The Search for General Principles of Social and Economic Evolution*. Chicago, IL, and London: University of Chicago Press.

Jo, Tae-Hee. 2021. "A Veblenian Critique of Nelson and Winter's Evolutionary Theory." *Journal of Economic Issues* LVI(4), pp. 1101–1117.

Lawson, Tony. 1997. *Economics and Reality*. London and New York: Routledge.

Lawson, Tony. 2003. *Reorienting Economics*. London and New York: Routledge.

Marshall, Alfred. [1890] 1920. *Principles of Economics*. Eighth Edition. London: McMillan and Company.

Marx, Karl. [1859] 1904. *A Contribution to the Critique of Political Economy*. Translated by M.L. Stone. Chicago, IL: Charles H. Kerr and Company.

Mayr, Ernst. 2001. *What Evolution Is*. New York: Basic Books.

Meek, Ronald L. 1976. *Social Science and the Ignoble Savage*. Cambridge: Cambridge University Press.

Mill, Johnathan Stuart. 1824. "On the Definition of Political Economy and the Method of Investigation Proper to It." Pp. 309–339 in *The Collected Works of Johnathan Stuart Mill, Volume IV: Essays on Economics and Society Part I*, edited by John Robson. Toronto: University of Toronto Press.

Nelson, Richard R. 2018. "Evolutionary Economics from a Modern Perspective." Pp. 1–34 in *Modern Evolutionary Economics: An Overview*, edited by Nelson, Richard. 2008. Cambridge: Cambridge University Press.

Pinker, Steven. 2003. *The Blank Slate: The Modern Denial of Human Nature*. New York: Penguin Books.

Poirot, Clifford. 2007. "How Can Institutional Economics be an Evolutionary Science." *Journal of Economic Issues* XLI(1), pp. 155–180.

Poirot, Clifford. 2008. "Is Pragmatism Good for Anything: Towards an Impractical Theory of Economics." *Forum for Social Economics* 37(1), pp. 61–76.

Rousseau, Jean Jacque. 1759. *Discourse on Political Economy* in Rousseau, Jean Jacque. 1923. *The Social Contract and Discourses by Jean-Jacques Rousseau*. Edited by G.D.H. Cole. London and Toronto: J.M. Dent and Sons.

Schumpeter, Joseph. 1954. *History of Economic Analysis*. New York: Oxford University Press.

Smith, Adam. [1776] 1904. *An Inquiry into the Nature and Causes of the Wealth of Nations by Adam Smith*. 2 volumes. Edited with an Introduction, Notes, Marginal Summary and an Enlarged Index by Edwin Cannan, London: Methuen.

Steiner, Phillipe. 2011. *Durkheim and the Birth of Economic Sociology*. Translated by Keith Tribe. Princeton, NJ: Princeton University Press.

Veblen, Thorstein. 1919. *The Place of Science in Modern Civilization and Other Essays*. New York: B. W. Huebsch.

Webb, James. 2007. "Pragmatisms, Plural. Part I.: Classical Pragmatism and Some Implications for Empirical Inquiry." *Journal of Economic Issues* XL(4), December, pp. 1063–1086.

Webb, James. 2012. "Pragmatisms, Plural. Part II: From Classical Pragmatism to Neo-Pragmatism." XLVI(1), March, pp. 45–74.

Wilson, Edward, O. 1975. *Sociobiology and the New Synthesis*. Cambridge: Cambridge University Press.

Wolf, Eric. 1982. *Europe and the People without History*. Berkeley: University of California Press.

1 The Origins of Evolutionary Social Theory

Introduction

The 16th through the 18th centuries were characterized by several interdependent processes which influenced efforts to understand the nature of the social order (see, Arrighi 1994; Darwin 2008; Neal and Cameron 2016; Smith 1991; Wallerstein 1974 and Wolf 1982 for useful analyses of these processes):

1. The commercialization of the social structure of most of Western Europe;
2. The creation of a world commercial system in which the international division of labor and terms of trade favored the colonial powers of Europe;
3. A shift in maritime hegemony over this commercial system away from the Italian city states, toward Spain and Portugal, and later to Holland and ultimately to England;
4. The rise of France as the strongest military power on the Continent;
5. The fragmentation of Christianity and an increase in the powers of secular rulers with respect to the power of the Pope;
6. The failure of any single power in Europe to assert dominion over the various political entities of Europe and the gradual consolidation of the power of individual states over more defined territories, or more put more succinctly, the origins of the nation-state system;
7. Extensive conflict over what specific form, whether Aristocratic, Royal Absolutist or Constitutional Monarchy, the governmental structure of these emerging nation states would take.

Given the extent of these changes, it is not surprising that traditional sources of authority and knowledge came under increased scrutiny. Multiple writers in the late Renaissance and Enlightenment adapted the methods of Philosophy to the study of the Natural World, giving rise to Natural Philosophy. Though Natural Philosophy encompassed multiple variants, the general trend was toward the displacement of both Thomism and

DOI: 10.4324/9781003170679-2

the earlier Renaissance idealization of the natural world and emphasis on texts as a source of knowledge. In contrast, Natural Philosophers, following the successes of Copernicus, Kepler and Galileo placed increasing emphasis on the importance of direct observation in combination with the philosophical method and rejected explanations couched in terms of entelechy and vitalism, especially in Physics. Natural Philosophy viewed the Universe as orderly, stable and rational. It sought to explain observable, natural phenomena as an unbroken chain of cause and effect, absent the use of concepts such as entelechy, vitalism, essentialism or final cause (Russell 1972, pp. 525–545).

This in turn gave rise to Civil or Moral Philosophy, which incorporated Political Economy. Two approaches to Moral Philosophy emerged: Social Contract Theory and what is sometimes termed Speculative, or Philosophical History. The first was based primarily on mythological explanations, while the latter sought to ground inquiry in the historical and comparative method. The former provided little understanding of the nature of the problems of the era, while the latter was to prove insightful in many respects. It is also in the latter that we find the origins of Evolutionary Social Theory.

Natural Philosophy and the Newtonian World View

The advances in Chemistry by Boyle, based on experimental methods, and the publication of Newton's *Principia* in the late 18th century were pivotal points in the development of Natural Philosophy. Both Boyle and Newton, however, in a sense kept two sets of books. Chemistry and Physics both explained observable phenomena in terms of mechanistic principles, and in the case of Boyle atomistic principles as well. At the same time, both also held views that were contrary to this approach to Chemistry and Physics. But it was the former view that defined Natural Philosophy. By the mid-18th century, Newton's Physics was considered to be the hallmark of good science and was associated as much with a World View as with Physics in particular. Though there were differing interpretations of Newtonism, the one that triumphed in England and France was strongly influenced by Empiricist interpretations of Newton.

Empiricism is a term that has multiple different meanings (Markie 2017; Russell 1972; Sober 2008), and in many circles, it carries with it negative connotations. For the purposes of this chapter, I will focus on Empiricism as it was articulated by Locke and Hume. If it is possible to reduce Empiricism to a simple postulate, it is that all knowledge derives from experience. However, this postulate is not as simple as it might seem at first glance. In Locke's (1689a, p. 28) view, we experience the world via sensory impressions based on our interaction with the world and initially form simple ideas: for example, we have an experience of "red" and an experience of "ball". We then formulate compound ideas such as "red ball".

While Berkeley took Empiricism to an idealist extreme, Locke's version was closer to materialism. For Locke, there is an external environment that actually impressed itself on our sensations.

Empiricism in this sense faces at least two related problems: that of substance and that of skepticism. As indicated above, and discussed later on as well, Empiricists in general have rejected the idea of "substance" behind reality. This is an issue that will resurface at multiple later junctures in this study. Locke's version is associated with an atomistic perspective in that it treats the world as if it is composed of discrete objects. But this does not necessarily mean that the world is solely comprised of discrete objects or that there are no connections between phenomena. For Locke, in my view, the atomistic view was a convenience: it is difficult to explain a comprehensive relationship of all objects to each other, as our experience of the world is piecemeal. Locke clearly recognizes that the mind relates objects and concepts. Locke was one of the foremost proponents of Newtonian physics, which strongly implies that objects are real, knowable and that there is such a thing as constant causal law.

The problem of skepticism emerges more strongly in Hume (1777b, p. 22). Hume argues that because we cannot directly observe causation, we can only infer causation on the basis of the constant correlation of phenomena. Furthermore, in Hume's view, induction is ultimately unreliable. We cannot know that the connections we observe today will persist in the future. This position makes Newtonian physics as well as Hume's project of a comprehensive science of man difficult, if not untenable. There are several possible solutions to this problem.

One solution is Hume's solution or at least one interpretation of Hume. Order, for Hume, in the natural and social world emerge spontaneously. It is defined by habit (1777b, pp. 60–80). This view is expressed as well in his extensive writings on Moral Philosophy: In Hume's view, ideas about benevolence arise from sentiment and are solidified through experience (1777b, p. 172). Hume adopts the same position with respect to social institutions. They are expressions of custom and habit created by humans and consequently evolving (1777b, pp. 205–211). Hence in Hume's view, it is on the basis of habitual experience that we come to make inferences as to causal relationships, though at best, most of our inferences can only be known probabilistically. Thus, we can credit Hume with the idea that knowledge can be, and is in fact, held by degrees of confidence. We are justified, Hume tells us in his famous discussion of miracles, in taking reports of phenomena that violate our established experience as incredulous (1777b, pp. 109–132). That Hume's approach is evolutionary is buttressed by his consideration of the general problem of emergence without specific design in his *Dialogues* (1777d). The problem with Hume therefore in my estimation is not that he assumes a closed system, but that his occasional willingness to push his position to its logical conclusion potentially undercuts the ontological assumptions necessary for any kind of science to work, or even to get out of bed in the morning (see also, Russell, pp. 659–674). Part of the problem depends on what we call knowledge. If knowledge, in a philosophical sense, is only what we can know for certain, then we actually know very little. If on the other hand knowledge is something we can have by degree, then the problem of certain philosophical knowledge is actually not a problem.

However, two other possible solutions, excluding extreme Cartesian rationalism deserve attention: that of Kant (1781) and that of Reid (1764, 1788a, 1788b). I will address Kant's solution first. Kant attempts to resolve the problem by allowing a limited basis for a priori synthetic knowledge, primarily of basic physical problems of time and space, and by positing a distinction between noumena (things as they actually are) and phenomena (things as we perceive them). In Kant's view, there is a certain way that the mind is predisposed to think. This does suggest that there is a logical basis for inferring causation and connections between phenomena. Yet the solution is purely idealistic. It does not actually address whether we are, or are not, in actuality arriving at an accurate understanding of the external world. If what is in our heads is merely a projection of an external world that we do not fully and accurately perceive, then Kant's solution is not really on any stronger ground than Hume's. In addition, it posits the existence of a transcendent, unseen, and in principle unobservable reality lurking behind observable reality. Whether the solution to the problem is to through Kant and attempt to resolve this dilemma, or to go around Kant, is also an issue that will resurface in Chapter 5.

The second solution is the Critical Common Sensist solution of Reid and others in the Scottish Enlightenment. This solution leads us toward Empirical Realism, and in my view, potentially to depth realism. Here again, this issue will resurface later in this study. Reid's argument was that with respect to Hume's skepticism, we should just simply not take it seriously (1764, pp. 1–11). Rather, we are justified, Reid tells us, in taking as given certain "common sense" propositions about the external world: these include such propositions as the external world exists, that we perceive the external world, and that our senses are reliable (1785, pp. 17–21). In addressing the issue of "causation" Reid makes the argument that we should abandon the term "causation" as a scientific term while permitting its usage in normal conversation. In contrast, Reid argues, we should reason in terms of explaining phenomena by general law (1788b, p. 5: Barrantes and Duran 2016).

In Reid's view, there are certain ways in which the mind is predisposed to think, and that these ways of thinking, generally lead us to reliable conclusions. Common sense propositions are those that we know to be true as basic aspects of the world that we learn as children. Yet as in all matters, Reid emphasized the importance of judgment as well as will. Not every common sense proposition is necessarily true (Barrantes and Duran 2016). In contrast to Hume, Reid was a theist and advocate of the argument to design. Belief in an ultimate designer is among the views that Reid sees as "common sense". According to Reid, the mind works because it is made by God. However, Reid's argument does not depend on an ultimate designer: the argument works as well with respect to a mind that is a product of natural selection. This view of the mind as active in organizing knowledge is also a part of Reid's views on Ethics. As I discuss later in this chapter, other major figures in the Scottish Enlightenment argued for a sensualist basis for morality based on empathy. Reid does not entirely reject this argument though he also argues that humans possess an innate moral sense. Furthermore, in Reid's view, some social arrangements are more conducive to human flourishing than others. For Reid, and other figures in the Scottish Enlightenment, including Hume, this is an empirical question, and is a central component of the project of Moral Philosophy.

Which, if any of the above positions, Newton himself held to in entirety is unclear. Hume, Kant and Reid wrote after Newton, while Locke was contemporary to Newton. All of them were ardent Newtonians. Locke was probably Newton's strongest advocate in Britain and Newton never disavowed Locke's Empiricism. In addition, it is possible to interpret Newton directly as at least a moderate Empiricist. For example, in his paper on optics (1671), he established the properties of light via experimentation and observation. Similarly, *Principia* (1687) in which Newton put forward his theory of gravitation, stresses the experiential basis of reasoning. In Book III of *Principia* Newton lays out his rules of reasoning (pp. 383–384). Rule 1 tells us that we should not add speculative explanations or hypotheses that are not consistent with empirical evidence. Rule 4, that we should accept as true, hypotheses that are consistent with the evidence, unless and until we have a better hypothesis, and we should reject hypotheses that are not consistent with the evidence. An implication of rule 4 is that our understanding is fallible and subject to revision. Rules 2 and 3 imply that there is constant, causal law in the Universe. Explanations that apply to observations of phenomena on earth, will also apply to astronomical phenomena.

Newton's own explanation of these rules is instructive, especially with respect to his explanation of rule number 3:

> That all bodies are impenetrable we gather not by reason but by our senses. We find those bodies that we handle to be impenetrable, and hence we conclude that impenetrability is a property of all bodies universally. That all bodies are movable and persevere in motion or in rest by means of certain forces (which we call forces of inertia) we infer from finding these properties in the bodies that we have seen. The extension, hardness, impenetrability, mobility, and force of inertia of the whole arise from the extension, hardness, impenetrability, mobility, and force of inertia of each of the parts; and thus we conclude that every one of the least parts of all bodies is extended, hard,

> impenetrable, movable, and endowed with a force of inertia. *And this is the foundation of all natural philosophy.*
>
> (p. 384. Emphasis added)

In other words, our knowledge of impenetrability comes from our experience. Via induction, we are able to generalize to properties of all bodies. Yet clearly, Newton's system is not limited to induction alone, and no major figure in Empiricism ever argued that observation and induction took placed independently of context or that theory and deduction played no role in knowledge. Newton's *Principia* presents us with a portrait of a Universe in which causation is both universal and necessary and that relevant principles can be derived via formal mathematics. This allows us to calculate planetary motion with an increased degree of accuracy. Deviations from an idealized ellipse are then explained by disturbances of the gravitational pull of other objects. More importantly, Newton's explanation clearly implies that general properties are actually real. Hence there is a common sense aspect to Newton.

The term "causation" in this context is potentially vexing. As the term was understood prior to Newton, by Newton and later empiricist interpretations of Newton, causation was mostly thought of in terms of proximate, mechanical causation. To use a very rough analogy, we can think of proximate causation in terms of billiard balls propelled by an external force, crashing into other billiard balls and generating motion, yet doing so in accordance with constant and universally valid general laws. Though again, Hume's position makes even this much problematic. But the mechanical concept of causation presented some difficulties for Newton's system. In Leibniz's view, planetary motion and deviation from pure orbits were explained by the variation in fluid vortices that governed the motion of planets (Russell, pp. 581–595). Newton rejected this explanation. Though some have alleged that Newton resorted to occultic forces to explain the idea of gravitation, this is not so. Newton clearly viewed gravity as a force that could act at a distance. But force in Newton's view is just the attraction of objects to each other: there is nothing else behind force (Smith 2008). The reader may note that we are back to the rejection of the concept of substance.

Before proceeding to a discussion of Moral Philosophy, a brief digression on the state of biology, or Naturalism of the era is in order. Biological analogies regarding society were by no means absent during this era. The problems for Naturalism were how to explain the distinction between living and non-living phenomena and how to classify different plant and animal species, including humans (Mayr 1982). While the idea that plants did not possess any properties of internal motion became increasingly accepted, the study of Nature and living organisms during this period continued to be defined by vitalistic and teleological conceptions of living things. Similarly, Linnaeus' system of classification, for example, rested on a sharp division between living and non-living entities. It also posited fixed boundaries of species. In some respects, Linnaeus has more in common with Aristotle, than with Newton and Boyle.

Yet at the same time, the ideas of change, progress and perfectibility were embedded within the Enlightenment. Naturalists struggled with how to explain apparent changes in the forms of living organisms over time. Rationalists such as Leibniz theorized the great chain of being as temporal, leading to gradual, continuing perfection (Mayr 1982, p. 326). Despite its imperfections, the Linnaean system of classification and its recognition of diversity was to later provide a conceptual framework in which Darwin, as well as precursors to Darwin, developed theories of biological evolution. Simultaneously, the discoveries of the diversity of flora and fauna and stratigraphy challenged the view of nature as static. In the mid-18th century, while continuing to maintain the idea of the fixity of species, the French Naturalist Buffon argued that specific species had separate origins. Though Buffon's theory was not an evolutionary theory in the modern sense, it did nevertheless posit change over time. These ideas, as I will note below, are present in the writings of both Rousseau and Condorcet, and provided a foundation for Lamarck's theories of evolution in the early 19th century.

From its inception, Natural Philosophy was intended as a vehicle through which human life could be improved. Given the above, understanding the place of humans in the Natural World and in relation to other animal species was central to the Enlightenment project. Yet this raised a disturbing contradiction in Enlightenment thought. On the one side, Enlightenment philosophers viewed humanity as united by a capacity to reason. This capacity placed humans both within the animal kingdom but also above and outside of nature and the animal kingdom. But with the partial exception of writers such as Condorcet and Wollstone Craft, they also placed males above females and Europeans above all other civilizations. European writers in the Enlightenment might express admiration for China and grudging respect for the Ottoman Empire but continuously placed Africans and indigenous Americans at the bottom of the hierarchy. This theme is echoed in Kant's lectures on Anthropology, as well as elsewhere, in which following Linnaeus, Kant classifies by both national and racial types, and places Europeans at the top, Asians and other groups lower on the scale and Africans on the bottom while simultaneously making rather absurd generalizations about the differences between males and females (Kant 1798, pp. 195–251).

I am not, I stress, arguing that Empiricists were better: they were not. Though atrocities by European Imperial powers as well as other Imperial powers in world history pre-date the Enlightenment, the idea of an allegedly scientific, biological, racial classification was new. In part, this was a function of efforts to systematize species as well as efforts to account for biogeographical variation. Humans in Kant's view were one species and his use of the term race is in reference to biogeographical variation. However, Kant's essentialistic and hierarchical view of systems of classification, in concert with the self-perception of Europeans as innately superior, shared by Kant and multiple other important writers in the Enlightenment, lent false claims of scientific validity to racism, and other similar ideologies. Hence it can be fairly argued that the modern concept of "race" was in part a product of the Enlightenment (Eze 1997). Similarly, while ethnocentrism, xenophobia and the idea that civilizations other than one's own are inferior have been common in human affairs, the idea of a specific, progressive, hierarchy of societies and civilizations is also a product of the Enlightenment.

At the same time, however, as I will discuss below, Kant and other Enlightenment theorists posited common origins of the human species, and were often critical of the exercise of arbitrary power, unwarranted social hierarchies, war and Imperialism. The concept of humans possessing a Universal human reason was central to the Enlightenment as were the concepts of progress, liberty and equality. In the pens of some, the critical nature of the Enlightenment could be turned toward analysis and critique of the social order. Though Enlightenment theorists were not united on the basis of ethics, both Kantian as well as Humean ethics require the humane treatment of all human beings. The racist and ethnocentric assumptions of multiple Enlightenment theorists therefore should be viewed as contradictory to the overall Enlightenment project, rather than as intrinsic to, or as an indictment of Enlightenment philosophy. In my discussion below on social theory in the Enlightenment, and also in subsequent chapters, I will address these contradictions as they arise.

Civil, or Moral Philosophy

Overview

The method of Natural Philosophy, both prior to and after Newton, was applied to the study of society in the form of Moral Philosophy. The goal of Moral Philosophy was to discover the principles which would lead to human prospering. One way to approach this issue was through Social Contract Theory. Though as I illustrate below, there were differences amongst the Social Contract Theorists on multiple points, what united them was the view that social order had to be created by agreement amongst humans, and that social order depended critically on the existence of a formal state. Though most Social Contract Theorists were Empiricists, with the partial exception of Montesquieu, their contribution had little empirical content. Consequently, Social Contract theory has a mythological quality. The idea that a formal state, or any other institution emerges as a result of deliberate action and agreement amongst humans, or that such an institution might be imposed on some by others, is not contrary to the idea of social evolution. But in addressing the state, the Social Contract theorists did not address this as a concrete era, did not address the possibility of precursor institutions and equated the state with social order.

Social Contract Theory

Hobbes

Though Hobbes wrote prior to Newton, his writings nevertheless illustrate many of the trends addressed above, and he is generally considered to be an Empiricist. Nevertheless, his arguments have a strong geometric and deductive character. What little empirical evidence there is in Hobbes, is primarily by way of generalization based on limited observations. Both the physical and social aspects in Hobbes' view are defined by discoverable Natural Law. In Chapter IX (pp. 64–65) of *Leviathan* (1651) Hobbes draws a distinction between knowledge of facts and knowledge of consequences of affirmations, the latter which Hobbes terms "Science" or Philosophy. Hobbes then makes a further distinction between Natural Philosophy and Politiques, or Civil Philosophy. Hobbes groups most of what we today would label as the physical and natural sciences under this former heading, though he places the study of ethics, rhetoric, poetry, logic and contracts under this heading as well. He divides the category of Civil Philosophy between the consequences of the duty and rights of the sovereign and the duty and rights of the subject. It is these issues that he addresses in *Leviathan* and elsewhere.

Where the Classical Political Theorists viewed the polis as emerging out of the natural sociability of humans, Hobbes presents a view of the State, or as he terms it, Common Wealth, as coming into being as a consequence of a deliberate, purposive act of humans. Though Hobbes does not address when and where this Common Wealth comes into being, the powers that he ascribes to it in Chapter XVII (pp. 128–132) are clearly those that we associate with the concept of a formal State. Yet at the same time, Hobbes' concern is also with the problem of social order more generally. For Hobbes, social order does not exist without the presence of a coercive state. Though this State may be unnatural, the creation of the State is in accordance with reason, and it is by reason we know that the State is owed obedience.

In Chapter XIII, Hobbes asserts that out of the state of Civil Society, people are naturally prone to quarrel with each other due to competition, diffidence and glory. Though there is indeed violence in this state, this state of being in Hobbes' view is characterized by a state of war. As an example of the State of Nature, Hobbes references indigenous Americans, Europe's feudal past, the state of relations between states, civil conflict in general, and specifically, the English Civil War. His arguments with respect to indigenous Americans are of course recognized today as inaccurate. Tribal, or Kinship-based societies, as well as Chiefdoms, clearly have a social order. The view that there is no social order absent in a coercive state is empirically wrong. He also references feudalism as an example of the State of Nature. Yet it could be argued that the multiple Baronies, Dukedoms, petty principalities and city states of the feudal era and of the Holy Roman Empire were mini-states. There was also clearly a social order in such entities. Paradoxically, Hobbes does recognize the Greek City States as Common Wealths.

In general, Hobbes is not concerned with the actual origins of the State. He does not explain the nature or origins of Absolutism as a specific form of the State. He does not specify any particular size or scale for classifying a Common Wealth. Curiously, he does not distinguish between Civil Society, the Common Wealth, or the State, but instead runs these categories together. His analysis really tells us nothing about the context of the problems of the State as an actual entity in 17th-century Europe. It can be argued, however, in partial defense of Hobbes, that the above is not his concern. He had witnessed the immense destruction of the English Civil War as well as of the Thirty Years War. His interest lies in explaining the consequences of disobedience to the State.

In sum, Hobbes limits his analysis of the problems of early modern states to the problem of stability and order, which for Hobbes takes precedence over all other factors. Hobbes does not have any particular conception of Political Economy per se, though he does assign a material motive, even if only in part to violence. The idea that human institutions come into being by design is not inherently anti-evolutionary, and as I discuss in many instances throughout this study, many after Hobbes proposed that the state in some sense emerged in such a fashion, albeit with some important precursors. But a one-time change in social organization, followed by an excessive focus on the problem of maintaining social order, is not a theory of social evolution.

Locke

In contrast, while Locke's (1689) argument for the rise of the State falls short of an evolutionary theory, Locke does at least, albeit to a limited degree, address the issue of social change. Locke ties the emergence of the Social Contract, and hence of a formal State, to the increasing complexity of commercial exchange. As with Hobbes, the Social Contract emerges as a conscious, deliberate decision. There is clearly a Political Economy in Locke, in the sense that property, production, commerce and contract are fundamental to the social order. But for Locke, Political Economy exists prior to, and outside of society. Similarly, Locke continues the treatment of both the state of nature and the emergence of a Common Wealth as abstractions.

Locke grounds his arguments in a theory of natural rights and natural law (Book II, Chapters I–III). Like Hobbes, Locke views humans as inherently asocial in the state of nature. The first and most important freedom in Locke's view is the right by virtue of natural law to retain the fruits of one's labor from which follows the freedom to engage in voluntary contracts (Book II, Chapter V). However, Locke never addresses how contracts can be negotiated, interpreted and enforced, outside of the existence of a state that can take on these functions. The asociality of humans however does not in Locke's view result in a state of war. Locke argues that in the state of nature people engage in peaceable trade with each other and enter into voluntary contracts. However, the growing complexity of commercial exchange necessitates the creation of an entity that can provide stability for the commercial order: that entity is the State (Book II, Chapter VIII). Once created however, humans owe the State obedience and loyalty, unless the State departs from the social contract (p. 97).

Locke's arguments are foundational to Classical Liberalism and exhibit the inherent contradictions of Classical Liberalism. Locke defines liberty in both economic and political terms and in addition to his treatises on government, also wrote coherently on economic, and specifically on monetary issues. In some interpretations, Locke has a kind of primitive labor theory of value (Locke Book II, Chapter V; Rima 2009, p. 48). In his *Treatise on Money* Locke presents an early version of the quantity theory of money and argues against the use of lowered interest rates as a means of stimulating economic activity. As was the case with many other, later British and French writers of the 18th century, what we today term "economic policy" was an extension for Locke of his theory of society and governance. Hence Locke defines economic liberty as freedom of contract and political freedom as ordered liberty, which means the right to be free from interference from government provided one is adhering to the law. His views on liberty are further reflected in his arguments for religious toleration, even with respect to heretics, and against prior censorship. This position is clearly evident in Locke's treatment of the social contract as a means to limit the power of arbitrary government, his view that the social contract applies to both the Sovereign and the people and his clear preference for Constitutional Monarchy.

Yet his willingness to extend the theory of natural rights and natural law was limited. Locke was a direct participant in the administration of Britain's Empire and accepted the existence of the institution of slavery, though writing against slavery as unnatural. Similarly, his references to the indigenous tribes of the Americas as illustrative of the State of Nature echo the ethnocentric biases of Hobbes. As with Hobbes, the argument is mostly normative. Nevertheless, as noted above, there is a partial theory of the rise of the state as rooted in the protection of property and the growing complexity of society and exchange. It is equally instructive however to note what Locke does not do: he does not trace the actual history of the State to make his case. As in Hobbes, the state of nature and the social contract are both fiction and the nature of the state is also similarly nebulous. In positing contract as the basis for the state, Locke ignores that the institution of contract requires a social framework to be meaningful. Hence logically and empirically, organized society and the State must precede the institution of contract.

Whether there is a direct link between Locke's argument and the Glorious Revolution of 1688 is unclear. Locke's essay on the social contract is generally viewed as having been written prior to the Glorious Revolution and hence was not necessarily a post hoc justification. That noted, Locke was a participant in the Glorious Revolution and the system that emerged from it is consistent with Locke's overall view of the appropriate relationship between the governed and government. Both the Glorious Revolution, as well as the much later creation of the U.S. Constitution were influenced by Locke's arguments and both might to some extent be pointed to as actual examples of consciously designed social contracts. But this only addresses a very specific, historical form of the State. It does not explain the origins or evolution of the State nor does it address the evolution of commercial society in any detail. Consequently, it presents us with very limited progress toward an evolutionary account of the social order.

Rousseau

In his *Discourse on the Origins of Social Inequality*, Rousseau (1754) begins by asserting that natural law cannot be understood by examining current law, but rather must be understood by examining humans in a state of nature. As with other social contract theorists, both the social contract and the state of nature do not refer to any definable historical era. However, in both the *Discourse* and *The Social Contract* (1762) he provides a quasi-evolutionary account of the emergence of both, while simultaneously positing them as mythological states. Rousseau makes the interesting argument that there was a time in which humans existed even prior to the state of nature. The state of nature for Rousseau is a time in which humans exist outside of the context of civil society, but nevertheless, possess human capacities. Rousseau's state of nature is a state in which humans are neither Noble nor Ignoble—they are innocent. Humans are not necessarily violent in this state as they are also motivated by the principle of sympathy.

Interestingly, Rousseau implies that there was a time prior to the State of Nature when humans resembled animals in their capacities but gradually learned to reason (1754, pp. 171–173). Like Hobbes, Locke, Montesquieu and multiple other Enlightenment writers, Rousseau refers to the indigenous Americans as an example of humans in the state of nature. He then notes that indigenous Americans are closer to civilized peoples than animals (pp. 175–179 and 180–189). Yet on this point, Rousseau is a bit ambiguous. The portrait he presents of indigenous Americans is distinctly unflattering and he presents it as a rather brute existence. But there are also differences between indigenous Americans and humans in the State of Nature. In *The Social Contract*, he notes that a representative Aristocracy had emerged amongst Native Americans and praises their system of government. In other words, Rousseau acknowledges, at least tacitly, that a social order can exist outside of a formal State and hints that there could be a progression of stages in human history.

Another interesting point in Rousseau is that he acknowledges the role of power in the formation of the State. Those with more power and wealth forced it on those without power and wealth. The state of war does not exist in the state of nature, but in the context of a state-ordered society. In both the *Discourse* and *The Social Contract* Rousseau argues that the social contract comes into existence by human convention. The argument in *The Discourse* is somewhat more detailed. Like Locke and Montesquieu, he attributes the rise of the social contract to growing complexity in human affairs, including, technological innovations (p. 215). In *The Social Contract*, he adds that it arises due to the inability of people to protect their own existence. Consequently, people agreed to alienate their freedom to the entire community (p. 64). As with other social contract theorists, Rousseau does not draw a clear distinction between social organization and the existence of a formal State.

Though Rousseau's view about how the Social Contract comes into existence is abstract and idealized, it does nevertheless give us a reasonably clear picture of his views on property, social equality and commerce. Rousseau argues that while a person has a natural right to security in property acquired by one's labor, no person has a right to claim more than that person is able to actually use. Rousseau's vision of the ideal society is that of a small community of individual farmers, shopkeepers and artisans. Rousseau does not argue for complete equality of possessions or even of rank. Some level of inequality in his view is natural. Yet extremes of inequality are incompatible with liberty. He defines equality as a condition in which no person is forced to sell himself due to extreme poverty and no person is in a position to buy another due to extreme wealth (1754, p. 94).

Where concepts such as the State, Popular Sovereignty and General Will are vague in his earlier writings, in *The Social Contract* Rousseau goes to considerable lengths to attempt to clarify these ideas though he places a strong emphasis on what the State should do, and less on what it actually does. Liberty is of course essential to his overall schema. No person in Rousseau's view has the right to enslave another, even in war. Liberty in Rousseau's view is inalienable. In *The Social Contract*, Rousseau does not necessarily treat the social contract as an imposition on people. The social contract is not a contract between the government and the people but an agreement amongst all the people. Hence Sovereignty, rather than residing in the State, resides in the people.

Rousseau draws a distinction between the particular will of individuals and the general will of the people as a whole. The general will is not simply an amalgam of particular wills: it is an abstract concept of what is genuinely in the interest of the people as a whole. At the same time, it is objective. The State is the executor of the people and government is the actual mechanism through which laws are enacted and mediates between the Sovereign (the general will of the people) and the State (1762, p. 50). Government and laws are legitimate only in so far as they are an expression of the general will and the government actually follows the laws.

Rousseau then addresses specific forms of government and on this point follows Montesquieu, whom I discuss below, in distinguishing between Aristocracy, Monarchy and Democracy. Any of these forms of government in Rousseau's view can be legitimate, provided the law is an expression of the general will and the ruler acts in accordance with the law. The preservation of forms requires virtue on the part of those who govern. Each system in Rousseau's view is prone to corruption. Hence Monarchy may devolve into tyranny or despotism. This occurs when a monarch usurps authority and governs in a way that is not in accordance with the law. Aristocracy has the potential to degenerate into Oligarchy and Democracy into what Rousseau terms Ochlocracy. Democracy does not guarantee that the General Will of the people will be enacted, but it does increase the probability. However, Democracy is only truly possible in a relatively small community in which wealth is relatively limited. Rousseau then illustrates his arguments by referencing to ways in which the above forms of government developed and decayed in Ancient Rome. Yet there is a critical feature missing from Rousseau's analysis. Despite his critique of Despotism, he never concretely addresses the rise of the Absolutist State as a specific form emerging out of Europe's feudal past.

Rousseau's views on the relationship between the state and the economy are better understood by an examination of his *Discourse on Political Economy* (1759). With respect to Political Economy, Rousseau is primarily concerned with the issue of policy and also subordinates the economy to politics. In my interpretation, though Rousseau is not as enamored with the market and division of labor as Smith and the Physiocrats, his arguments do not reflect those of a romantic innately opposed to commerce and industry. Rousseau echoes in part the Aristotelian view of Economics as Oikonomia (household management) applied to the affairs of the State in its management of resources. He draws an analogy between the head of State and the head of the Patriarchal household. For Rousseau however, this analogy has its limits. The functions of the State will depart significantly from the functions of a male head of household due to the increased levels of complexity in managing the affairs of the state and the differing foundations of both (p. 249).

Here again, Rousseau jumps directly from a descriptive or positive theory of how economic policy is carried out, to a normative argument regarding its foundations and goals. Just as the law should be an expression of the general will, public administration should follow that principle (p. 258). Similarly, he argues that the administration of the state should aim at virtue (p. 264). Rousseau locates the foundation of the production of wealth in the land, a point which echoes the Physiocratic doctrine. Notably, Rousseau did not oppose the development of industry but rather presents an argument for what economists today term "balanced growth", in which the growth of agriculture does not retard the development of the industry. On this point as well, we should take note of Rousseau's agreement with the Physiocrats. Nor is his argument here necessarily anti-Smithian. As I discuss below, Smith and others in the Scottish Enlightenment generally viewed the development of agriculture prior to commerce and industry as the normal case. In contrast, they viewed Europe's history of developing commerce and industry prior to agriculture as an abnormal case that had created significant distortions in Europe's pattern of development.

Unlike Turgot, the Physiocrats and Smith, Rousseau does not systematically address the issue of the relative shares of different social classes in production, though he does address the problem of economic inequality. Rousseau's ideal society, as expressed in *Discourse on Political Economy* is one in which every person had sufficient property to provision their household and is largely self-sufficient. The objective of the State in Rousseau's view should be to ensure security in property, prevent the means through which large-scale social inequalities can arise and insure proper management of public finances. The State should focus on receiving duties, rather than receiving bounties. Rousseau regards the organization of the State for conquest as inherently oppressive. His views on public finance also appear to follow that of the Physiocrats as he opposes taxes on land but proposes a luxury tax on items such as household servants and other similar features.

In my analysis above I have noted both the mythological and abstract aspects of Rousseau's analysis, as well as those aspects that point in a more concrete, evolutionary direction. Though the latter is present, it is not carried through. His argument that the foundations of the state as a specific political form lie in inequality of property and force does imply that the state as a form has a specific historical origin and that it plays a functional role—that of maintaining and enforcing social inequality—though this is clearly not Rousseau's ideal of what the State should do. The argument of Rousseau, as well as of Hobbes, Locke and others, that the State emerges by design, is not of necessity inconsistent with an evolutionary view, but the process and mechanisms through which this occurred are never addressed. While the history of Rome is looked to in part as a source of historical data and in part as a moral lesson, the line from the dissolution of Rome to the rise of the Absolutist State is never drawn. We have also noted that Rousseau addresses the economic foundations of the State and the economic role of the State while subordinating economics to politics. Yet, the concepts of a state of nature and of an original contract remain abstract fictions and his focus on the forms of government are also overly abstract. Hence while Rousseau made some progress toward an evolutionary view of society in comparison to Hobbes and Locke, his progress was strictly limited by his adoption of the abstract and mythological concepts of the State of Nature and the Social Contract.

Kant

The concept of an orderly, stable and law-like Universe, as I have noted above, exerted a significant influence on the development of Social Contract Theory. In Kant's treatment, physical laws and the formation of the Universe are interpreted in a dynamic sense. But Kant's concept of evolution is abstract, teleological, typological and idealist. In his *Universal Natural History* Kant (1755) had presented a rationalist and teleological account of Newtonian physics. As an admirer of Newtonian physics Kant found Hume's mitigated skepticism to be damaging to the orderly and rational world of causal relations implied by Newton's physics, yet also conceded that Hume had aroused him from his dogmatic slumber. In response to Hume, Kant (1781) modified his previous position and set forth his critical method in *Critique of Pure Reason*. The critical method is to use reason itself as a means to inquire what are the actual capacities and limits of reason. This critical method leads to the conclusion that the ability of the faculties to comprehend the external world is limited.

In order to make this argument work, Kant must draw his well-known distinction between noumena and phenomena, and between analytic and synthetic statements in order to arrive at his conclusion that a limited us of the a priori synthetic is possible. Though Kant does not directly stipulate that he is applying his critical method to social theory, its influence throughout his political essays is nevertheless pervasive. Consequently, Kant's arguments, though in some respects attractive as normative propositions, exhibit the same defects of Rousseau: that is Kant can only treat social forms as abstractions, not as concrete changing entities. Kant's metaphysical history, as we will see in the next section, stands in direct contrast to the actual empirical history of multiple contributors to the Scottish and French Enlightenment.

In his essay, "Idea of a Universal History", Kant (1784) articulates the foundations of his transcendental idealist views of politics. Kant argues that in spite of the apparent disorder in human affairs, it is "possible to discover a regular march" (p. 3). This march toward the realization of the manifestations of humanity will take place in accordance with Natural Law in the same sense that the weather is regulated by Natural Law to take care of nature. Kant argues that the principle directing this march is human reason. This reason is manifested in what he argues is the species' "unsocial sociability" (p. 10). This "unsocial sociability" leads to struggle and development and the creation of morality in turn leading to a progressive realization of freedom. Though Kant stresses autonomy as the basis for freedom, when Kant talks about autonomy and freedom, he is stressing a definition of freedom as consistency with the nature of humans, which is defined by reason. Freedom in Kant's view is not anarchy and license. In order for freedom to be realized, humans require a master in the form of the State to assure that individuals do not impinge on the freedom of others. This master can increase the freedom of all, but the master in turn must be regulated by Law, which is also the embodiment of reason. Just as the State necessarily emerges out of the struggle within society, so too the eventual establishment of an international Federation of states under International Law is destined in accordance with the plan of nature. Kant acknowledges that his argument is contradicted by the facts of history and that his argument is a priori. In his defense, he contrasts what he terms metaphysical history with the empirical narration of history.

This view is further developed in his essays "Political Right" (1793a) and "Political Progress" (1793b). The Social Contract comes into existence as a specific form of agreement and the conditions of it are Liberty, Equality and Self Dependency (1973a, p. 35). Kant does not address how and why this kind of social organization comes into existence. There is an economic aspect to this society in that the distribution and control of property should not be one that inhibits the development of property by others. Similarly, there should be significant social mobility for people to choose occupations that they are qualified for (pp. 79–90) Kant acknowledges that the concept of the Social Contract is a fiction. It does not require reference to a specific event or era, but is rather, based on reason (p. 90). But it is a fiction that expresses the mutually agreed-upon obligations of citizens as expressed in the general will. In contrast to Hobbes, Kant argues that the State has obligations to the citizens, but that the citizens are obligated to obey the State even if the State does not adhere to the contract. However, citizens must be free to criticize the State's departure from the Social Contract.

In "Political Progress" (1793b) Kant takes up the issue of whether or not humans should be loved, and whether or not progress is occurring. Here again, Kant views the development of Republican forms of government as inevitable and asserts that progress is occurring. Progress, Kant argues must occur due to the love of humanity because if humans are not capable of progress, they are not worthy of love. The appearance of the lack of progress in Kant's view is not evidence that progress will not occur. In addition, the apparent lack of progress is owed to the general improvement of human expectations. Consequently, the creation of a system of International Law that embodies these principles is predetermined.

In his essay on "Perpetual Peace" (1795), Kant outlines his schema and requirements for the creation of this system. Kant argues, in contrast to Hobbes and Machiavelli, that politics must be guided by moral action and that there should be no moral distinction made in the exercise of domestic politics or in international politics. Kant articulates these articles in the form of Preliminary and Definitive Articles. The articles Kant proposes are derived from his general view of morality as duty and his categorical imperative for ethical standards. The articles can be summarized as requiring states to act in a way that will not undermine the international rule of Law, establish Republican government and respect the sovereignty of all peoples. Notably, in his Definitive Article 3, Kant criticizes colonialism as inconsistent with the Universal principle of sovereignty. The system, it should be noted will be based on a confederation, rather than a Union, as the principle of a confederation retains respect for sovereignty.

Though one might doubt that this development is guided by an underlying teleology of unfolding reason, the principles which Kant lays out, if enacted, would clearly represent an advance in international relations. Kant's argument, to a limited degree, works as a purely normative argument. Yet it is not truly Universal, as in Kant's hands, it applies only to European states. Nevertheless, in defining justice, Kant begins from the abstract and moves to the concrete as he does with politics and the form of the State. Reason, and its unfolding in history, is consequently separated from actual concrete experience in Kant. Furthermore, in grounding his ethics in abstract reason, Kant cannot address the importance of custom and habit in defining what part of our ethics should be based on duty and what part should be based on experience. As with other social contract theorists both the state of nature and the social contract retain a mythological quality. Finally, it should be pointed out, Kant has no theory of Political Economy whatsoever.

Montesquieu

In contrast to the abstract and deductive character of Social Contract Theory as articulated by Hobbes, Locke, Rousseau and Kant, Montesquieu's (1748) approach provides a bridge between the former method and the empirically and historically grounded approach that gave rise to Evolutionary Social Theory in the form of Philosophical History. Though Montesquieu wrote prior to Rousseau, his arguments are sufficiently distinct and also influential on later theorists, that he merits separate treatment. Meek (1976), for example, argued that Montesquieu is the source of the social evolutionism that characterized much of late 18th-century Scottish and French Moral Philosophy and Political Economy. Though Montesquieu is most often treated as a Political Theorist, his writings are in actuality more comprehensive. His objective is clearly to articulate a comprehensive approach to Moral Philosophy. Nevertheless, he falls short of fully developing an evolutionary approach.

In *The Spirit of the Laws* (1748) Montesquieu presents an argument that laws should reflect the spirit, or nature of the society in which they are enacted. In other words, laws should reflect the institutional makeup of society. His discussion is both positive and normative. It is positive in the sense that he emphasizes the way in which different forms of social organization and specific types of government actually shape the law. It is normative in the sense that he addresses the kinds of laws that should be enacted to prevent corruption. Montesquieu distinguishes between the laws set by God, which in his view men are likely to forget, natural law, and laws created by humans. Philosophy, as the search to understand both natural and human law, enables humans to correct for their tendency to forget God's law.

In Montesquieu's view, there is a way in which it is best for humans to live. That way is discoverable via the application of Philosophy to human affairs. In contrast to other Social Contract Theorists, in Volume I, Book II Montesquieu argues that people are formed to live in society. Like other Social Contract Theorists, Montesquieu looks to the Savage societies of his day as similar to what humans would have been like in the state of nature. However, in Book I, he rejects Hobbes' view of the State of Nature as one in which people strive for dominance. He identifies the State of War with the existence of the Social Contract. It is in the stage of Civilization where classes struggle with each other and in which a social equilibrium emerges. Yet he remains pessimistic about human nature in general, seeing it as prone to corruption. In the opening of Book I, Chapter III he states that "As soon as mankind enters into a state of society they lose the sense of their weakness, equality ceases and then commences the state of war" (p. 6). The purpose of Law is to ameliorate this conflict.

In Book III, Montesquieu argues that law should function in a way as to best serve the characteristics of a people. These characteristics are shaped by multiple factors. While Montesquieu's argument is empirically grounded, he uses that empirical grounding to articulate a normative argument about how to best meet this goal. Laws should reflect the nature of the specific form of government. In a Monarchy, a single person governs, constrained by laws. The principles of the Monarchy are honor, ambition and esteem. In a Despotism, the will of the tyrant is the defining principle. The principle of the Despotism is fear. In a Republic, sovereignty lies in the body of the people and the principle of the Republic is equality before the law and virtue of the people. Montesquieu's ideal society is one in which a benevolent Monarch rules in keeping with the law, constrained by both the common people and the Aristocracy, an idea that had an obvious impact on much of 18th- and 19th-century political theory, including arguments for separation of powers.

All forms of government in Montesquieu's view are prone to corruption and this theme surfaces throughout Montesquieu's works. Hence, we might ask whether Montesquieu has a theory of evolution, or a theory of degeneration, or both. Montesquieu notes the actual changes in the political structure of his era, particularly, the rise of Absolutism as a form of governance. Montesquieu is particularly critical of the tendency of Absolutist Monarchs to destroy the power of intermediate classes, in particular, that of the Aristocracy, so as to increase the power of the Monarch over the people. The French Structuralist Marxist, Louis Althusser (1972), argued that Montesquieu's analysis is constrained by his class position in society and that Montesquieu is presenting an argument for the interests of the Aristocracy. Though there is some merit to this view, it ignores the extent to which Montesquieu is engaging in a critique at the conduct of the French Monarchy which was in the process of consolidating power, often at the expense of the Aristocracy. Both in the *Spirit* and in *Grandeur* (1721) Montesquieu notes how monarchs cynically exploit the common classes, directing them against the Aristocracy, not as a means of promoting Republican Government, but as a means of creating a Despotism.

Montesquieu provides some hints toward a theory of the rise of the State as a form of organization but does not develop it. In Volume I, Books XIV–XIX, Montesquieu distinguishes between three forms of social organization, Savagery, Barbarism and Civilization, each of which corresponds to a way of organizing production. He equates Savagery with hunting, Barbarism with pastoralism and civilization with settled agriculture. These forms of social organization are in his view sequential stages as well as contemporary forms of social organization. This classification, with some modifications, notably continued to be the standard method of classification well into the 20th century. Meek (1976, pp. 32–33) argues that subsequently, theorists in the Scottish Enlightenment added a stage of Commercial Society. Though Montesquieu does not formally label Commercial Society as a stage, we should surely credit Montesquieu with an awareness of the far-reaching nature of the commercial changes of the era. Similarly, as with later theorists, Montesquieu equates Commerce with Liberty and peaceful relations between states while at the same time noting the potential corruption that Commerce may bring inside a polity.

As is the case with all unilinear stage theories, Montesquieu's classification poses significant problems. In addition, his opening discussion of the influence of climate on social structure and personality in Book XIV by modern standards is rather absurd. Furthermore, as was the general case with European writers of the era, Montesquieu's portrayal of other societies often suffers from ethnocentrism and assumptions of European superiority, though some of this is owed to the sources available to him. In addition, to a limited degree, Montesquieu acknowledges both the potential shortcomings of European societies as well as the accomplishments of other societies.

Montesquieu's *Persian Letters* are noteworthy as they present European society as strange and exotic from the perspective of non-Europeans, while also exhibiting typical European exoticism of other cultures. In the *Spirit of the Laws*, Montesquieu repeatedly praises liberty and opposes slavery, though he argues for possible exceptions in countries where the climate is excessively hot. Though his writings on non-European societies exhibit the ethnocentric bias that is characteristic of European writers of the time, he held up Chinese and Ottoman polities as comparable to Europe with respect to its level of social organization. At the same time, he viewed these societies as prone to despotism. Unfortunately, his description of Africa as lacking any significant development of arts or society beyond the level of Savagery is both wrong and thoroughly racist. With respect to International Relations, he supported the right of nations to self-defense and argued that the only actual relations states could have was defense against each other and was opposed to Imperialism.

Another theme in Montesquieu's writings that surface in later writings in the Scottish and French Enlightenment is the connection he draws between commerce, liberty and international peace. Montesquieu emphasizes the ways in which commerce most often leads to peaceable relations between nations and to mutual improvement for both parties. However, his views on the beneficence of commerce are mitigated. Commerce has a tendency internally to break down traditional connections between people and he notes what in today's terms are the generally negative impacts of commodification. His argument is not really for free trade, but rather for balanced trade, or for a kind of controlled mercantilism. In some instances, he argues, that trade can actually lead to a loss of liberty and prosperity.

Another important contribution of Montesquieu to development of Evolutionary Social Theory is his pioneering method of what today is often referred to as philosophical or speculative history. In Volume II, Books XXVII–XXXI, Montesquieu traces the development of feudal law, out of the fall of Rome due to the Barbarian migrations and destruction of Rome. Like most European writers of the era, Montesquieu clearly accepts the premise that a significant part of Europe, as opposed to Mediterranean Europe, was at one point in time Barbaric. This makes feudal society in Europe not so much a stage in historical development, but a particular form of decentralized, agrarian society, ruled by an Aristocratic class. Both commercialism and Absolutism then developed together over the course of 16th, 17th and 18th centuries. It is not quite a theory of the transition from feudalism to Capitalism, but it is close. In this respect at least, Montesquieu's approach is clearly evolutionary.

Though the Spirit of the Laws recapitulates some of the arguments Montesquieu makes in *Grandeur and Declension* (1721), the arguments in the latter work merit discussion as they help to illustrate how Montesquieu treats issues of structure and agency. It is also instructive as it sets the tone for subsequent 18th-century European analyses of Rome, the stage of Barbarism in Europe and the ultimate rise of centralized states and commercial society. Though as with later histories there is an element of a moral tale in the collapse of Rome, Montesquieu's analysis is on the whole grounded in an analysis of the relationship between the specific forms of government and the social structure of Rome. Hence it provides for a critical understanding of the nature of the Roman society and its transition from Monarchy, to Republic, to Empire, and ultimately collapse. There is nothing flattering or glorifying in Montesquieu's portrait of Roman society.

In *Grandeur and Declension*, Montesquieu (1721) begins by attributing the greatness of Rome to the greatness of its leading men. However, he then makes the interesting statement that humans create political systems by design, but that once created, these systems create individuals (p. 3). There is a strong aspect of structural determinism in Montesquieu's writings. Montesquieu paints a picture of Rome, not so much as a society, but as a vast machine organized for warfare and plunder. The relative success of Rome in Montesquieu's view was due to its warlike organization, its ability to copy the technology of other societies and to adopt their techniques in ways that neutralized their opponents' attacks against Rome's potential weaknesses. The strategy of Rome according to Montesquieu was not always to directly conquer outright, but in multiple instances to draw other civilizations into its orbit and slowly reduce their independence.

The demise of the Common Wealth was an inevitable outcome of the structure of Rome's institutions, as was the fall of the Roman Empire in the West. Rome was founded as a Monarchy but the power of the people was increased at the expense of the monarchs. The monarchs were expelled and Rome became a Common Wealth. However, the institutional structure of the Common Wealth inevitably led to its corruption and transformation into despotism and Empire. The ultimate fall of the Western Empire was due to the gradual decline of central power, the inability of the barbarians to enter the East, a tacit alliance between the Barbarians and the Eastern Empire, and the power of the barbarian tribes to whom land had been ceded. While this is not necessarily an economic (in the narrow sense of the term) explanation for the decline of Rome, it is nevertheless a material explanation.

In contrast to Althusser, my critique of Montesquieu centers on three points. Firstly, in maintaining the concept of a social contract and a state of nature, Montesquieu perpetuates the myth of society as "unnatural" and of humans as asocial. This is reflected in his argument that there is no government in the state of Savagery. This is contradictory to his argument that humans are by nature formed to live in society. Secondly, in positing his stage theory as both synchronic and diachronic, he can offer no explanation for the failure of some societies to develop into subsequent stages other than geographical determinism. And again, in some instances, his theories of the impact of climate are simply absurd. Nevertheless, the basic point that ecology and demographics play a role in shaping social forms and hence politics and the law, is an important insight in Montesquieu's writings. Furthermore, Montesquieu's treatment of the issue of corruption does serve to illustrate that social evolution is not always an upwards march of progress and that social retrogression is always a possibility. On the other hand, a theory of corruption is not the same as a theory of evolution, regardless of whether or not social evolution entails progress. Thirdly, while Montesquieu addresses the role of structure in shaping human action, he lacks a coherent theory of agency, primarily relegating it to those circumstances in which institutions are initially created. Hence, he tends to lapse into "great man" explanations. Yet I agree with Meek that Montesquieu deserves credit for positing a general materialist theory of social evolution and for setting the stage for subsequent discussion. In addition, he draws the relationship between this process and Political Economy.

Philosophical History and Political Economy in the Scottish and French Enlightenment

Overview

Where Hobbes had labeled the study of society as Civil Philosophy, in the Scottish Enlightenment, the application of Philosophy to the study of society was referred to as Moral Philosophy. Regardless of the label, the scope of the subject was the same. Moral Philosophy was clearly intended as Hume put it, to be a comprehensive theory of man. Hence, multiple Scottish writers sought to answer the question of what set of social arrangements would be most conducive to human well-being. Though this question was one that in their view could be answered empirically, it rested on the normative assumption that human well-being was premised on liberty and material prosperity. The result was an empirically grounded "moral philosophy" that incorporated all of the contemporary social sciences under one general umbrella and provided a theory of social evolution that was grounded in empirical inquiry.[1]

Hutcheson, Ferguson and Hume

Francis Hutcheson's writings set the tone for later developments in Moral Philosophy. Moral philosophy in the view of Hutcheson must be "one of those commanding arts" (1747, p. 180) that tells us how to pursue the other arts. Hutcheson defines those things that promote happiness as good, and those that promote misery, evil. Our initial ideas of good and evil arise from our experiences (1747, p. 181). But Hutcheson also argued that humans are constituted in a certain way and that happiness depends on living in that way. Furthermore, a benevolent Deity would have ordered the world in such a fashion (p. 188). Later, Hutcheson addresses the source of our feelings of goodwill toward our fellow human beings, locating that in our capacity for empathy, a position also taken by Hume and Smith. In sum, Hutcheson synthesized Aristotle's views on ethics with Utilitarianism. Though Hutcheson might be thought of as an Empiricist, he is not necessarily inconsistent with Reid's argument that people have an innate moral sense, a capacity for individual moral choice and a more general rationality through which to shape laws in general (Reid 1788, p. 1). The idea that humans have an innate moral sense is prevalent throughout the writers in the Scottish Enlightenment.

Nevertheless, Hutcheson maintained aspects of Social Contract Theory in his approach. He also rejected the idea that the origins of the State lie in violence. As I discuss below, later writers in the Scottish Enlightenment rejected the idea of a social contract. Furthermore, the idea that the origins of the State were in violence was similarly prominent. Nevertheless, with the exception of Millar (1771), most writers in the Scottish Enlightenment, by stressing the importance of habit and custom in addition to pure reason, tended toward conservatism in the sense of stressing the need to maintain established institutions, absent compelling reasons to reform them.

The rejection of the concept of a social contract is prominent in Ferguson's (1767) essay on the *History of Civil Society*. Whether or not Ferguson's arguments were intended to be specifically directed at Hobbes, the essay is clearly anti-Hobbesian in structure and tone. Ferguson opens his essay with a critique of the concept of a state of nature as well as the tendency of social contract theorists to generalize on the basis of a few ad hoc generalizations. Instead, Ferguson argues, as in all other areas of inquiry, we should form our views of general human characteristics by a careful investigation of facts. After tracing through the progression of societies in different stages, Ferguson argues that political establishments emerge naturally on the basis of human beings to herd together (p. 204). Moreover, Ferguson notes, human action often has unintended and unforeseen consequence (p. 206). Like multiple other writers in the Enlightenment, Ferguson (1857) also addresses the causes and consequences of the collapse of Roman authority in the West, an issue which I will address further in relation to others below.

Similarly, David Hume's (1778) *History of England* emphasized the turbulent and violent character of English history while at the same time his criticisms of the demands of Parliament during the English Civil War often led to his being accused of advocating Monarchism. The view of the State as arising in violence but persisting on the basis of custom and habit is prevalent throughout his *Essays on Morals* (1777a) but stated succinctly and explicitly in his essay "On the Origin of Government" (Book V). Morality, in Hume's view, is a combination of instinct, experience and social duty. It is solidified via social habit. Hume specifically rejects a contractual origin for the State as not justified by actual historical experience. The State arises in Hume's view out of chieftainship and is established by violence and gives rise to a shared social habit of obedience to the State. Though Hume's argument could be interpreted as a critique not only of the origins of the English State but indeed of all states, Hume's emphasis on the importance of social habit leads him (as well as many in the Scottish

Enlightenment) to argue for the preservation of social habits. Thus, in Hume's view, we should obey the sovereign because the results are otherwise disastrous, an argument, that in some respects, echoes Hobbes, but from a different foundation. Hume's skepticism of unbridled power, however, is clear in his Essay on the Perfect Common Wealth (1777c).

A further point that should be noted is that in general, following Montesquieu, Hume and other Scottish Enlightenment theorists drew a general connection between the spread of commerce and the establishment of a government based on laws. The general preference was for Constitutional Monarchy and separation of powers, a view that of course exerted significant influence on the founders of the American Republic (Hume 1777c). The connection between the economic and political is pervasive though it remains a matter of dispute as to how much they ascribed causal influence from the economic to the political (Meek 1976; Winch 1978, chapters 1 and 4). Hume in particular wrote extensively on issues related to political economy but due to space constraints, I will not pursue that issue herein but will instead focus a bit later on Smith's contributions. Before turning to my discussion of Smith, however, I will first address the centrality of the development and application of an explicitly historical sociology, or as it was termed then, "Philosophical History". In this regard, the contributions of Johnathan Millar and of William Robertson are of particular importance.

Smith's Stage Theory in Millar's Writings

The use of the historical and comparative method was central to the Scottish Enlightenment's understanding of Moral Philosophy. As noted above, Montesquieu had laid the foundations for a theory of variation and change over time in human social organization in relation to ecological, demographic and technological features of society. Not surprisingly, the influence of Montesquieu on the writings of Scottish Enlightenment philosophers was pervasive even as they developed Montesquieu's basic three-stage classification of societies further by adding a fourth stage, that of commercial society. Again, whether this is an addition or a clarification, can be disputed. This connection Montesquieu and the Scottish Enlightenment has been addressed extensively by Meek. Meek (1976, chapter 1) argues convincingly that the articulation of the four-stage theory originated with Smith's Lectures on Jurisprudence, rather than with Millar. Though as I discuss below, Smith integrates the theory into his work, Millar's treatment is nevertheless instructive due to his comprehensive development of it.

In the preface to his original version of *The Origin of the Distinction of Ranks*, Millar (1771) asserts that there is a general uniformity to human nature, but that the differences in social characteristics are due to the influence of society and its institutions. We can only understand human nature and the differences in human conduct Millar argues by "real experiments, not by abstracted metaphysical theories". Millar recognizes the impossibility of conducting actual experiments in human societies but in his view this does not preclude the use of the experimental method. As he notes:

> It is therefore by a comparison only of the ideas and the practice of different nations, that we can arrive at the knowledge of those rules of conduct, which, independent of all positive institutions, are consistent with propriety, and agreeable to the sense of justice.
>
> (p. 287)

Again, we should take note that as was generally the case in the Scottish Enlightenment, Millar has a normative theory about rights, justice and liberty, but views the analysis of the evolution of the above to be an empirical undertaking. Justice in Millar's view is refraining from harm and correcting harm. Beneficence was based on empathy. Justice could be achieved and compelled, while Beneficence could not. Though his schema is implicitly critical of social hierarchy, his primary objection is to unearned privilege and servitude, not to inequalities of wealth per se. That noted, Liberty is central to Millar's scheme. His own politics were strongly Whig. He was supportive of the cause of the American colonists, among the most vocal critics of slavery and similarly one of the few defenders of the ideals of the French Revolution, in contrast to more conservative figures such as Burke. Millar also viewed the creation and evolution of rights as evolving in the context of a social framework: in other words, the proper system of laws was instrumental in Millar's view to the realization of Liberty.[2]

In the body of his work Millar traces the rise of social hierarchy by placing societies in a progressive technological sequence of hunting, pastoralism, agriculture and commercialism which overlap the social organizational stages of savagery, barbarism and civilization. These stages in Millar's view are universal. Millar's stage theory is intended to be generally descriptive of the normal case of social evolution, though in his view all societies in existence had passed through the stages of savagery and barbarism. While existing savage and barbaric societies were similar in organization to the earlier stages of contemporary civilizations, Millar did not necessarily see them as mere atavisms. Social Evolution, in Millar's view, or the lack thereof, was dependent on multiple factors (p. 64). Notably, Millar placed significant emphasis on the influence of laws and customs, rather than climate, in determining levels of development. Thus, in Millar's view, it was possible to draw on data from existing societies as one source of evidence of the social organization of contemporary civilizations.

As was pervasive in the Enlightenment, Millar looks to the state of indigenous American tribes as a model of "Savagery" and to contemporary herding societies, such as the Tatars and Arabs as exemplars of the stage of

Barbarism. Unfortunately, Millar's data was not based on careful, ethnographic study of non-European societies and in multiple cases expresses the clear biases characteristic of Europeans of the era. That noted, in his treatment of sources, Millar endeavors to weed out the fantastical from the reliable and warns against associating values with the terms "Savage" and "Barbarian". Furthermore, he notes that modern civilized societies can also be savage and barbaric. It is necessary in Millar's view to weigh the virtues and benefits to humans of subsequent stages. As with others in the Scottish Enlightenment, Millar's view is clearly progressivist: on balance, he views the Commercial stage of society as the best for human beings.

In the earliest stage of savagery Millar asserts that societies are egalitarian, have no concept of private property and though there is a lack of emotional bond between the sexes, there is nevertheless a rough equality between the two. Millar traces the rise of formal social hierarchies to the rise of storable wealth and barbarism, which also leads initially to a diminution in the status of women. The origin of formal states in Millar's view lies in the extended family or clan. Thus, the institution of the chief increasingly gives rise to the institution of the monarch as society becomes more complex and the chief becomes more powerful. The power of the monarch however in Millar's view is often more limited than many might suppose as Monarchs are subject to councils that have their roots in tribal councils and laid the basis for the later rise of Parliaments in European history.

Like multiple other Europeans of his day, Millar provides special attention to Roman history and to the collapse of the Roman Empire. In doing so, he provides a similar schema to that of some contemporary historians in trading the passage from the world of the Roman Empire to the rise of the feudal system in Europe. Millar's definition of feudalism is political: he identifies it with the institution of vassalage and the holding of land on condition of military service due to the relative weakness of the King. Feudalism in Millar's view is not uniquely European but exists in multiple times and places. Millar also notes how the rise of feudalism in the political sense was tied to the institution of serfdom, a form of labor that Millar considered to be only slightly better than slavery. This system gradually broke down due to the establishment of towns and cities and the spread of commerce. Though initially this was tied to the increasing power of the Monarch vis-à-vis the nobility, it also aided with the accumulation of wealth. In turn, the accumulation of wealth raised the demand for labor, providing incentives for the ending of servile obligations and the rise of various forms of cash tenancy and sharecropping, and ultimately, to free labor. Like other writers of the Scottish Enlightenment, Millar argues that commerce and the spread of wealth are conducive to the spread of liberty, as it undermines the servile relationships of vassalage and serfdom. These ideas of course, form the backbone of a considerable part of Smith's argument in *The Wealth of Nations.*

Robertson's Application

While Millar's history is in a sense speculative and general, others, such as Robertson (1740a, 1740b), applied the comparative and historical method to address the origins and functioning of the emerging nation-state system and the relations of European powers to their colonies. This approach to history, including the concrete problems of state formation and the evolution of the international system, had been pioneered by Voltaire (1751) in his *History of Louis XIV.* Robertson's work is particularly instructive, given the fashion in which it addresses multiple issues of contemporary concern such as the origin and evolution of the nation-state system, the rise of feudalism and its eventual transformation. Robertson begins his multi-volume work with an extensive history of the decline of the Roman Empire and the evolution of the feudal system (1840a). The vehicle that Robertson used to advance his arguments is a multi-volume analysis of Charles I of Spain (1840b), also known as Charles V in his capacity as Holy Roman Emperor. The goal of Charles V according to Millar was to create a unified, European Empire, an endeavor which ultimately failed. In addressing this issue, Robertson places the coronation and later acts of Charles V in the context of a broader comparative history.

The problem faced by Charles V, as well as other early modern European Monarchs, is that of curtailing the power of the nobility, unifying a defined geographical area, creating and paying for a standing army and projecting power against other Monarchs. Robertson's portrait of Charles V is sympathetic though Robertson notes his ultimate failure due to the similar abilities and powers of other early modern European monarchs. The failure of Charles V is in Robertson's view a product of overambition and overextension of power.

In analyzing the efforts of Charles V to unify Europe, Robertson addresses the emergence of Spain's colonial relationship with the Americas. As with Millar, much of Robertson's portrait of most of the Americas, with the exception of the Aztecs and Incas, as dominated by hunting societies with limited development of agriculture is now known to be inaccurate. These inaccuracies, though clearly reflective of European ethnocentric biases, are owed to the paucity of Robertson's sources. Robertson's analysis of the impact of Spanish colonialism on indigenous societies pays significant attention to the deliberate efforts of Spanish settlers to enslave the indigenous Americans and describes a practice of genocide and environmental destruction. However, Robertson does not attribute this to conscious, deliberate policies by the Spanish Crown, but rather to the inability of the Spanish Crown to reign in its colonial subjects. Unfortunately, in his discussion of English Colonialism, Robertson is generally apologetic for English policies.

The preceding discussion should serve to illustrate that regardless of its specific shortcomings, the Scottish Enlightenment established Moral

Philosophy as a comprehensive social science or as Hume termed it as a "Science of Man", with the ultimate goal of attempting to answer, via the process of empirical inquiry, what would lead to the greatest state of happiness for humans. The conclusion reached was that generally, humans were made happiest by the combination of wealth and liberty. This leads to the practical question of what a Sovereign can do to promote both wealth and liberty, a question which is addressed via Political Economy. Though there were multiple contributors to Political Economy other than Adam Smith, we have come to regard Smith's contributions as the most systematic and thorough. Of particular note is the close connection in Smith between Evolutionary Social Theory and his Political Economy.

Adam Smith

The topic of *The Wealth of Nations* is the causes of the progress, or lack thereof, of opulence (or wealth) and the relationship of opulence to issues of Liberty and Justice (Winch 1978, 1992). Though the work is generally regarded as a treatise on Political Economy, Smith (1776) actually uses the term only twice: in his introduction (p. 3) and at the beginning of Book IV in Volume 1 (p. 395). Smith defines Political Economy as follows:

> Political Economy, as a branch of the science of a statesman or legislator proposes two distinct objects. The first object of political economy is to provide a plentiful revenue or subsistence for the people, or more properly to enable them to provide such a revenue or subsistence for themselves; and secondly, to supply the state or commonwealth with a revenue sufficient for the public services. It proposes to enrich both the people and the sovereign.
>
> (Volume I, p. 395)

Defined in this fashion, Political Economy is both normative and an art. What underlies this art however is a detailed, empirical analysis which is grounded in the historical and comparative method. In other words, following Meek, I agree that Smith's Political Economy is derived from his theory of social evolution. However, Meek identifies Smith's Political Economy primarily with theories of value and distribution, which while of obvious importance to Smith, are not the sum total of his political economy. In inquiring into the causes of opulence Smith divides the work into five books, each of which treats a specific topic that is of relevance to the others (the division of labor, the accumulation of capital stock, the policy of Europe with respect to commerce, systems of Political Economy and revenue and expenditures of government).

In Volume I, Book 1, Smith begins by providing a description of the division of labor in the nascent industrial system of the commercial society of his day. Though Smith's arguments are often held to depend on the analysis of exchange rather than on production, Smith's description links the two together. Specialization and division of labor lead to an augmentation of the productivity of labor, hence increasing the total output of society. As an illustration of the concept, he first addresses the division of labor in a specific productive unit, where he provides his famous example of the pin factory. He then proceeds to explain how the division of labor functions in society as a whole. In the civilized state of society, production is too complex to be organized under one roof and consequently, coordination must take place amongst different productive units based on specialization and division of labor.

Specialization and division of labor in Smith's view increase as society become more complex and the market becomes more extensive (Volume I, Book I.2). Smith then traces the historical evolution of the division of labor through the four different stages of human history. He begins by asserting that humans in all societies have an innate propensity to truck, barter and exchange, and that these exchanges are based on voluntary self-interest, rather than beneficence. People engage in exchanges because such exchanges will allow them to enjoy more than they could if they relied only on themselves. The division of labor, and particularly its coordination function in society distinguishes humans from animals and begins with the rise of reason and language.

This raises two interesting questions about Smith. One, is Smith positing a universal homo economicus? Two, is he abandoning his emphasis in *The Theory of Moral Sentiments* (1759) on beneficence? Answering these two questions requires a short digression. In both cases, in my view, the answer is no. In Volume II.V.1.1 Smith presents a different picture of the coordination of production and exchange in Savage and Barbarous societies than he does in Volume I, Book I. He notes that in such societies all men are both hunters or shepherds and warriors. He also describes the communal organization of production in such societies. Nor does he limit the circulation of goods only to barter but notes elsewhere the pattern of what contemporary anthropologists term reciprocity, redistribution and tribute in such societies, though he does not use these terms (II.V.I.2).

Similarly, like other philosophers of the Scottish Enlightenment, Smith's enthusiasm for the division of labor is tempered. Toward the end of *The Wealth of Nations* (Volume II, Book V, Art III. Part 2) in his discussion on education, Smith argues that the division of labor destroys the intellectual, social and martial virtues (p. 267) unless government undertakes efforts to remedy these effects. This state, Smith argues, is characteristic of the laboring class in civilized societies. Hence, Smith argues, there is a need for the State to attend to their education (269). The division of labor is therefore not without its costs to society, but it is an ill that can be ameliorated and in Smith's view, the benefits from the division of labor are substantial.

Like other prominent figures in the Scottish Enlightenment, Smith derives his understanding of ethics from an empirical and sensualist base in which moral principles are derived from empathy as well as innate moral sense, a view that is consistent with those of Reid. As is well known, in *The Theory of Moral Sentiments* Smith emphasized the importance of benevolence. Furthermore, he noted that our tendency to admire and emulate the wealthy lessens our sense of empathy. But he had also argued that we should not force people to be benevolent and hence could not base justice on an expectation of benevolence. Hence Smith's emphasis on our inability to depend on the benevolence of our fellow humans to supply our wants and needs, but instead on the necessity to look to self-interest is not inconsistent with Smith's view of human nature articulated in *The Theory of Moral Sentiments.* In addition, in Smith's view, basing Justice on an expectation of benevolence also leads to subservience. This interpretation is notably supported by Donald Winch (1978).

Nor is Smith blind to the potential pitfalls of untrammeled selfishness. Smith does not posit self-interest as a search to gain an unfair advantage over our fellow human beings. In his much later passage in Book IV, Chapter 2, as well as elsewhere, Smith excoriates the search for monopolies and special privileges on the part of merchants. Hence self-interest, at least under conditions of fair competition, operates in Smith's view as a search for what is normal. For Smith, normal is defined at least in part by habit and custom, even if in the last instance it depends on the cost of production. It is in this context that Smith asserts that the pursuit of self-interest, rather than consciously trying to sell or trade in the public interest, will promote the wealth of society.

> But the annual revenue of every society is always precisely equal to the exchangeable value of the whole annual produce of its industry, or rather is precisely the same thing with that exchangeable value. As every individual, therefore, endeavours as much as he can both to employ his capital in the support of domestic industry, and so to direct that industry that its produce may be of the greatest value; every individual necessarily labours to render the annual revenue of the society as great as he can. He generally, indeed, neither intends to promote the public interest, nor knows how much he is promoting it. By preferring the support of domestic to that of foreign industry, he intends only his own security; and by directing that industry in such a manner as its produce may be of the greatest value, he intends only his own gain, and he is in this, as in many other cases, led by an invisible hand to promote an end which was no part of his intention. Nor is it always the worse for the society that it was no part of it. By pursuing his own interest he frequently promotes that of the society more effectually than when he really intends to promote it. I have never known much good done by those who affected to trade for the public good. It is an affectation, indeed, not very common among merchants, and very few words need be employed in dissuading them from it.
>
> (Volume I, p. 421)

Having defined the principle underlying the division of labor, Smith then traces the evolution of money, including the various commodities used as money through the stages of increasing complexity and division of labor in Book V. Money, in the form of coinage, arises during the stage of civilization, defined by settled agriculture, urban artisan production and extensive commerce, due to the need for a universal medium of exchange and requires state coordination. Yet money prices in Smith's view are not real. Smith then argues that the only invariant standard of value is labor. Hence the price of commodities, over the long run, will converge to rough labor equivalents, even as prices in the short run may diverge from labor values.

This leads us to another question about Smith. Is his theory of value a reversion to a natural law theory of value, as Veblen was to argue over a century later? In my estimation, this is a misunderstanding of Smith. In the rude state of society, according to Smith, prior to the rise of a capital stock, labor receives the full value of its produce. However, as soon as capital stock and later private property in land appear over the course of history in the context of what Smith terms an improved society, the price of a commodity must divide into the wages of the worker, the profits of the owner of the capital stock and the rent of the land. This price in turn can be decomposed into the amount of labor expended by the owners of each resource. In the process of the progress of manufacture Smith tells us some commodities will incorporate only wages and profits, but over the general course of improvement, a considerable portion of annual income will be devoted to maintaining the idle (Vol. I, p. 57). In the next section, Smith explains that the normal, or customary price will be equivalent to these three components.

In stressing this aspect, Smith is not, in my estimation proposing the existence of equilibrium or market clearing prices per se. Rather, as habit and custom arise out of our general sense of what is necessary for maintenance and people are unlikely to sell below what is necessary, prices will consequently tend to converge to labor equivalents. It is important to note that Smith is not just providing us with history, he is placing the determination of relative prices and relative shares in the context of historical sociology in which social groups emerge with distinctive roles and in which rewards are largely determined by this social role. Smith's view was that in the absence of restrictions that created domestic monopolies, the well-being of all social groups, aside from merchants protected by domestic monopolies, would improve. Similarly, since rewards would be determined via competition, such a system, were it to exist, could be considered fair. Smith is not defending the existing distribution of wealth.

Smith then turns to explain what he terms "the policy of Europe", by which he means the favoring of commerce and cities over the towns. He applies the four-stage theory of hunting, pastoralism, farming and commerce to explain his views on the increasing complexity of social organization and the course of European social and economic development.

Based on his understanding of history, Smith argued that the normal progression was for improvement to take place in agriculture first and then lead to improvement in commerce and industry. However, Europe's progress had departed in part from this natural or normal sequence due to the collapse of Roman authority and the feudal system. This created a system of servile relationships between nobles and monarchs, and peasants and nobles. The creation of towns and commerce provided an area of freedom and the growth of towns and commerce gradually eroded the nature of servile relationships. Hence commerce in Smith's view on the whole led to increasing liberty, though again, Smith noted that increasing specialization and division of labor could lead to a diminution in people's overall quality of life. This reversal in European history actually slowed the progress of increasing the productive capacity of European society. On that basis, Smith concludes that efforts to actively promote industry and place restrictions on commerce would inhibit progress.

It is not until Book IV that Smith directly addresses the topic of systems of Political Economy, directly which he divides into two camps: "the system of commerce, the other, the system of agriculture", or in other words, the two schools conventionally referred to as Mercantilism and Physiocracy. Smith critiques the advocates of the Mercantile System (see also, Rima 2009, chapters 2 and 3) for equating the wealth of a nation with money. In contrast, Smith defines wealth by what today we term per capita GDP. Hence the wealth of a nation is determined by the productive capacity of the country, which in turn is a function of the productivity of labor, which is determined by capital, specialization and division of labor. Smith traces the evolution of mercantile legislation throughout Europe, with primary emphasis on England, as arising due to the arguments of the merchants, which he labels as partly solid in arguing for the free export of gold and silver, but as sophistical for arguing that governments needed to take active steps to augment the inflows of gold and silver and that the high price of foreign exchange led to an unfavorable balance of trade (p. 400). Over time Smith argues, merchants adopted Munn's argument that the promotion of exports and discouragement of imports would lead to favorable flows of gold and silver. This system in Smith's view had led to a situation that created domestic monopolies which benefited the merchants but actually depressed domestic consumption.

Smith's attack on the Mercantile system is an attack both on the existing set of policies as well as the intellectual foundations of those policies, which Smith regards as fallacious. In Smith's view the entire system of State-sponsored trading companies such as the East India companies of England and Holland, efforts to direct and control trade, restrictions on entry into professions—in sum the whole system of what Smith viewed as a directed effort to promote large merchants and industrialization over the interests of small merchants, rising industrialists and laborers—had restricted the creation of wealth. Similarly, Smith also critiques the colonial system. He notes that the colonial system had created wealth for particular individuals and that much of this wealth had been directed back to the colonial powers while at the same time, impoverishing many of those areas that had been colonized. This colonial system in Smith's view was an extension of the Mercantile system. Though this whole structure had been accompanied by an era of improvement of wealth in Europe, in Smith's view, wealth creation would have been greater and more evenly shared in the absence of this system. Smith repeats these points in Volume II, Book 5 when he attacks the costs of state subsidies to joint stock companies.

In his discussion of the Physiocrats, Smith begins by critiquing the mercantilist policies of Colbert for favoring industrial development over agriculture and for supporting a system which prevented free domestic trade in grain. The result was to depress the overall productivity of French agriculture. Smith then outlines the system of the Physiocrats which he argues has done no actual harm since it has never been adopted and is unlikely to ever be adopted. He then outlines the Physiocratic doctrine. The Physiocrats had held that agriculture produced a return over and above that necessary for its maintenance, while manufacturing and commerce were barren, as they only produced sufficient revenue to replace the underlying costs of reproduction. However, the Physiocrats also held that specialization and division of labor enabled the rural sector to purchase needed goods from the industrial sector and to be more productive by focusing on cultivation. Hence, the Physiocrats opposed the system of Colbert which had favored industry over agriculture and argued for a system of free trade, or "laissez faire".

Smith's critique took aim at the Physiocratic assertion that only peasants and landlords engaged in productive labor and that agriculture was the sole source of wealth. Smith argued in contrast that industry was capable of producing a surplus and he generally regarded landlords and servants as unproductive, and manufacturers and laborers as productive. Nevertheless, on the whole, Smith was favorable to the Physiocrats program and there are clear Physiocratic influences on Smith.

Smith then engages in a historical and comparative study of the impact of policies that have favored agriculture over the industry. His analysis of India and China is on the whole, favorable to these societies in that he recognizes the productive accomplishments and comparative levels of development. He is critical of the policies of the Ancient Greeks and Romans which depressed industry and notes that slavery is an impediment to technological progress. Smith argues that these societies could benefit from freer trade, which would lead to greater improvement in manufacturing. Efforts to favor one area over another however Smith argues ultimately lead to a depression of conditions. The solution for Smith is for the State to confine itself to national defense, the promotion of public works and the administration of Justice.

In Book V Smith addresses the issue of government revenues and expenditures, and again, compares and contrasts the needs of different forms of social organization. Smith traces the process of changes in societal organization and its impact on the ability of a society to fight and fund wars. Smith provides a trenchant analysis of the rise of nation states and the growth of standing armies. In his analysis of the relationship of State societies to societies of Hunters and Barbarians, Smith notes that in general, State societies have an advantage with respect to these societies, in large part due to the ability of such societies to benefit from the division of labor and have a specialized class of soldiers. The exception of course was that prior to the creation of modern (to Smith's era) standing professional militaries armed with firearms, pastoralists did on occasion overcome and conquer state societies.

But the rise of the State in Smith's view was also negative. The growing complexity and wealth of society along with an increasing division of labor requires greater state outlays and increases in state financing, leading in turn to a greater ability of a state to project power. The state, in Smith's view, arises on the basis of property and inequality. Smith argues that there are four sources of inequality, personal inequality, age, fortune and distinctions of birth. Smith attributes the greatest difference to the latter two and traces the origin of the State to the rise of inequality amongst shepherds. The State, according to Smith, exists primarily to protect property.

> Civil government, so far as it is instituted for the security of property, is in reality instituted for the defence of the rich against the poor, or of those who have some property against those who have none at all. (Volume II, p. 207)

Smith's arguments in *The Wealth of Nations*, as with others in the Scottish Enlightenment, provide us with a concrete, empirical, historical and comparative analysis of the problems related to social organization in the 18th century. Though the issues of valuation and of state policy are not neglected in others, Smith provides us with the most rigorous treatment of these issues. But Political Economy is derivative of Evolutionary Social Theory. This approach was not confined to the Scottish Enlightenment but was also prevalent in France.

Turgot and Political Economy

Where Voltaire's *History of Louis the XIV* is specific, Turgot's contributions to history echo the efforts in Scotland at writing a comprehensive universal history of human societies and tying that to a theory of political economy. It is likely that Turgot exerted some influence on Smith, and vice versa. However, Turgot's efforts at a universal history remained relatively undeveloped and incomplete. Consequently, his works in this area don't really add to the preceding discussion of the four-stage theory. In contrast, his views on Political Economy, while reflective to some extent of Physiocratic doctrine, are in multiple respects, quite illuminating and as in the case of Smith, are derived from his broader theory of social evolution. Consequently, in spite of their incomplete and speculative nature, Turgot's views on societal evolution are worthy of brief discussion for that reason alone. In addition, Turgot's contributions also set the stage for the development of similar ideas later in France by Condorcet and also by Comte in the 19th century.

Turgot's first effort at a universal history was his *Philosophical Review of Successive Advances of the Human Mind* (1750a). That work was never completed. His second work *On Universal History* (1750b) is also relatively abbreviated. In *Universal History*, Turgot, following Montesquieu provides a sketch of how geography, climate and modes of subsistence set the parameters of systems of government. Both *Universal History* and *Advances* stress the role of intellectual progress as well as progress in the arts in general. Both works, it should also be noted, in contrast to Voltaire's willingness to challenge some conventional European tropes, suffer from an uncritical reliance on standard European self-portraits as free and distinctive from Eastern despotism, as well as from Biblical Literalism.

In contrast, his major work on Political Economy (1766), *The Formation and Distribution of Wealth* tie Turgot's theory of history and his analysis of commercial society together. After tracing through the development of Agriculture, Turgot provides an analysis of changes in the class structure of Agrarian society. Though the analysis is articulated as a structural-comparative argument, the sequence in which he treats its development is clearly historical. He begins with wage labor and then successively analyses slavery, serfdom, sharecropping, renting and entrepreneurial farming, and analyses these forms of rural social organization in relation to his theories of rent and value.

Whether Turgot can be classified as a Physiocrat can be debated, but there are clear areas of overlap between Turgot and the Physiocrats. He argues that all value ultimately derives from land. Landlords, in Turgot's view, live off the bounty of nature as the peasant is paid in some form a sufficient amount to allow the peasant to reproduce, after paying advances and other expenses. The rest goes to the landlord. This agricultural surplus then provides for the greater specialization and division of labor which allows for the development of both commerce and industry. Turgot does not tell us directly that peasants are exploited, but the implication can easily be drawn from a reading of Turgot. Turgot then proceeds to provide a fairly cogent analysis of capitalist production, which he ties to a theory of money, credit and capital accumulation. Whether Turgot regards workers as exploited is not clear, since technically, neither workers nor capitalists produce value, but rather produce commodities whose value is ultimately tied back to a specific unit of land. The produce of agriculture, expressed in monetary terms, provides a fund for advances that the capitalist can use to organize production.

The parallels between Smith and Turgot are obviously striking, in spite of their different views on value. Both provide a history of the rise of Capitalism and both provide an analysis of nascent Capitalism, though neither clearly distinguishes Capitalism as a stage that is subsequent to the era of Commercialism. Both identify the system of mercantile privileges enforced by the State as an obstacle to progress. Turgot actively sought to reform the French taxation system as well as the system of land tenure in France in a direction that would have promoted freer commerce as well as stimulated agricultural productivity. In that sense, Turgot shared with Voltaire the tendency to curry favor with absolutist monarchs as a means of enacting their envisioned reforms. In contrast to Voltaire, Turgot sought to reverse the mercantilist policies engaged in by the predecessors of Louis XVI. Yet these very reforms could be argued to illustrate the problems inherent in the theory of laissez faire. It was the breaking down of internal barriers to trade in agricultural markets that was to lay the basis for the creation of famine and general social conditions that led to the French Revolution.

Condorcet's Revolutionary Evolutionism

Even prior to the French Revolution, British writers for the most part, with the exception of Millar, were generally conservative in their approach to the maintenance of established institutions, a conservatism that is echoed in the contributions of Voltaire and Turgot and their tendency to curry favor with Absolutist Monarchs. However, other French writers, such as Helvetius and others combined the revolutionary zeal of Rousseau, with the concrete empirical approach of the previous writers. I will focus in this chapter on the contributions of the Marquis de Condorcet, and his expression of the Enlightenment ideal of progress culminating in the perfectibility of humanity. In the subsequent chapter, I will address the response to Condorcet by Malthus. Condorcet's dedication to liberty, his opposition to the terror of the French Revolution, his opposition to slavery and his support of early feminist contributions, on the whole, place Condorcet on the side of those whose views were sharply critical of invidious distinctions.

In his *Outlines of an Historical View of the Progress of the Human Mind*, Condorcet (1796) provides a sweeping vision of human history, which builds on the previous contributions of Turgot. The goal of his *Outline* is to demonstrate that there are no limits to what humans can accomplish through the growth of the mind and its application to human improvement via technological and social improvement. In his introduction, Condorcet provides an overview of the nature of the human mind. Following Locke and Hume he asserts that knowledge arises from experience. The capacity of the human mind to reason develops from childhood to adulthood and through interaction with other human beings through language. Having defined the nature of the human mind, Condorcet then sets out to provide a history of the development of the human mind. In doing so, he tends, as do many later writers in the 19th century, to equate the biological evolution of the human mind with the evolution of society. Condorcet's writings pre-date the explicitly biological evolutionary theory of Lamarck in biology by less than two decades and his position on the development of the human mind bears a striking resemblance to later Lamarckian interpretations.

Though Condorcet has ten, instead of four, stages, there are strong parallels between his schema and that of Turgot and the stage theorists in the Scottish Enlightenment. Again, Condorcet does not begin with a state of nature. He posits that the first human societies were based on the family which either by a natural increase in population or combination grew into the horde. Custom and tradition, rather than formal law defined this stage of society. The technology of production during this stage was limited primarily to hunting, gathering and fishing and the cultivation of a few plants. As people developed an attachment to the horde, they also increasingly defined the identity of their own horde in opposition to enemy hordes. Governance in this stage was via a tribal council. However, this precluded the participation of women and the requirement of brute strength led to the confinement of women to a status that is equivalent to slavery. This led to warfare and the rise of the institution of the chief. In this stage, some men are more prone to reason than others and discover some useful knowledge but this knowledge is also accompanied by superstition and quackery. As society divides into a quasi-priestly class and those who believe the quasi-priestly class, the priestly class uses its authority to manipulate others.

The second stage was pastoralism. The rise of food production allowed for the increasing complexity of human societies and the production of a surplus. This led to the rise of a laboring class, the creation of the institution of slavery via warfare, to the solidification of the authority of the chief, the origins of class society, commerce between groups, a general softening of manners and a small improvement in the status of women. Despite the improvement of technology, political authority and religious authority combined and cemented the power of some people over others. Gradually, the cultivation of plants led to the rise of agriculture. However, some societies, owed in part to climate or the overall ambition of the people failed to develop past this stage.

The third epoch is the epoch of the rise of civilizations and the invention of writing. Society became more complex and stratified, and specialization and division of labor arose. Technological progress led to the rise of metallurgy and other new arts. The status of women continued to improve. Merchants and artisans were now added to the previous classes of owners, domestics and slaves. Formal states arose in towns as powerful chiefs began to call themselves king. Some kings were able to establish their authority despite resistance from others and in addition became tyrants. In some cases, Kings were able to conquer other societies, thus giving rise to empires and the imposition of tribute. At the same time, a new class of nobles arose. Though the origin of priests was in the application of human reason, the priests and their reasoning became essentially corrupt and their practices were oriented toward deceiving people. Some early civilizations, such as China, in Condorcet's view, became stuck in this stage.

Having up to that point focused on the rise of Civilization in a general sense, Condorcet then turns to tracing the history of Europe. Republican forms of government arose in Greece along with the rise of Philosophy and the expansion of the arts. Knowledge and the Sciences generally expanded under the Roman Empire followed by the retrogression of the feudal era. They began to revive again following the Crusades. This revival continued throughout the Renaissance and accelerated after the invention of the printing press at which time humans threw off the yoke of authority. This led to the tremendous expansion of human knowledge during the Enlightenment and gave rise to the French Revolution. The final, or tenth stage is the future of mankind which will be one of constant improvement via the continued growth in the capacity of the human mind.

In summary, there are two, not entirely consistent aspects to Condorcet's scheme. Condorcet advances our understanding of social change through his emphasis on scientific reasoning leading to technological change. However, on this same point, Condorcet lapses into idealism and teleology while at the same time incorporating the error of late 18th-century naturalism to equate social evolution with changes in the human mind itself, rather than stressing the cumulative nature of scientific progress. His schema is primarily a history of ideas and as such is useful. Condorcet and others do not explain how and why this way of thinking came to be more prevalent during this era and it lacks explanatory power with respect to articulating an explanation for changes in the structure of human society. Condorcet's dialectic is between scientific thinking and dogma and superstition. Ultimately, the triumph of the former is pre-ordained and it is on that point that respect Condorcet lapses into teleology.

Conclusion

In assessing the contributions of social theory in the Enlightenment toward a genuine evolutionary analysis, it is possible to point to both areas of shared progress as well as shared failings of multiple theorists. As we have seen, social contract theory provided only a limited understanding of the origins of social institutions, of the mechanisms for change in social institutions, or even of the concrete, practical engagement with the nature of the challenges of the era. In contrast, the Social Newtonism of the Scottish and French Enlightenment, with its empirical, comparative and historical emphasis presented a significant step forward in the development of evolutionary social theory. The chief virtue of this approach was its progress toward developing an early version of evolutionary social theory that was grounded in comparative and historical analysis, though the sources of this analysis were clearly inadequate. By stressing the role of the progress of commerce as peaceful and leading to increased liberty through the dissolution of servile social structures they made initial strides toward a theory, albeit inadequate of the rise of Capitalism. In stressing the importance of Political Economy as an area that was derived from, but nevertheless still informed by an evolutionary theory of society writers such as Smith and Turgot laid the foundations for a later and more extensive theory of the functioning of industrial capitalism. If their contributions on this score were incomplete, we should note that the rise of industrial capitalism was at this point also incomplete. Finally, though their collective methods displayed ethnocentric biases and were in multiple instances apologetic for social hierarchies, that same method could also provide the foundations for a trenchant critique of social hierarchies. All these issues, as I argue in the succeeding chapters, resurfaced in both the 19th and 20th centuries, and continue to be of relevance today. It is to those issues that I now turn.

Notes

1 My interpretation of the Scottish Enlightenment draws on multiple sources, in addition to my own reading of the cited texts. See for example Dow (2002), Rima (2009), and Winch (1978, 1992).

2 See the account of Millar's life by Aaron Garrett in the above cited version of Millar's work a useful summary and overview of the life and social ideas of Millar (pp. 17–64).

References

Althusser, Louis. 1972. *Politics and History: Montesquieu, Rousseau, Hegel and Marx.* Translated by Ben Brewster. London: New Left Books.

Arrighi, Giovanni. 1994. *The Long Twentieth Century: Money, Power and the Origins of Our Times.* New York and London: Verso.

Barrantes, Manuel and Juan M. Duran. 2016. "Thomas Reid on Causation and Scientific Explanation." *Journal of Scottish Philosophy* 14(1), pp. 51–67.

Condorcet, Marquis de and Marie-Jean-Antoine-Nicolas Caritat. 1796. *Outlines of an Historical View of the Progress of the Human Mind, Being a Posthumous Work of the Late M. de Condorcet.* Translated from the French. Philadelphia, PA: M. Carey. https://oll.libertyfund.org/titles/1669

Darwin, John. 2008. *After Tamerlane: The Rise and Fall of Global Empires: 1400–2000.* New York: Bloomsbury Press.

Dow, Sheila. 2002. "Historical Reference: Hume and Critical Realism." *Cambridge Journal of Economics*. 26(6), 683–695.

Eze, Emanuel Chukwudi, ed. 1997. *Race and the Enlightenment: A Reader.* Makon, MA: Blackwell.

Ferguson, Adam. 1767. *An Essay on the History of Civil Society.* Fifth Edition. London: T. Cadell. https://oll-resources.s3.us-east-2.amazonaws.com/oll3/store/titles/1428/1229_Bk.pdf

Ferguson, Adam. 1857. *The History of the Progress and Termination of the Roman Republic.* Philadelphia, PA: Willis P. Hazard.

Hobbes, Thomas. [1651] 1901. *Leviathan.* Oxford: Clarendon Press.

Hume, David. 1777a. "Of the Origins of Government." Pp. 37–41 in *Essays, Moral, Political, Literary,* edited by Eugen F. Miller. Revised Edition. Indianapolis, IN: Liberty Fund.

Hume, David. [1777b] 1992. *Enquiries Concerning the Human Understanding and Concerning the Principles of Morals by David Hume,* edited by L. A. Selby-Bigge, M. A. Second Edition. Oxford: Clarendon Press.

Hume, David. [1777c] 2016. "Idea of a Perfect Commonwealth.". Pp. 521–529 in *Essays, Moral, Political, Literary,* edited by Eugen F. Miller. Revised Edition. Indianapolis, IN: Liberty Fund.

Hume, David. [1777d]. *Dialogues Concerning Natural Religion.* Volume II, Pp. 419–548 in Hume, David. 1828. *The Philosophical Works of David Hume. Including All the Essays, and Exhibiting the More Important Alterations and Corrections in the Successive Editions by the Author.* 4 Volumes. Edinburgh: Adam Black and William Tait, 1826. https://oll.libertyfund.org/title/hume-philosophical-works-of-david-hume

Hume, David. [1778] 1983. *The History of England from the Invasion of Julius Caesar to the Revolution in 1688.* Foreword by William B. Todd, 6 vols. Indianapolis, IN: Liberty Fund.

Hutcheson, Francis. [1747] 2007. *A Short Introduction to Moral Philosophy.* Edited and with an introduction by Luigi Turco. Indianapolis, IN: Liberty Fund.

Kant, Imanuel. [1755] 2008. *Universal Natural History and a Theory of the Heavens. Or, an Essay on the Constitutional and Mechanical Origin of the Entire Structure of the Universe Based on Newtonian Principles.* Translated by Ian Johnston. Arlington, VA: Richer Resources Publications.

Kant, Immanuel. [1781] 1986. *Critique of Pure Reason.* Great Britain: Guernsey Press.

Kant, Immanuel. [1784] 1891. "Idea of a Universal History from a Cosmopolitan Point of View" Pp. 1–30 in Kant, Immanuel. *Kant's Principles of Politics Including his Essay on Perpetual Peace,* edited by Hastie, B. D. Edinburgh: T. and T. Clark.

Kant, Immanuel. [1793a] 1891 "Principles of Political Right" Pp. 31–62 in Kant, Immanuel. *Kant's Principles of Politics Including his Essay on Perpetual Peace,* edited by Hastie, B. D. Edinburgh: T. and T. Clark.

Kant, Immanuel. [1793b] 1891. "The Principle of Progress" Pp. 63–76 in Kant, Immanuel. *Kant's Principles of Politics Including his Essay on Perpetual Peace,* edited by Hastie, B. D. Edinburgh: T. and T. Clark.

Kant, Immanuel. [1795] 1891. "Perpetual Peace" Pp. 77–148 in Kant, Immanuel. *Kant's Principles of Politics Including his Essay on Perpetual Peace,* edited by Hastie, B. D. Edinburgh: T. and T. Clark.

Kant, Immanuel. [1798] 1978. *Anthropology from a Pragmatic Point of View,* edited by Franz Rudnik. Carbondale and Edwardsville: Southern Illinois University Press.

Locke, John. 1689a. *The Works, vol. 1 An Essay Concerning Human Understanding Part 1*. London: Rivington.

Locke, John. 1689b. *Two Treatises of Government; Books I and II*, edited by Thomas Hollis. London: A. Millar et al.

Markie, Peter. 2017. "Rationalism vs. Empiricism." In *The Stanford Encyclopedia of Philosophy*, edited by Edward N. Zalta. Fall 2017 Edition. https://plato.stanford.edu/archives/fall2017/entries/rationalism-empiricism/ accessed on 8/6/2020.

Mayr, Ernst. 1982. *The Growth of Biological Thought. Diversity, Evolution and Inheritance*. Cambride, MA, London: Bellknap Press.

Meek, Ronald L. 1976. *Social Science and the Ignoble Savage*. Cambridge: Cambridge University Press.

Millar, John. [1771] 2006. *The Origin of the Distinction of Ranks; or, An Inquiry into the Circumstances Which Give Rise to Influence and Authority in the Different Members of Society*. Edited and with an Introduction by Aaron Garrett. Indianapolis, IN: Liberty Fund.

Montesquieu, Charles Louis Secondat de la Brede. 1721. *Grandeur and Declension of the Roman Empire*. In Montesquieu, Charles Louis Secondat de la Brede. *The Complete Works of M. de Montesquieu* 4 volumes, Volume 3. London: T. Evans. https://oll.libertyfund.org/title/montesquieu-complete-works-4-vols-1777

Montesquieu, Charles Louis Secondat de la Brede. 1748. *The Spirit of the Laws*. In *The Complete Works of M. de Montesquieu*. 4 volumes, Volumes 1 and 2. London: T. Evans. https://oll.libertyfund.org/title/montesquieu-complete-works-4-vols-1777

Neal, Larry and Rondo Cameron. 2016. *A Concise Economic History of the World. From Paleolithic Times to the Present*. Fifth Edition. New York, Oxford: Oxford University Press, 2016.

Newton, Isaac. [1671] 2017. *A New Theory of Light and Colors*. In the version presented at www.earlymoderntexts.com Johnathan Bennett: https://www.earlymoderntexts.com/assets/pdfs/newton1671.pdf

Newton, Isaac. [1687]. *Principia. The Mathematical Principles of Natural Philosophy*. www.globalgreyebooks.com. Global Grey ebooks, https://www.globalgreyebooks.com/ebooks1/isaac-newton/principia-mathematica/principia-mathematica.pdf accessed on 8/6/2020.

Reid, Thomas. 1764. *An Inquiry into the Human Mind*. In the version presented at www.earlymoderntexts.com, Johnathan Bennett. https://earlymoderntexts.com/authors/reid

Reid, Thomas. 1788a. *Essays on the Intellectual Powers of Man*. In the version presented at www.earlymoderntexts.com, Johnathan Bennett. https://earlymoderntexts.com/authors/reid

Reid, Thomas, 1788b. *Essays on the Active Powers of Man*. In the version presented at www.earlymoderntexts.com, Johnathan Bennett. https://earlymoderntexts.com/authors/reid

Rima, Ingrid. 2009. *Development of Economic Analysis*. Oxon, New York: Routledge, Taylor and Francis.

Robertson, William. 1840a. *A View of the Progress of Society in Europe, from the Subversion of the Roman Empire to the Beginning of the Sixteenth Century* in *Works of William Robertson, D.D. to Which Is Prefixed, an Account of the Life and Writings of the Author, by Dugald Stewart*, 8 volumes. London: T. Cadell. Vol. 3. https://oll.libertyfund.org/titles/2776

Robertson, William. 1840b. *The History of the Reign of the Emperor Charles V, book 1.* in *The Works of William Robertson*. Vol. 3. https://oll.libertyfund.org/titles/2776 accessed on 5/27/2020.

Rousseau, Jean Jacque. 1754. *A Discourse on the Origin of Social Inequality*. Pp. 156–246 in Rousseau, Jean Jacque. 1923. *The Social Contract and Discourses by Jean-Jacques Rousseau*, edited by G. D. H. Cole. London and Toronto, ON: J.M. Dent and Sons. https://oll.libertyfund.org/titles/638 accessed on 8/6/2020

Rousseau, Jean Jacque. 1759. *Discourse on Political Economy*. Pp. 247–287 in Rousseau, Jean Jacque. 1923. *The Social Contract and Discourses by Jean-Jacques Rousseau*, edited by G. D. H. Cole. London and Toronto, ON: J.M. Dent and Sons. https://oll.libertyfund.org/titles/638 accessed on 8/6/2020

Rousseau, Jean Jacque. 1762. *The Social Contract*. Pp. 1–123 in Rousseau, Jean Jacque. 1923. *The Social Contract and Discourses by Jean-Jacques Rousseau*, edited by G. D. H. Cole. London and Toronto, ON: J.M. Dent and Sons. https://oll.libertyfund.org/titles/638 accessed on 8/6/2020

Russell, Bertrand. [1945] 1972. *A History of Western Philosophy*. New York: Touchstone.

Smith, Adam. [1759] 1852. *The Theory of Moral Sentiments and on the Origins of Languages*. Edited with a Biographical and Critical Memoir of the Author, by Dugald Stewart. London: Henry G. Bohn. https://oll.libertyfund.org/titles/2620 Accessed on 8/06/2020. https://www.adamsmith.org/the-theory-of-moral-sentiments

Smith, Adam. [1776] 1904. *An Inquiry into the Nature and Causes of the Wealth of Nations by Adam Smith*. 2 volumes. Edited with an Introduction, Notes, Marginal Summary and an Enlarged Index by Edwin Cannan, London: Methuen. https://oll.libertyfund.org/titles/171

Smith, Alan K. 1991. *Merchant Capital, Colonialism, and World Trade; 1400–1825*. Boulder, CO: Westview Press, 1991.

Sober, Elliot. 2008. "Empiricism." Pp. 129–138 in *The Routledge Companion to the Philosophy of Science*, edited by S. Psillos and M. Curd, 2008. New York: Routledge.

Turgot, Anne Robert Jaques. 1750a. *A Philosophical Review of the Successive Advances of the Human Mind* in Meek, Ronald L. 1973. Ed. *Turgot, On Progress, Sociology and Economics*. Cambridge: Cambridge University Press.

Turgot, Anne Robert Jaques. 1750b. *On Universal History* in Meek, Ronald L. 1973. Ed. *Turgot, On Progress, Sociology and Economics*. Cambridge: Cambridge University Press.

Turgot, Anne Robert Jaques. 1766. *Reflections on the Formation and Distribution of Wealth* in Meek, Ronald L. 1973. Ed. *Turgot, On Progress, Sociology and Economics*. Cambridge: Cambridge University Press.

Voltaire. [1751] 1901. *The Age of Louis XIV*. In *The Works of Voltaire*. Vol. XII. New York: E.R. Dumont. https://oll.libertyfund.org/titles/2132

Wallerstein, Immanuel. 1974. *The Modern World System: Capitalist Agriculture and the Origins of the Modern World System*. 4 volumes. New York: Academic Press.

Winch, D. 1978. *Adam Smith's Politics: An Essay in Historiographic Revision*. Cambridge: Cambridge University Press.

Winch, D. 1992. "Adam Smith: Scottish Moral Philosopher as Political Economist." *The Historical Journal* 35(1), pp. 91–113. Retrieved June 5, 2020, from www.jstor.org/stable/2639481

Wolf, Eric. 1982. *Europe and the People Without History*. Berkeley: University of California Press.

2 The Development of Evolutionary Social Theory
1815–1871

Introduction

Following the Napoleonic Wars, the 19th century witnessed significant breakthroughs in the application of technology to production, giving rise to Industrial Capitalism in North Western Europe, while other areas of Europe, as well as the rest of the world, lagged significantly behind. Though the slave trade came to an official end as the abolitionist movement gained strength, overtly coercive forms of social relations persisted: for example, slavery persisted in the Southern U.S. and other areas of the world and serfdom maintained its grip on the peasantry of Russia. Whether laissez faire, in any meaningful sense, ever actually existed is debatable. However, the era was marked by increasing economic integration, the spread of international trade as well as specialization and division of labor in production, regionally and on a global scale.

In many respects, the period is one of the contradictions. Latin America gained independence and the era is generally viewed as that of free trade imperialism, rather than formal imperialism. But European powers forced open the doors of China to the Opium trade and the Ottoman Empire was increasingly pushed back. Company Rule over India intensified and European powers began to fill the vacuum created by Ottoman decline and European powers were already administering areas of Africa by the end of the era. Europe experienced revolutionary upheavals followed by reactions on the part of the Ancien regime. The major powers attempted, sometimes successfully, sometimes not, to manage the peace and attempt to stem the tide of nationalism and Constitutional government. The year 1871 marks the culmination of multiple trends. In 1871, Charles Darwin published *The Descent of Man*, Bismarck unified Germany, the Paris Commune was crushed, but Bonapartism came to a decisive end.

Though the events of the end of the French Revolution in some cases tempered the exuberance of the more ambitious Enlightenment theorists, the spread of industrialization and technological progress reinforced the trend toward conceiving society as an upward march of increasing complexity and integration. The Philosophy of Science continued to be

DOI: 10.4324/9781003170679-3

strongly influenced by Empiricism and its close cousin, the Positive Philosophy of August Comte. These trends strongly influenced Social Evolutionary Theory. However, Political Economy was increasingly defined as a separate area of inquiry with its own unique method. Though Evolutionary Social Theory was sometimes characterized by speculative excesses, it was more grounded than the increasingly abstract approach of Political Economy. In Biology, Darwin succeeded in challenging what had been a Lamarckian consensus in both Biological and Social Evolutionism and did so by grounding his theory in observation, induction and rigorous theory.

Philosophy of Science in the Early and Mid-19th Century

Empiricism and Positive Philosophy

In 19th-century Britain, with the partial exception of Spencer, both Empiricism and its close cousin, the Positive Philosophy of August Comte (1896) dominated views on how to conduct scientific inquiry. Much of this work focused on providing a comprehensive account of Science that explained common principles of all of science, including mathematics, the physical and natural sciences, and the emerging social sciences. The scientific method was generally held to consist of a search for general causal law via a process of observation, induction, deduction, verification through experiment and, where necessary, revision.

The term induction itself was a matter of some controversy between two important figures in British Philosophy of Science, Johnathan Stuart Mill (1843a, 1843b) and William Whewell (1849). Mill is generally acknowledged as the chief heir of the Empiricist tradition, and in some respects, Mill's Empiricism was extreme. For example, Mill held that logic was based on the most general aspects of experience and was a guide for discerning the truth or falsehood of statements, rather than a guide to reasoning. In some respects, Whewell's approach departed from strict Empiricism and exhibited considerable influence by Reid. For example, Whewell assigned a greater role to the mind in organizing knowledge than did Mill. Whewell's views are also of particular note given that Whewell himself was a well-respected Naturalist, who also wrote extensively on Political Economy (1862), and along with Charles Lyell (1830), exerted the most direct influence on Darwin's approach to Science. In addition, where Mill was more reserved about the role of hypotheses leading to valid claims, Whewell was in general more permissive.

Mill (1843a, p. 287) viewed induction in the sciences as continuous with everyday inquiry yet drew a distinction between observation and induction. In Mill's view, a genuine induction added information to observation. For example, Mill argued that Kepler's description of planetary orbits as elliptical was not a true induction, but rather a description based on observation of what was actually present. In contrast, Whewell (1849) drew a stronger distinction between everyday activities and induction in science. The latter in Whewell's view required training and refinement as well as a more active role of the mind in organizing knowledge. In Whewell's view, Kepler's arrival at describing the orbits of planets as ellipses required both hypothesis as well as training in the sciences. Thus, Kepler's description of elliptical orbits in Whewell's view was a true case of induction (Whewell 1849, pp. 18–19).

This difference in the definition of induction was also reflected in their respective views on hypothesis formation and its reliability. Mill (1843b, pp. 643–647) argues that many observations are in actuality inferences. These inferences lead to a colligation of facts, which might then form the basis for a hypothesis. Mill is skeptical that the predictive value of a hypothesis is truth indicative of the hypothesis. In contrast, Whewell (1849, pp. 58–60) is more permissive of the role of hypotheses and argued that they are based on concepts. Whewell criticizes Mill for arguing that more than one hypothesis can truly be consistent with the same set of facts. Moreover, Whewell argues that the ability of a hypothesis to predict accurately is truth indicative of a hypothesis. In reading these debates between Mill and Whewell, the reader may be struck by the ways in which the two converged to some degree over time and how for the most part, their differences were matters of emphasis, rather than of kind. That said, Whewell's approach is clearly more permissive than Mill's in asserting what we are justified in believing and places more emphasis on the role of judgment in science, reflecting, in my view, the influence of Reid.

This raises the issue of what makes induction reliable. In order for induction to be reliable, there must be constancy with respect to the underlying laws of nature or, in the case of reasoning from analogy, at least a strong similarity between diverse phenomena. Hence constant natural law will produce the same effects under the same conditions or slightly different effects under variable conditions. For example, if we observe that water erodes a particular kind of stone at a particular rate, we are justified in assuming that the same rate of erosion applied in the past while simultaneously noting that different kinds of rock will erode at a different rate. This principle, which came to be known as uniformitarianism was central to Charles Lyell's contributions to Geology. In Lyell's view, Uniformitarianism allows us to make the inference that current geological formations are a result of a step-by-step process of the operation of constant causal law which operated in the same manner as in the past. Based on this assumption, Lyell (1830) was able to demonstrate that the earth was significantly older than previously thought and to gradually displace, at least amongst naturalists, the catastrophism implied by flood geology. In addition, Lyell also drew a direct connection between the application of the concept of cumulative causation in Natural History, and human history (p. 1), though Lyell does not use either the term "evolution" or "cumulative causation". Like Whewell, Lyell was initially an advocate of the argument to design. Nevertheless, his work helped to set the stage for Darwin's later contributions.

This raises the questions of what is and is not meant by causation, under what conditions we are justified in making an inference about causation on the basis of observations of constant conjunction, and whether or not it is possible for there to be an uncaused cause. Mill's treatment of this issue is particularly helpful. Firstly, Mill argues that it is necessary to distinguish between incidental correlations and actual laws. For example, in Mill's view, it is wrong to infer that the setting of the sun causes the rising of the sun: both are in actuality caused by the rotation of the earth. Similarly, Mill argued against the concept of an uncaused cause. In Mill's view, the world was the result of an unbroken chain of causation, hence all current states of the world result from previous states (1843b, pp. 348 and 371). Furthermore, Mill also argues that it is possible for a single phenomenon to have multiple causes. In Physics and mechanics, causation is summative of the vectors of forces acting on an object. In chemistry, however, it is possible in Mill's view for causation to be a result of interactions. Similarly, he argued that novel properties could emerge as a result of complex interactions.

Another aspect of Mill's views on Philosophy of Science is that while Empiricism is generally associated with nominalism, at least some aspects of Mill strongly imply a commitment at least to empirical realism, though not necessarily to transcendental realism. Mill argued that both proper names and predicates could describe real things and real properties. In Mill's view, the sentence "snow is white" does not mean that snow possesses "whiteness", but that snow possesses a property that leads to it being perceived as white by the observer. Mill also argues that the properties of general law are both actual and real, even when they are not activated. To illustrate this point, Mill used the example that gunpowder always possesses the potential to explode, but that the explosive property of gunpowder is only activated under specific conditions (p. 337). Thus "explanation" in terms of general law and cause in Mill's view were equivalent. For example, if one observes an explosion, one might conventionally say that the lighting of a fuse was the proximate cause of an explosion yet take this as a specific instance of more general explanation in terms of the properties of the elements of gunpowder and matches.

The idea of explaining causation in terms of properties, rather than as just correlation, raises the issue of metaphysics. Empiricism in general, and Comte's Positive Philosophy especially, are generally viewed as hostile to metaphysics. Yet the term metaphysics has multiple meanings. Comte rejected explanations couched in terms of causation and metaphysics. Whewell was critical of Comte's rejection of cause and metaphysics as in Whewell's view, these were necessary concepts for science (Whewell 1849, p. 6). But while Whewell was a strong theist and advocate of the argument from design, he also rejected superstitious and occultic explanations for phenomena. Mill viewed this dispute as owing to a semantic misunderstanding of

Comte by Whewell. What Comte was rejecting in Mill's view was not metaphysics per se, if by metaphysics one means ontology in the form of the study of the general properties of entities. If anything, Comte was more cognizant and permissive of the role of theorizing in hypothesis formation than Mill. Comte's system makes little sense without explanation based on actual properties of phenomena. What Comte was rejecting was bad metaphysics: or in other words theological and animistic explanations offered in place of actual explanations of phenomena.

Comte's views on metaphysics are further illustrated by his division of the history of Science and Civilization both into three stages: theological, metaphysical and positivistic (Vol. 1, Chapter 1). In Comte's view, these stages were both sequential and necessary. In the theological stage, causation was attributed to specific spirits and supernatural actions. In the metaphysical stage, causation was attributed to the internal essences of phenomena. In the Positivist stage, explanation was given in terms of general law. It is because the Theological and Positivist ways of approaching knowledge are diametrically opposed, that human understanding must pass through the metaphysical stage. In elaborating on this point Comte uses Newton's theory of gravitation as an example. He argues that trying to define further concepts such as weight and mass as innate and in terms other than attraction results only in circularity (Vol. 1, p. 31). In his later discussion (Vol. 2, p. 5) on the foundations of Biology, Comte elaborates on these distinctions and argues that the Positivistic approach to Biology begins with the external world and places humans in this external world, rather than starting from the premise of abstract human consciousness. This Positive method in Comte's view can and should be extended to what he termed Social Physics.

What unites the sciences in Comte's view is method (Chapter 2). The method of science in Comte's view is observation, observation by experiment, comparison, and in the case of "Social Physics" or Sociology, history. Explanation in Comte's view was in the form of consilience, which has two complimentary applications. One application is that multiple sciences can be brought to bear on a particular area, thus strengthening the argument for a particular explanation or hypothesized law. A similar application was in the argument that multiple lines of evidence could also be used to illuminate a particular phenomenon. Comte's view that the physical, natural and social sciences shared a method, was accepted by Mill and Whewell as well, except as I discuss below, in Mill's case, not necessarily in Political Economy. While Mill was to set forth a distinctive method for Political Economy and paid significant attention to the problem of value, Comte rejected much of Political Economy with its emphasis on value as metaphysical and laid out a holistic and evolutionary vision for the social sciences, a point I will return to shortly.

Comte's vision of the sciences and their relationship to each other was both comprehensive and also rooted in his Positivist view of Science.

Comte divided knowledge into the abstract, or general, which subsumed specific cases and applications under its umbrella, and the concrete, or practical areas of knowledge. Comte's concern in *The Course* lies in explaining the relationship of the sciences in terms of the former aspect of Science (Vol. I, p. 45). The Course is not intended as a Science text, but rather as a presentation of a specific Philosophical method: i.e., Positivism. Hence in developing a hierarchy of knowledge Comte proceeds in ascending order from the most general and simple to the most complex and particular: i.e. Mathematics, Astronomy, Physics, Chemistry, Biology and ultimately, Social Physics. Though Comte does argue that more specific applications should in principle be derivable from more general principles, he clearly recognizes limits to this kind of reductionist strategy. At each successive level, Comte argued that additional, specific laws were required, which might differ from the laws of more basic sciences but could not contradict those laws. Though Comte did not use the term, he clearly had a concept of emergence. In addition, Comte divided successive areas of science into Statics and Dynamics, the latter of which forms the basis for Comte's evolutionism in both Biology and Social Physics. Yet Comte's evolutionism, at least in Biology, was derivative of the contributions of Lamarck, whose writings set the parameters for evolutionary theorizing in general, both before and after Darwin. Consequently, a brief discussion on Lamarck will serve to place the evolutionism of Comte and others in context.

Evolutionary Theory: Biological and Social before Darwin

The Influence of Lamarck

The idea of biological evolution, or rather "transmogrification" of species gained widening acceptance before Darwin's publications. Yet much of evolutionary theorizing both prior to and after Darwin in the 1^{9t}h century was speculative in nature. Similarly, the influence of Lamarck's ideas on inheritance often led theorists to draw a direct connection between Biological and Social Evolution. Moreover, ideas about social evolution exerted significant influence on Biological theories of evolution. Hence in the 19th century, it is not really possible to entirely disentangle their respective threads. Consequently, an overview of Lamarck's ideas will help to explain the trajectory of both biological and social theories of evolution in the early and mid-to-late 18th centuries.

Lamarckism is often characterized as a theory of evolution by acquired characteristics. Though this is an aspect of Lamarck's position, there is more to Lamarckism than just the inheritance of acquired characteristics. Notably, the idea of acquired inheritance is not inconsistent with Darwin's emphasis on the role of variation and selection. Though I will address

Darwin in more detail later in this chapter, in explaining Lamarck it will be helpful to contrast Lamarck's theory with Darwin's theory. Lamarck's view is that the environment created a need for adaptation in species, leading to a gradual change in the nature of the organs and physical structures of species through use. In other words, the environmental pressure came first, and the adaptation followed. This is in direct contrast to Darwin's view that variation comes first and selective pressure second (Mayr 1982, p. 354). Lamarck viewed non-human animal species as simpler forms than humans, and also emphasized the uniqueness of the human brain as the most significant differentiating factor between humans and non-humans. In addition, Lamarck's view of evolution was progressivist, and perfectionist and confined evolution to a single line, again, in direct contrast to Darwin's branching, non-teleological framework for evolution. These concepts shaped much of 19th-century Biological and Social Evolutionism and often shape contemporary popular misunderstandings of Evolutionary Biology. Both Comte and Spencer had views on both biological and social evolution that were closely similar to Lamarck's.

Comte's Evolutionism and Social Physics

Like Lamarck, Comte held to a progressive evolutionary view of the human species in general, which was evident in his three-stage approach to both science and history reviewed above. Comte begins by placing human beings in the natural world and rejects Cartesian dualism (Vol. 2, p. 5). He argues instead that the mind is a complex set of faculties, present in all humans, and a product of evolution Comte's philosophy of biology is holistic in the sense that he views biology as concerned with the whole organism and the functional relationship of its structures and parts, as well as changes in the structure of a species over time. Comte devotes several pages to a discussion of the differences between Cuvier, who argued for the fixity of the species, and Lamarck. His support for Lamarck is qualified however and he asserts that the environment can have only a limited impact on the form of a species, but he accepts that it can be modified over time. Both with respect to classification schemes and humans, Comte takes a hierarchical and progressivist view. However, he argues that extensive modifications of a species will ultimately lead to the destruction of the species (Vol. 2, pp. 50–59).

Comte's Sociology, or as he termed it "Social Physics" draws heavily on biological analogies and looks to biology as the foundational science for Social Physics. Comte extended these ideas to his study of society to argue for analysis of both the structure and function of institutions as well as the social forces that maintained such institutions and those that led to social change. Like Condorcet, Comte's evolutionism contains a strong idealistic streak in the sense that he ties progress to changes in ways of thinking to the development of the mind. Similarly, like Condorcet,

Comte held out the hope that scientific thinking, if applied to society, could lead to improvement in social conditions.

In articulating his Social Physics, Comte viewed the contemporary state of the Social Sciences as dismal, due to the lack of the application of the Positive Method to the study of society. Comte's hostility to metaphysics is also reflected in his views on Political Economy. Social Physics in Comte's view was intended as a unified science of society, in both evolutionary and static sense, and could therefore address the concerns of Political Economy without recourse to a separate theory or method. The proper method for the study of the social sciences was consequently historical and comparative. Comte rejected most of the discussion of value theory in Political Economy as unnecessarily metaphysical. Comte further argued that the social sciences had gone through both the theological state and the metaphysical state. In the theological state, the union of the military and theologians prevented progress. In the metaphysical state, the problem was one of abstract, metaphysical doctrines of revolution as exemplified by Rousseau which tended to oscillate between revolutionary terror and corruption. Consequently, Comte did not entirely share Condorcet's view of the infinite perfectibility of humans but instead drew a distinction between the forces of order and progress and argued for the need for both. Comte's view that science, if applied to society could lead to improvement, while maintaining order was reflected in his generally positive view of industrial society.

Unfortunately, he did not share Condorcet's opposition to racism or sexism and he regarded Industrial societies as more advanced than other societies. Comte makes an argument for a strong state that can be guided by the principles of Positive Philosophy. In Comte's view, conflict in industry arose as a result of poor coordination. Comte views industrial society and industrial technology as progressive. His ideal society is one in which enlightened factory owners, guided by philosophers, are able to win the loyalty of the working class through rational and humane management as a means of maintaining the system. It is difficult to place Comte politically as he is neither clearly on the left nor the right of his era, though he was definitely an opponent of laissez faire. He had witnessed the instability of the 1830s and 1840s in France as well as the legacy of Bonapartism, which he rejected. His overall social vision is one that could fit with any form of managed capitalism but in that respect also has an authoritarian and elitist aspect and proved useful to the Brazilian top-down, authoritarian model of economic development in the 20th century.

The Influence of Spencer

The idea that evolution leads to progress and increasing complexity in both biology and social organization was prominent in the writings of Herbert Spencer. Spencer's writings span several decades over the mid- and late-19th century, and he continued to be influential well into the late

19th century. Nevertheless, his views on biological and social evolution predate Darwin's publications, and despite significant differences between his views and those of Darwin, he was clearly an influence on Darwin. The core of his ideas was present by the early 1850s, though they were fleshed out in more detail in *First Principles* (1862b). Like Comte, Spenser articulated a unified evolutionary approach to all the sciences, including the social sciences (see also, Carneiro, pp. 3–5).

The key to understanding Spencer in my estimation lies in his approach to ontology and epistemology, much of which Spencer appears to have developed out of Kant and Hegel. From Kant, Spencer adopted the distinction between noumena and phenomena as well as his argument that the noumena is unknowable (1862b, p. 110). Similarly, he argued for a priori synthetic truths though what he means by it differs from Kant's meaning. In Spenser's view, once basic axioms were established, such as the laws of physics, it was possible to derive logically necessary arguments on the basis of those axioms. He did not argue that such axioms were pre-existent in the brain independent of experience. He also held that once articulated, the conclusions derived from the axioms still require verification through the process of induction. From Hegel, he took the idea of the Universe as an unfolding process, moving toward higher levels of complexity integration and development. (p. 159). Though Spencer was not a theist in the strong sense, he argued that the truths of religion and science were ultimately compatible at the most abstract level and his views on the whole place him in the Deist camp. Space and Time in Spencer's view were abstract and unknowable while Matter and Motion were experiential and knowable, while Force was primordial (p. 110). Yet at the same time Spencer adopted the Newtonian view that there was no internal essence or anything beyond Matter, Motion and Force that required explanation. Truth, in Spencer's view, is what guides "us to successful action and the consequent maintenance of life...while error...is the absence of such accurate correspondence" (p. 87). The real for Spencer is that which is persistent.

This leads us to further discussion of Spencer's views on evolution. To understand his definition, we first have to note that Spencer begins from what he calls the general law of continuous redistribution of matter and motion (287): matter and force can be transformed but cannot be destroyed. Matter tends to follow the law of least resistance, flowing first into unoccupied spaces. What leads to combination in Spencer's view is not clear, but Spencer argues that there is an inherent tendency in the Universe for matter to combine and form ever higher and more complex compounds. Spencer's conception of this is of the entire Universe as an ever-widening spiral, drawing more and more elements together, in an oscillating process leading to higher and higher levels. Contrary to what is often argued about Spencer, he did not deny the second law of Thermodynamics but recognized that eventually, this process would reach a final equilibrium and that final equilibrium would be death.

Spencer devotes three full chapters in *First Principles* to developing his definition of evolution and finally arrives at the following:

> *Evolution is an integration of matter and concomitant dissipation of motion; during which, the matter passes from an indefinite, incoherent homogeneity to a definite, coherent heterogeneity; and during which, the retained motion undergoes a parallel transformation.*
>
> (p. 407: emphasis added)

Organic evolution follows this same law. As populations increase, organisms migrate into new areas. As is widely recognized, it was Spencer who first coined the term "survival of the fittest". His ideas on evolution were developed independently of Darwin and his Lamarckism notwithstanding, Spencer does have a concept of "natural selection". However, variation in Spencer's view arises from the pressure of the environment. As empty spaces decline and organisms compete for resources, nature will eliminate those organisms least adapted to life. Though Spencer emphasizes the struggle for life and competition for resources amongst organisms, he also advances an idea similar to that of an ecosystem in recognizing that increased complexity leads to tighter integration and interdependence of multiple species and the environment.

These ideas are carried over into Spencer's views on social evolution which in Spencer's view is also process of increasing complexity, heterogeneity and consequent integration (1862a, p. 227; 1873, pp. 50–60). This process is driven by population growth, which leads to the need for more tightly administered integration in the transition from Savagery, to Barbarism to Civilization. There is a clear recognition in Spencer of the interdependence of political, social, economic and demographic factors. Spencer uses the example of European society as progressing from feudalism to monarchy to modern states, and ultimately to alliances between states. At the same time, industrialization required tighter integration across industries as well as in the process of production itself. The process of European expansion in Spencer's view would break up the less complex non-European societies, eventually absorbing them into European societies.

Though Spencer was not shy about resorting to biological analogies and portrayed society as a social organism, his ideas about both biological and social evolution were based on his understanding of physics. Spencer argues that technological advances are predicated on increasing energy capture from the environment (1862b, pp. 228–230). Spencer was a reductionist in the sense that he saw the laws of social development as ultimately derived from, not just analogous to, the laws of physics, and explainable in terms of matter, force and motion.

Spencer is often portrayed as a methodological individualist, a view that is supported by his treatment of society as an aggregation of individuals. But his views on this matter were more complex. An aggregation in Spencer's view was significantly more than just an adding up of the properties of individuals. Spencer also provided an early and coherent concept of the relationship of Institutions to Social Structure. Structure, in Spencer's view, was found in the relationship of social institutions to each other and could not be separated from function. These structures could change over time and this process in Spencer's view would over time lead to progressive change. Spencer regarded industrial society as leading to the progressive amelioration of social ills. However, Spencer rejected the idea that conscious coordination and application of science could hasten or improve this process and Spencer opposed state intervention as a means of bringing about social evolution. Spencer's view that state intervention could damage the process of social evolution by precluding later, more beneficial adaptations was at times taken to extremes, as in his criticism of public sanitation (1873, p. 60)

In spite of Spencer's view that the state and the mechanism of military coordination arose with increasing complexity, Spencer was clearly anti-State. There is a kind of dialectic in Spencer between the mechanism of military coordination and the mechanism of industrial coordination. The two in Spencer's view are opposed. Military coordination and military societies in Spencer's view were ultimately destined to stagnation, while societies founded on the industrial principle would prosper. How Spencer resolves the issue of coordination and conflict in society is not clear. A partial answer is found in his view that over time, people's inherent nature evolved with society, leading to a society of people more fit to coordinate themselves on the basis of the industrial principle, absent the coercive power of the State. Ultimately, this would lead in Spencer's view to the withering away of the state.

While Spencer and Comte share a similar, though not identical view on the nature of evolution, Spencer diverged from Comte's view that the application of scientific reasoning could improve social evolution. Much of what later came to be associated with "Social Darwinism" would be better thought of as "Social Spencerism". The term is generally interpreted as basing an argument for laissez faire in biology, with particular reference to the concept of survival of the fittest. Given this definition, the accusation against Spencer does have some merit. In Spencer's view, natural law contained within it a drive to increased complexity and progressive improvement. It was not possible in Spencer's view to improve on that process. Hence, he opposed State action to attempt to improve existing social arrangements.

However, Spencer's views were not entirely biologized: Spencer's views on society were for the most part derived from his advocacy of individual freedom and his opposition to the State. There is a strong anti-authoritarian and anti-militarist vein that runs through Spencer's views on social and political philosophy and in multiple respects, he can be viewed as a precursor to contemporary Libertarianism. In some cases,

Spencer's opposition to state intervention was extreme, as exemplified in his opposition to public sanitation. However, we should also note that Spencer opposed Imperialism on the same grounds. Spencer's views were further developed and articulated by Spencer's disciple, William Graham Sumner, whose contributions I will address in the next chapter.

Thus far, while noting underlying differences in approach and interpretation, we have seen that a basic theoretical framework in the 19th century was solidified with respect to social evolution in which societies moved progressively through stages of increasing complexity and integration, and from relatively informal modes of social organization to formal modes of social integration. This was echoed, for example, by others such as Henry Maine, who emphasized the distinction between societies based on custom and societies based on formal law. This framework incorporated many of the same themes and methods of classifying societies of 18th-century social evolutionism. But where the 18th-century social evolutionists had focused on the rise of commercial society, the emphasis of Comte and Spencer was on the rise of, and problems associated with, the industrial society of 19th-century Europe and the United States. Though both are often referenced as founders of modern Sociology, their respective contributions went well beyond contemporary disciplinary boundaries. Other social evolutionists of the era incorporated the same themes and level of generality into their work, while placing more emphasis on the study of past and present non-industrial societies, and consequently, are often viewed as early founders of archaeology and anthropology, though again, we should be cautious of applying contemporary disciplinary boundaries to 19th-century theorists.

Evolutionism in Archaeology and Anthropology: Tylor and Morgan

Where 18th-century Evolutionary Social Theory was based entirely on second-hand reports, Henry Lewis Morgan, despite significant shortcomings, advanced Evolutionary Social Theory to at least a limited degree by being among the first to engage in actual ethnographic research. In his studies of Native American tribes, Morgan was among the first to go beyond traveler's reports and second-hand information. Similarly, in contrast to the 18th-century social contract theorists, Morgan acknowledged the existence of the political organization of Native American social groups, especially that of the Iroquois federation. Unfortunately, Morgan's methods were undermined by his support for the forced assimilation of Native Americans and his failure to advocate for Native American rights. Similarly, as with other prominent figures in 19th-century social evolutionism, he too fell prey to racially biased and ethnocentric errors in thinking. Nevertheless, in my estimation, Morgan did help to advance analysis by drawing an explicit connection between technological change, scientific thinking, social organization and the evolution of the State, even if the analysis suffers from a near-exclusive focus on the evolution of European institutions. Morgan's analysis of the origins of the State was later incorporated into the historical materialism of Marx and Engels, whose contributions I will address in the following chapter (see also, Harris 1968, pp. 180–216).

In his discussion of institutions, Morgan draws a distinction between society, organized via the mechanisms of kinship and the State, organized on the basis of property and territory. Though Morgan does not clearly define institutions, it is clear that by the institution he means organized and habitual ways of organizing society. Morgan's account of the rise of organized political life begins with a view of humans as both social and reasoning beings that interact with their environment. Transitions from one phase to the next in Morgan's view are a result of the co-evolution and interaction of technology and institutions (Morgan 1877, chapter 1). Because technology in Morgan's view is closely connected to inventions and discoveries, he also places considerable emphasis on how different forms of thinking either promote or inhibit technological innovation.

Morgan expands on these ideas throughout the book. He adapted the three-stage division of human history into Savagery, Barbarism and Civilization and further divided these three stages into lower and upper Savagery, and lower and upper Barbarism based on technological capacities. Civilization and the State in Morgan's view are a result of a long process of increasing complexity from the communal and matriarchal family, through the extended kinship group and tribal confederations. Morgan's view, that patriarchy had been preceded not just by matrilineal descent but by matriarchy, was to be echoed later by Engels and many other late 19th-century social evolutionists, though this point has been largely rejected amongst contemporary archaeologists and anthropologists. Morgan discusses and compares kinship organization amongst contemporary (to his era) Native Americans as well as Ancient Greeks and Romans and notes the multiple parallels in the organization. The state emerges in Morgan's view when a specific kinship group is able to establish hereditary rights to rule and establish property over productive resources. Civilization then passes through multiple stages of integration from the city state through the modern, territorial state.

The relationship between technology, scientific thinking and social complexity is also prevalent in the approach of Tylor. Though Tylor's ideas were similar to those of Spencer and Darwin, Tylor makes clear in his preface that his views were developed independently of them (p. viii). As was the case with the 18th-century theorists, Tylor makes extensive use of the comparative method in arguing that contemporary Savage and Barbarous societies could shed light on the history of European and other civilizations. Unfortunately, Tylor did not adopt Morgan's emphasis on ethnography but instead formulated his position primarily on secondary sources. Nevertheless, Tylor is extremely detailed in his analysis of cultural traits and the detail is organized into a theoretical framework.

But where Morgan focused on the evolution of institutions, Tylor (1871) emphasized the role of culture. Tylor defines culture as

> that complex whole which includes knowledge, belief, art, morals, law, custom, and any other capabilities and habits acquired by man as a member of society. The condition of culture among the various societies of mankind, in so far as it is capable of being investigated on general principles, is a subject apt for the study of laws of human thought and action.
>
> (p. 1)

Tylor uses the term "civilization" to refer to a specific stage beginning with the use of writing and the rise of organized states yet also equates the term civilization with culture in general. In that sense, all humans, in Tylor's view, even in the stage of Savagery, possess a civilization or culture. Contemporary European and American civilization in Tylor's view was a consequence of an unbroken sequence of events, leading from Savagery, to Barbarism to Civilization as a result of a connected and unbroken sequence of events throughout history.

Tylor clearly envisioned the study of Cultural Evolution as at least potentially scientific. The goal of Tylor's science of culture was to search for general laws that can explain both the study of existing as well as past cultures. This raises the interesting question as to how, or whether, Culture and Cultural Evolution can be studied scientifically. Tylor makes two arguments that in his view permit the scientific study of culture. One is that human behavior is sufficiently uniform to permit the classification of what he terms "species", by which he means a category or type of *society*. In Tylor's view, all humans, at all times and places share the same underlying cognitive capacities. Hence the human mind, in responding to specific circumstances, will arrive at the same or similar solutions to problems under the same or similar circumstances. In arguing that both human cognitive capacities and ways of thinking impact behavior, and consequently Cultural Evolution, Tylor is not in my estimation resorting to an idealist argument. Rather, he is drawing attention to the interaction of technology and ways of thinking. The second feature that makes the scientific study of Cultural Evolution possible in Tylor's view is the existence of cultural parallels given the same states of societal organization and technology. Differences in societies thus arise through the process of cultural evolution. Hence Tylor has a branching theory, at least to some extent, of Cultural Evolution.

Through successive chapters, Tylor also addresses some specific mechanisms of cultural evolution. Cultural Evolution according to Tylor takes place through progress, degradation, survival, revival and modification. In his discussion of Native American groups, Tylor strongly criticizes those who view Native Americans as "degenerate" people. Instead, Tylor acknowledges their "achievement" of culture and also notes that European contact had a negative influence on Native Americans. The purpose of civilization in Tylor's view is to promote overall human goodness and happiness. In Tylor's view, modern European Civilization can be judged superior to other civilizations. However, for Tylor, this judgment is a general trend and he notes that advances are not uniform in all areas. He also acknowledges that there are multiple instances in which more "advanced" civilizations are less humane than less advanced civilizations and he also notes again the ways in which some European practices, such as Slavery, were less moral than other similar institutions in the past.

Tylor also exhibits some awareness of what today is referred to as the structure agency problem and has an emergent concept of culture. Tylor notes that people may act for their own interests and against the interests of society. But he also notes that this action produces culture. Consequently, both the study of individual action as well as macro analysis are needed in the study of culture. Tylor notes that while humanly devised habits and customs may embody wisdom, it is also possible that they may embody other less admirable traits. However, once established, cultural traits may continue to persist long after a society has transitioned from one stage to the other. Tylor calls this persistence, "cultural survivals". In observing cultural survivals, it is possible in Tylor's view to trace the origins to its historical roots. Thus, the persistence of common grazing rights in Medieval Europe in Tylor's view is owed to a period of time when all land was held in common by the kinship group.

Like the other social evolutionists, Tylor held to a progressivist theory of culture change, and he classifies stages of culture in accordance with the overall state of industrial arts, manufacture, scientific knowledge, religion, morality and complexity of society. In classifying societies on this scale, he of course ranks Europeans at the pinnacle and non-Europeans in successively lower stages. Consequently, it is fair to critique Tylor for adopting racially biased and ethnocentric judgments. As with Condorcet and Comte, Tylor's discussion of the role of ideas and ways of thinking does not necessarily imply idealism, but rather points to the consequences for social of ways of thinking, and the consequences for ways of thinking that arise from social action. Here again, Tylor was interested in the broader implications of ways of thinking for human action and the consequences of human action on social organization. Hence the application of Scientific thinking in Tylor's view will lead to technological progress and to cultural advancement. Tylor's progressivism is most prominent in his discussion of religion which he traces through its earliest stages of animism through the rise of Christianity. Like Condorcet and Comte, Tylor contrasts the matter of fact and problem-solving nature of modern science with the animistic, mythological and in his view, retarding effect of religious thinking.

Tylor concludes his *Primitive Culture* with the following:

> Yet it is evident that, notwithstanding this all profound change, the conception of the human soul at its most essential nature, continuous from the philosophy of the savage thinker that of the modern professor of theology...The divisions which have separated the greater religions of the world into intolerant and hostile sects are for the most superficial in comparison with the deepest of all religious schisms, that which divides Animism from Materialism.
>
> (pp. 501 and 502)

Hence Tylor's contributions, while inadequate, and vulnerable to legitimate criticisms of racial and ethnocentric bias, went significantly beyond simply an atheoretical exposition of history. In contrast to the Cultural Materialist Marvin Harris (1968, pp. 202–204), I do not regard Tylor and Morgan as idealists or as atheoretical. Carneiro (2003, pp. 1–9) has a more positive view of Spencer, Tylor and Morgan than does Harris. In my own interpretation, an important insight of Tylor is the rise of, and consequences of, scientific ways of thinking. This way of thinking contrasts with an explanation based on supernatural or dogmatic methods and is prevalent from the Enlightenment through the entire panoply of 19th-century Social Evolutionary Theory and beyond. It is not coincidental that this corresponds to the rise of modern industrial society. One can be a good materialist and still recognize the interaction of thinking with feeling and acting and the ways in which acting leads to changes in social organization, which in turn exerts an influence on ways of thinking and feeling.

Thus far we have noted that Anthropology and Sociology emerged as all-encompassing evolutionary disciplines, prior to and contemporaneously with the publication of Darwin's major works on biological evolution. Their theorizing encompassed areas we today classify as Political Science, Sociology, Anthropology and even Political Economy under one general umbrella modeled, for the most part, on an understanding of biological evolution. The partial exception to this was Spencer's model, which was the most physics based of the early 19th-century social theorists. Darwin clearly did not invent the idea of evolution, in either its cultural or social sense. Indeed, as I discuss further below, the influence goes from Comte and the other social evolutionists such as Maine, and even Smith and Malthus, to Darwin—not the other direction. This is of course not to deny that Darwin made original contributions and innovations on the concept of evolution. This view is also supported by Harris (1968, pp. 105–107), though as the reader will note later in my discussion of Darwin, I take issue with some of Harris' characterizations of Darwin on race. Before proceeding to my analysis of Darwin's contributions to evolutionary theory however, there is one puzzle that must be addressed:

the increasing separation of British Political Economy from Evolutionary Social Theory, as well as the interesting connection of Darwin's theories of biological evolution to ideas in Political Economy.

The Trajectory of Political Economy

Where Political Economy, as understood by Smith and Turgot, was derived from Evolutionary Social Theory, over the course of the 19th century, Political Economy, at least in Britain, came to be viewed as a distinctive area of inquiry unto itself with its own unique method. This did not however imply rejection of Evolutionary Social Theory per se, but rather an emphasis of Political Economy on a narrower range of issues related to the pursuit of wealth, in the context of an industrial, privately owned and commercial economy. In other words, what was proposed was a division of labor between the broad emphasis of Evolutionary Social Theory and the narrow focus of Political Economy. This trend continued into the late 19th and early 20th centuries. At present, however, I will focus on the development of mainstream, British Political Economy beginning with Malthus and then Ricardo and Johnathan Stuart Mill.

Malthus as Social Evolutionist

Malthus (1798) is often cast in the role of arch reactionary and misanthrope, though some scholarship on Malthus provides reason to question this interpretation (Winch 2013). But to a limited degree, some of Malthus' arguments are understandable in the context of the British response to the French Revolution as well as to writers like Condorcet and Godwin (Malthus 1798, Vol. 2, pp. 1–38) who stressed the possibility of unlimited progress. Unfortunately, the tendency in Britain was to interpret all efforts at social improvement through the prism of the violence of the French Revolution. With the exception of Millar, whose contributions were addressed in the previous chapter, we can draw a line from the relatively cautious and measured defense of ordered liberty of multiple writers in the Scottish Enlightenment and their emphasis on the importance of habit and custom as checks to pure reason, to the conservatism of Burke and Malthus.

We can also draw a line from the evolutionism of the Scottish Enlightenment to Malthus' evolutionism. Malthus' argument against the idea of improvement or melioration of social misery through public policy was grounded in historical and comparative analysis. In this regard, Malthus' original contribution is to point to the limiting role of population and ecology. Yet it is questionable whether Malthus' policy recommendations actually follow from his analysis. A society that is doomed to underconsumption, general gluts, overpopulation and in which a substantial section of the population is condemned to persistent poverty could just as easily be seen as one which is in need of radical change.

With respect to method, Malthus' stressed the role of induction, deduction and verification as a means of arriving at valid conclusions, and like the earlier Scottish and French theorists, made use of both historical and comparative examples. Contrary to arguments that Malthus' population principle ignored institutional and social factors, Malthus examined the relationship between population and food production, and the distributive consequences of that interaction, in differing forms of social organization and localities (Vol. 1, pp. 259–514). Malthus notes how human populations have increased food production in each successive stage due to technological change. However, population increase in Malthus' view blunted whatever improvements had occurred as a result of increases in productivity. As is well known, Malthus' argued that as human populations reached the carrying capacity of a given form of social organization, it would be subject to positive checks on population such as war and famine, and negative checks on population such as delayed marriage and child birth. Population growth, according to Malthus placed a burden on society, which was inevitably borne by the poor.

Because efforts to improve the lot of the poor in Malthus' view would lead to faster population growth, Malthus' was skeptical of schemes to ameliorate poverty via social relief. Malthus was particularly critical of the English poor laws and regarded them as having an overall negative impact on the lives of the poor (Vol. 2, pp. 63–117). Because the poor laws subjected those receiving relief to a system of monitoring and surveillance, Malthus regarded them as contrary to liberty. Malthus makes two critical assumptions in this regard: one is that food production is fixed in the short run and the other is that distributive shares between classes are also fixed in both the short and long run. Hence any effort to actually alter the distribution of income would likely lead to a reduction in work effort while requiring a decrease in the consumption standards of the wealthy. Malthus' pessimism is similarly reflected in his argument against Say's Law that a general glut of commodities, due to a lack of effective demand would be possible.

Malthus' argument, which was to ultimately exert an influence on Darwin, that there is a struggle amongst human beings over resources, should be regarded as both a biological and social fact. However, Malthus' argument that this state of affairs cannot be rectified does not necessarily follow logically from his analysis. On the contrary, the argument that the system is rigged against the poor points to the very real structural impediments to substantive reform present not just in the social climate of the early 19th century, but in every social era. This does not however mean that humans could not learn to find better ways of organizing society as a means of both increasing productivity and achieving a more just distribution of resources. Yet in another respect, Malthus' pessimism might be seen as a necessary corrective to the overreach of late Enlightenment theorists and of radical, utopian schemes.

Ricardo

While Malthus' approach to Political Economy was consistent with that of the earlier 18th-century theorists, with the writings of Ricardo, Political Economy began to be defined by an emphasis on deductive analysis based on general, abstract principles, coupled with a set of doctrines about value and distribution and which in turn gave rise to policy prescriptions. Winch (2013) notes at several junctures in his analysis of Malthus the break both in terms of general approach to Political Economy as well as the difference between Malthus and Ricardo on the issue of general gluts. Multiple History of Economic Thought texts as well (see, for example, Rima 2009 and Hunt 1979) note the emphasis of Ricardo on the use of the abstract-deductive method as well Ricardo's incorporation of Malthus' population principle into his own analysis. My concern herein is notably not specifically with Ricardo's statement of his doctrines, but with the longer-run impact of Ricardo on the nature and practice of Political Economy. My argument herein is that the alleged Ricardian vice is a vice only when taken to excess.

This raises an interesting issue: Is the abstract deductive method itself the problem, provided the following are present? This is an issue to which I will return later in this study at several junctures.

1. The principles on which the analysis is based are generally descriptive of the actual features of the entity being studied;
2. The specificity of the institutional context is recognized and understood;
3. There is a further effort to corroborate, reject or at least modify the general principles in light of evidence garnered from empirical inquiry.

Ricardo's analysis meets conditions 1 and 2. Ricardo's theory of value and distribution is dependent on his recognition of the role of social classes in production and the average British reader would have recognized Ricardo's descriptions of conditions of landholding and social classes in Britain. Moreover, as did Smith, Ricardo also stressed the importance of capital accumulation and technological progress over time. Nor was Ricardo blind to the political ramifications and practicalities of his economic theorizing given his direct participation in the Manchester Liberals and his efforts at political reform of both the Poor Laws and the Corn Laws. And though Ricardo himself was a proponent of laissez faire, his doctrines also proved useful to others arguing for radical reform.

The failure of Ricardo's method for Political Economy in my estimation arises with respect to number 3. Hence, Ricardo set Political Economy on the path to adopting the method of reasoning from first principles to conclusions, with no need for efforts at actually verifying the theory through further empirical inquiry of the society and period being studied, and no effort to engage in historical and comparative analysis. This raises an interesting question about Marx's use of the abstract-deductive method and its relationship to his Historical Materialism, an issue which for the sake of the continuity of ideas, I address in the subsequent chapter. My immediate goal is to show how changing definitions of Political Economy led away from an evolutionary approach to social theory that up till this point had been the presumptive approach to social theory.

Johnathan Stuart Mill on Political Economy

Where Ricardo set Political Economy on the road to being a deductive science focused on the working out of long-run tendencies of a system based on general principles, Johnathan Stuart Mill accelerated the trend. Of equal importance in the case of Mill is the nature of the foundational postulates on which Mill sought to build Political Economy. Mill, in my view, would have certainly believed he had met all three conditions, but in my estimation, he did not. A justification for this assertion requires some detailed discussion.[1]

In his work on Logic, and elsewhere, Mill (1824; 1843a, pp. 354, 384, 454; 1843b, pp. 833–835) addresses the philosophical problems of what we today term the social sciences and how these problems relate to Political Economy. Curiously, Mill does not address these issues directly in his *Principles of Political Economy*, which for the most part is devoted to an analytical treatment of rent, prices, wages and other similar topics of Political Economy. Though Mill views himself as the heir to the Ricardian tradition, his incorporation of Utilitarianism and of the Utility Theory of Value, as opposed to Ricardo's initial formulation of the Labor Theory of Value (or if one prefers, a proto-labor theory, or cost of production theory of value) places him as a dubious heir to the Ricardian tradition on that point.

On the larger point of treating Political Economy as deductive discipline based on principles accepted as true, Mill is consistent with Ricardo. In his work on Logic, Mill criticizes Hobbes and the Benthamites for their use of the geometric method which he argues is based on overgeneralizations and not truly scientific. Mill accepts the legitimacy and importance of what Comte termed "Sociology" and Comte's unified evolutionary approach to Sociology. However, he criticizes Comte's restriction of that method as the only one appropriate for the social sciences as overly narrow. Another important distinction is that for Comte, the foundational science for the social sciences is biology, whereas for Mill, the foundational science for Political Economy is Psychology. Mill's argument on this point is in part semantic. In his essay on the method of Political Economy (1824) Mill argues that the issue of the appropriate method for a discipline is best understood after the discussion of the discipline itself and provides the following definition:

> the science which traces the laws of such of the phenomena of society as arise from the combined operations of mankind for the production

> of wealth, in so far as those phenomena are not modified by the pursuit of any other object
>
> (Vol. IV, p. 339)

Mill also adds that this applies only to human societies at the stage of social existence. Notably, Mill does not deny the presence of non-pecuniary motives nor is he an advocate of a universal homo economicus. Mill acknowledges that human action will be shaped by social institutions and the context in which action occurs. He does however posit the relevance of homo economicus for the study of industrial, market economies, in so far as one is addressing the implications of narrowly focusing on the pursuit of wealth. Mill then further distinguishes between the study of Political Economy as a science, and the applications of Political Economy in the form of policy, which he characterizes as art. Mill also makes a distinction between Social Economics, which corresponds to Evolutionary Social Theory and Political Economy.

Mill's work on logic provides some further insights into the basis of his argument. The method that Mill argues is appropriate to Political Economy is what he terms the "inverse historical" method in his Logic and also as the *a priori* method. When Mill uses the term "a priori", he does not mean that we can know Political Economy independently of experience. The method is composed of induction, ratiocination and verification (1843b, pp. 833–835). But experimentation in Mill's view is not possible in the Social Sciences. Hence the kind of induction that Mill is arguing for with respect to Political Economy is based on introspection and psychology—not a detailed comparative and historical study of the process of the creation and distribution of wealth. The basic premises of Political Economy in Mill's view are drawn from general experience, but not necessarily specific experience. Hence principles that are formulated on that basis can be employed to reach tentative conclusions about general tendencies of the direction of matters such as prices, wages, rents and other similar phenomena. While Mill's "a priori" method is primarily intended for Political Economy, he provides an illustration of his argument with an example drawn more narrowly from the study of politics. According to Mill, we do not need to engage in a detailed study of the specific forms of governance to know the consequences of specific forms of government—again, the general experience is sufficient. Though Mill does not address the possibility of any kind of rigorous testing of theories in Political Economy, he does acknowledge the role of verification and that such principles might need to undergo subsequent revision.

The above raises an interesting question: given Mill's general allegiance to Empiricism, is his advocacy of a separate method for Political Economy inconsistent with his emphasis elsewhere on induction? In Mill's view at least, he is not. As noted previously, Mill rejects the possibility of an uncaused cause. In addition, Mill argues that general laws control specific laws. The general law that controls human behavior in Mill's view is psychology, specifically, psychology with a utilitarian foundation. Mill argues that induction is possible in humans with respect to psychology and via induction to arrive at general laws of psychological motivation for human behavior. Through our knowledge of psychology it is possible in Mill's view to separate the motives of the acquisition of wealth from other motives. Yet social behavior, as a specific principle, should be viewed as controlled by the more general principle, which is psychological (Vol. VIII, p. 877). This can, as Mill acknowledges, lead to cultural bias. The other aspect is that Mill does not have high expectations for what kind of knowledge Political Economy leads to. In Mill's view, that knowledge is imprecise, inexact and culture-bound, a point that has also been emphasized by Hausman. Mill's a priori method for Political Economy was not intended as a "general theory" approach, it was put forth as a partial theory approach. This emphasis, as we will see in the next chapter, was also continued by Marshall.

That noted, Mill's argument for a separate approach to Political Economy and its separation from social philosophy is nevertheless vulnerable to at least three lines of criticism. One line of criticism centers on Mill's psychologism, and especially his reliance on utilitarianism. Even though Mill's utilitarianism departed from the crasser version of Bentham's Utilitarianism, the idea that human motivations can be reduced to sensations of pleasure and pain in any society, even in the arena of the pursuit of wealth, is contrary to the complexity and purposiveness of human behavior. Similarly, the idea that psychologism is, or can be, the foundation for the social sciences is contrary to the principle of the emergence. Thirdly, even though we should accept Mill's argument that controlled experiments are not possible in the social sciences, it does not follow that we should resort to more abstract reasoning and thought experiments. Such processes may serve the purpose of hypothesis formation and aid in guiding empirical research, but they cannot be taken as independently of actual inquiry. Rather, in order for a statement in any area of inquiry to be accepted as warranted, it must be confirmed via empirical inquiry. Our inability to conduct controlled experiments in the social sciences requires a greater degree of specificity. The search for verifiable general laws or more accurately general principles of analysis may then take the form of careful, cross-cultural and historical analysis as a means of discerning which, if any, general statements might be descriptive of human societies in general, which, if any, general statements might be descriptive of specific forms of society, and which, if any, are true only under specific circumstances. In doing so, we must of course recognize that our conclusions are indeed as Mill noted, imprecise and inexact in comparison to the natural and physical sciences.

Having noted the shortcomings of Mill's a priori method for Political Economy, Mill nevertheless in my estimation deserves considerable praise for the positions he took on multiple political and social issues, especially given the era in which he wrote. He was among the few to provide specific attention to the unequal status of women in society and to argue for gender equality, though some may disagree with Mill's emphasis on Liberalism as the foundation for gender equality. He was also a consistent opponent of slavery and a proponent in general of expanding the scope of political freedom. Moreover, he argued for a more just distribution of wealth. His views therefore should be at least partially distinguished from the stricter versions of Classical Liberalism. That noted Mill's positions did at times embody the kinds of contradictions inherent in Classical Liberalism of justification of the actions of the British East India Company of British Imperialism in general. These contradictions within the corpus of British Liberalism were to resurface in Darwin's major contributions to biology.

Darwin's Biology

Where some accounts of Evolutionary Social Theory stress the centrality of Darwin in the development of Evolutionary Social Theory, the narrative I have developed in this chapter emphasizes the development of both social and biological theories of evolution prior to, and independently Darwin. In addition, both social and biological theories of evolution that developed prior to or concurrently with Darwin's contributions exerted considerable influence on Darwin. As I address in the next chapter, social evolutionists writing after Darwin were influenced by Darwin, though not necessarily to the degree that is often believed. Yet understanding the place of Darwin in evolutionary theory in both the natural and social sciences is of immense importance. In this section, I focus primarily on Darwin's views and the potential ramifications of his views. I address his impact in more detail in the subsequent chapter.

The first issue to address is Darwin's understanding of Philosophy of Science, and how that influenced his work. Darwin was strongly influenced by the currents of 19th-century British Empiricism. However, as I believe is clear from the earlier discussion in this chapter, Empiricism was interpreted and applied quite liberally and the case of Whewell was more consistent with Reid's Common Senism. Hence while there were some disagreements about the meaning of induction and hypothesis, the emphasis was on observation and induction as the basic approach to science. This did not mean that scientists were preceded by ignorance of the context and relevance of observations. Darwin was a practicing Naturalist who spent decades observing Nature prior to formulating his theories. His approach can be clearly distinguished from the more speculative and deductive approach of Spencer. In stressing the role of observation and induction in Darwin's work, I do not mean to imply that there are no prior theoretical influences on Darwin. Quite the contrary: the idea of evolution in general was already prevalent in Darwin's time and it notably took

Darwin some time to arrive at his own acceptance of evolution, as well as to articulate his specific approach to evolution (see, for example, Mayr 1991, pp. 1–11).

In developing his arguments in *Origin* and *Descent*, Darwin drew on multiple sources of evidence as well as the arguments of other evolutionists in the era. In *One Long Argument* Ernst Mayr (1991) provides the following description of the method of naturalism and of Darwin:

> They observe numerous phenomena and always try understand the how and why of their observations. When something does not at once fall into place, they make a conjecture and test it by additional observations., leading either to a refutation or a strengthening of their original assumptions. This procedure does not fit well into the classical prescriptions of the philosophy of science, because it consists of continually going back and forth between making observations, posing questions, establishing hypotheses or models, testing them by further observations, and so forth.
>
> (p. 10)

Mayr's emphasis on Darwin's method of explanation as "one long argument" also merits specific attention. As I explain below, drawing on both Mayr's analysis as well as my own reading of Darwin's major works, Darwin's style of argumentation is on that draws together multiple threads of evidence while simultaneously considering the evidence and arguments of his opponents, and refuting those arguments. Darwin's theory of evolution is not one theory: it is rather, as Mayr notes, five mutually reinforcing theories: evolution as such, common descent, multiplication of species, natural selection (pp. 36–37). Both as a means of better understanding Darwin's method, the influences on Darwin and the ramifications of his contributions, it will be useful to briefly analyze Darwin's arguments in both *Origin* (1876) and *Descent* (1877), published originally in 1859 and 1871, respectively. Below, I summarize the main arguments of both.

The first four chapters of *Origin* provide the foundation of Darwin's argument. The explanandum of Darwin's argument is the extent of variation in both domesticated and non-domesticated species, which he details in the first two chapters of *Origin*. Where Lamarck had emphasized the role of the environment in creating needs for changes in structures, Darwin's explanation reversed the order: the variation came first and the environment acted as the force for selection. In Chapter 3, Darwin draws on Malthus' population principle to explain what he termed "the struggle for survival" amongst members of the same species, as well as different species, with an emphasis on species in the same genus. In Chapter 4, Darwin explains his principle of natural selection and other similar forms of selection and draws an analogy between the artificial selection of domestic breeding and natural selection: natural selection acts as a step-by-step process to eliminate structures that are not conducive to an organism's survival and preserve those that are. Chapter 5 sets out the "laws" of this process. But Darwin's laws are not laws in the Newtonian sense: they are general principles that guide the analysis. The remainder of the book sets out the various sources of empirical evidence and conceptual arguments for and against his theory. Darwin's explanans is that the diversity of species can be explained as a result of the above process. This process is non-teleological and results in a branching pattern of speciation.

In *Descent*, Darwin takes the operation of natural selection as established and devotes his attention to examination of the evidence for natural selection as an explanation for both human physical and cognitive evolution. This latter point is the most controversial aspect of Darwin's views and was notably the point on which Wallace and Darwin disagreed. Darwin initiates his argument in *Descent* with an examination of the existence of multiple homologous structures between humans and other animals with particular attention to the similarities between humans and mammals and especially between humans and other primates. He then explains his argument for the evolution of bipedalism in humans (p. 94) and also compares the development of reason in animals. At the time Darwin wrote, the availability of fossil evidence with which to demonstrate the step-by-step development of bipedalism amongst humans was limited. Consequently, Darwin relied strongly on comparative evidence to demonstrate the intermediate nature of limited bipedalism in primates and quadripedalism in other primates.

But Darwin goes beyond explaining the development of bipedalism and explains how human cognitive and ethical reasoning could arise as a result of a step-by-step process of variation and selection. In contrast, Wallace continued to emphasize a non-natural, or spiritual foundation for the cognitive capacities of the human brain. In his discussion of the human ethical sense Darwin directly cites (see, footnote, p. 106) Adam Smith's view of ethics as arising out of empathy in *The Theory of Moral Sentiments* as a given. He then explains how this capacity could arise via natural selection. In advancing this argument Darwin looks to examples of empathy in the animal kingdom and notes its higher development in the human species.

In *Descent*, Darwin addresses the differing views prevalent in his era on race. Amongst Creationists, some argued for a single creation of all humans. Yet others argued for the specific creation of the different races and saw in this a justification for slavery. Similarly, non-creationists were divided between those who argued about whether all humans were descended from a common ancestor or if the different races had different ancestors. There was also considerable argument between evolutionists and diffusionists. Diffusionists generally viewed non-European cultures as derived from other civilizations, and in the case of indigenous Americans, as degenerate cultures, that had once been civilized but had regressed.

In contrast, the evolutionist view stressed common descent as well as similar patterns of cultural adaptation to environmental circumstances. Both Tylor and Morgan, whose contributions I addressed previously in this chapter, argued that the human mind did not vary amongst cultures and that a common human mind arrived at common solutions to common problems, thus explaining cultural parallelisms.

In these debates, Darwin was an advocate of a single origin of the human species and an advocate of the evolutionist view. In advancing this point in *Descent*, Darwin draws on the writings of Tylor, Lubbock (1865) and other social evolutionary theorists of the era. Darwin stressed the separation of the lowest "savages" from primates in terms of intelligence. Nevertheless, Darwin also accepted the premise that there was a difference between the intelligence of Europeans and of Africans, and also that non-European societies were cultural laggards. At the same time, it also implied that Europeans had fairly recently been in the stage of "barbarism" and had been at least partially responsible for destroying civilization but had ultimately evolved from barbarism to civilization. Unfortunately, Darwin does not directly address whether the difference in civilizational complexity is owed purely to cultural factors, or whether biological and cultural evolution are strongly linked. On this latter point, we should take note that this reflects the influence of Lamarck's theories of inheritance. There can clearly be no question that Darwin's writings absorbed and reflected the racial biases of the era.

Though Darwin was subject to the biases of his era, his contributions ultimately point to the futility of trying to define humans in terms of fixed, unvarying and biologically pure concepts of race. His theory does provide for a way of thinking about biogeographical variation both within and between overlapping populations of humans. Firstly, we should note that the concepts of "race" and "species" were not always clearly defined in Darwin's era and were often employed in a typological and essentialist fashion. Human variation was taken as a given and humans were grouped on the basis of skin pigmentation, other observable physical characteristics and by Continent of origins. Some considered these differences to be fixed and discontinuous and also associated with a hierarchy of civilizational accomplishments with Europeans at the pinnacle. This kind of typological and essentialist view of race, which is rooted in folk taxonomy, is at odds with Darwin's definition of species and his emphasis on continuity and variation. Darwin himself does use the term "race", but his usage is with respect to observable physical differences between varieties of humans. One of Darwin's contributions was to provide us with a clearer definition of the term species, devoid of essentialism and based on population thinking which acknowledged variation within a species.

While Darwin clearly viewed all humans as part of the same species, he nevertheless accepted the basic premise that Europeans were more highly evolved and civilized than other human populations. In *Descent*, Darwin provides an explanation for the observable, phenotypic variation amongst human populations, and his explanation was based primarily on sexual selection. If Darwin accepted the premise of a racial hierarchy within a unified human species, he did not advocate the enslavement or elimination of other races by Europeans. Nevertheless, like Spencer, Darwin does explicitly argue that selection takes place at the level of civilizations when he argues that Europeans are likely to replace other races and civilizations. He clearly accepted the inevitability of European Colonialism and Imperialism. Though he did not actively oppose Imperialism, there is no evidence that Darwin celebrated or advocated this process. On the contrary, Darwin's passionate commitment to abolitionism is well known (Moore and James 2009).

The Ramifications of Darwin's Theories

This brings us to the issue of the ramifications of Darwin for social theory. It is useful to initially divide contemporary theorists who seek to draw a specific political philosophy from Darwin between those who view Darwin as providing the foundations for a "Darwinian Left", those who argue for Darwin as a contemporary, secular, moderate Conservative, or those who see in him the foundations for Libertarianism. But Darwin has more often been used as a punching bag for both the left and right. As a general rule, it is possible to group his critics into two camps: those who are afraid that Darwin leads us down the road to the dissolution of traditional Christian morality and those who are afraid he will not. Darwin has been alleged to be responsible for a wide range of positions such as sexism, racism, extreme laissez faire, imperialism and fascism, a defense of the patriarchal heterosexual family as well as views that are incompatible with the preceding such as Feminism, Socialism, Marxism and generalized assaults on the heterosexual nuclear family. Intelligent design advocate, Richard Weikart (2004) has argued that Darwin advocated an ethics of struggle and that his ideas led to the displacement of ideas about human equality. The anthropologist Marvin Harris, who was an advocate of both biological and social evolutionism, accused Darwin of being a racial determinist (1968, chapter 4). The issues however in my view are more complex.

In the first instance, there is a complex issue of whether or not should judge theories in biology on the basis of real or alleged ramifications for political ideology? The question of whether or not humans share an ancestor with other great apes, or more broadly, whether Darwin's theories of evolution or more to the point, the current Neo-Darwinian synthesis approach to biological evolution are true, are in my estimation independent of whatever actual ramifications there may or may not be for any of the above. With respect to the standards of his day, there can be no doubt as to Darwin's scientific integrity. Nevertheless, our understanding of biological evolution has advanced considerably since Darwin's era.

That said, Darwin did not write in a vacuum and there were clearly both social influences on his work and his work had ramifications for how we view humans. First, we should note how Darwin viewed the issue of ethics. Darwin's ethics were clearly and unequivocally most strongly influenced by Smith's views on sympathy, though he does not view evolution as leading to beneficent order. He does however draw a distinction, even if only one of degree, between biological instinct and social order. He views humans as social animals. In his discussion of the evolution of a moral sense in humans, he adopts Smith's view of morality based on the principle of sympathy and argues for a naturalistic basis for the adoption of the Golden Rule and views humans as social animals. He argues that human society should aim for the higher good. In doing so, he draws directly on both Hume and Smith (Darwin 1877, pp. 106, 109, 114 and 126, footnotes). He is critical of utilitarianism and argues that ethics should be devoted to the good of society, rather than the happiness of society.

Darwin's views on equality are somewhat more difficult to piece together. Desmond and Moore (2009) portray Darwin as a British Liberal. Liberalism is a complex political philosophy that has not always been consistent with its better principles in application. 19th-century British Liberalism was often particularly contradictory. Opposition to slavery and the slave trade, for example, was often accompanied by justification for Imperialism and laissez faire (see, for example, Scanlan 2020, chapter 1). Furthermore, in the context of Liberalism, the term equality requires definition. 19th-century Liberals, with varying degrees of consistency (Mill being among the most consistent), emphasized the equality of rights. It certainly did not mean, and never has been interpreted as an argument for perfect equality. Even Marx in his *Critique of the Gotha Program* argued that the slogan "from each according to his ability, to teach according to his need" could not be realized until the full attainment of the final stage of communism. Darwin was certainly not a socialist and was not an advocate of egalitarianism. To the contrary, he was a conventional British Whig, steeped in the Classical Liberal tradition, with all the contradictions that view entails.

This raises a further and interesting point about Darwin's theories: Is Darwin's emphasis on competition simply a reading of Smithian Political Economy and Victorian presumptions about gender into nature, only to then recapitulate it back to us? Darwin's emphasis on selection at the individual level, competition amongst individuals within a species and sometimes between species as well as some of his views on sexual selection do echo both. However, Darwin's views on these issues were more diverse than is sometimes appreciated. For example, Darwin acknowledged the possibility of group selection, the evolution of cooperation, as well as of female choice in sexual selection.

To the extent that we should reasonably attempt to evaluate the politics of 19th-century theorists by the standards of contemporary progressive, left politics of the 21st century, Darwin was clearly not on the side of the angels. Nor was anyone else in the 19th century in entirety on the side of the angels, including Marx. Nor were 19th-century Creationists and neither have 20th and 21st Creationists of varying stripes embraced ideas of human equality. Nor was Darwin on the most reactionary side. The challenge for contemporary theorists, in both the natural and social sciences, is to purge the theory of ideas that are both empirically wrong, and/or those ideas which reinforce invidious distinctions. In cases where ideas may have factual support but also the capacity to lend themselves to promoting invidious distinctions, we should certainly be clear as to our opposition to such distinctions. But When Darwin's theories are separated from his reactionary ideas, they are in actuality considerably strengthened. Yet this kind of emphasis on the subtleties and qualifications as well as contradictions of Darwin's views on society is not quite the stuff that can be used to scare off schoolchildren and parishioners from serious study of theories of biological and social evolution.

Similarly, we should recognize that as a process of empirical inquiry, science is fallible. This is equally true of Darwin. Nevertheless, Darwin's arguments have significant implications for the philosophy of science, including both the natural and social sciences. Though the natural philosophy of the Enlightenment had in principle rejected explanations couched in terms of final cause, entelechy and vitalism, it often smuggled such concepts in through the back door. In the case of Kant and Hegel, these ideas were driven straight through the front door. Darwin's theories decisively broke with the concepts of vitalism, entelechy, essentialism, beneficent equilibrium in nature and teleology (see, Mayr 1991). Similarly, in stressing the non-teleological nature of this process, Darwin can be credited with the consummation of the break from the vulgar Aristotelianism of medieval scholasticism set in motion by Francis Bacon.

One area where Darwin's approach does have clear ramifications is that it is entirely inconsistent with Hegelian idealism and the Kantian emphasis on the noumena-phenomena distinction and on typological classifications. Darwin's views on the species question undermined the prevailing view that species were composed of an unchanging "stuff" and instead shifted the focus of species as interbreeding populations with varying characteristics. His emphasis on evolution as a gradual, or step-by-step process of variation and selection established the principle of continua as a mode of analysis. His views of adaptation and natural selection presented the natural world as composed of struggle and competition, as opposed to benevolent balance. On this last point, Darwin's debt to Malthus was both clear and acknowledged. When he writes about nature acting as a selective force, he is using shorthand to describe the complex web of interactions that shape an organism's or species natural environment, which the organism or species also participates in creating. In other words, Darwin attributes force or causation to the structure of the ecosystem. Darwin's approach is clearly one that is consistent with the concept of emergence.

By stressing evolution as a consequence of a step-by-step process of cumulative change, leading to a branching pattern of speciation, Darwin at least in part, broke company with the general tendency of 19th-century evolutionists to view evolution as a progressive, goal-directed process leading to successively higher forms. On this point, however, it should be stressed that Darwin himself was not always entirely consistent and there are ways in which the language of teleology occasionally seeps into both *Origin* and *Descent*. One can still ultimately resort, if one chooses, to an argument to Design by postulating a creator as the designer of the evolutionary process. But the conclusions of *Origins* and *Descent* push the designer further back and make the designer superfluous for understanding the day-to-day operation of nature and entirely vitiates the need to search for some kind of force or entity lurking behind and directing observable phenomena. To what degree these ideas did and did not influence late 19th-century social evolutionary theory, is the issue to which I now turn.

Conclusion

The early and mid-19th century witnessed the rise of explicitly evolutionary approaches in both Biology and the Social Sciences. Empiricism and the Positive Philosophy of August Comte exerted significant influence on both. The critical idea in both was that the basic form of a biological species or type of social organization could change in fundamental ways. However, due to the influence of Lamarck, the emphasis in both areas was on transformation characterized by increasing complexity and integration. Much of Evolutionary Social Theory during this era was speculative, and often marred by ethnocentric and racist views of non-European cultures. Darwin's theories were articulated following a long period of direct observation and reflected this milieu. However, Darwin, for the most part, abandoned the idea of evolution as a process of increasing complexity and integration. The ramifications of Darwin's writings for society as a whole are often misunderstood. Darwin's views on society did influence his writings on biology though his science should be considered as sound by the standards of the era. Darwin did not however, found a new ethic based on struggle. Instead, his writings reflected both the positive and negative features of Classical British Liberalism. The characterization of Darwin having led to Hitler makes as much sense as arguing that Hitler was a logical consequence of Adam Smith.

Note

1 Daniel Hausman (1992) has made similar arguments regarding Johnathan Stuart Mill and his impact on Economics, though my views on Mill were for the most part developed in awareness of, but independently of Hausman's.

References

Carneiro, Robert L. 2003. *Evolutionism in Cultural Anthropology*. Boulder, CO: West View Press.

Comte, August. [1896] 2000. *The Positive Philosophy of August Comte*. Freely Translated and Condensed by Harriett Martineau with an Introduction by Frederick Harrison in Three Volumes. Original by George Bell and Sons. London: Batoche Books, Kichener.

Darwin, Charles. 1876. *The Origin of Species by Means of Natural Selection, or the Preservation of Favoured Races in the Struggle for Life*. London: Murray. Sixth Edition. In Whye, ed. http://darwin-online.org.uk/converted/pdf/1876_Origin_F401.pdf

Darwin, Charles. 1877. *The Descent of Man, and Selection in Relation to Sex*. Second Edition, revised and augmented. London: John Murray.

Desmond, Adrian and James Moore. 2009. *Darwin's Sacred Cause*. London: Penguin.

Harris, Marvin. 1968. *Rise of Anthropological Theory*. New York: Crowell.

Hausman, Daniel. 1992. *The Imprecise and Separate Science of Economics*. New York: Cambridge University Press.

Hunt, E. K. 1979. *A History of Economic Thought: A Critical Perspective*. Belmont, CA: Wadsworth Publishing Company.

Lubbock, John. [1865] 1878. *Prehistoric Times as Illustrated by Ancient Remains and the Manners and Customs of Modern Savages*. Fourth Edition. London: William & Norgate.

Lyell, Charles. 1830. *Principles of Geology. Being an Attempt to Explain the Former Changes in the Earth's Surface by Reference to Causes now in Operation*. Vol. 1. London: John Murray. http://darwin-online.org.uk/content/frameset?pageseq=1&itemID=A505.1&viewtype=text

Malthus, T. [1798] 1826. An Essay on the Principle of Population. Vols. 1 and 2. Sixth Edition. London: John Murray.

Mayr, Ernst. 1982. *The Growth of Biological Thought. Diversity, Evolution and Inheritance*. Cambride, MA, London: Bellknap Press.

Mayr, Ernst. 1991. *One Long Argument: Charles Darwin and the Genesis of Modern Evolutionary Thought*. Cambridge, MA: Harvard University Press.

Mill, Johnathan Stuart. 1824. "On the Definition of Political Economy and the Method of Investigation Proper to It." Pp. 309–339 in *The Collected Works of Johnathan Stuart Mill, Volume IV: Essays on Economics and Society Part I*. Edited by John Robson. Toronto: University of Toronto Press. https://oll.libertyfund.org/title/mill-the-collected-works-of-john-stuart-mill-volume-iv-essays-on-economics-and-society-part-i

Mill, Johnathan Stuart. 1843a. *The Collected Works of Johnathan Stuart Mill- Volume VII. A System of Logic: Part I*. Edited by John Robson. Toronto: University of Toronto Press.

Mill, Johnathan Stuart. 1843b. *The Collected Works of Johnathan Stuart Mill- Volume VIII. A System of Logic: Part II*. Edited by John Robson. Toronto: University of Toronto Press.

Morgan, Henry Lewis. [1877] 1944. *Ancient Society or Researches in the Lines of Human Progress from Savagery through Civilization*. Reproduced from the "First Indian Edition" published by BHARTI LIBRARY, Booksellers & Publishers, 145, Cornwallis Street, Calcutta. Transcribed for www.marxists.org by Ibne Hasan. Accessed at: https://www.marxists.org/reference/archive/morgan-lewis/ancient-society/index.htm

Rima, Ingrid. 2009. *Development of Economic Analysis*. Oxon, New York: Routledge, Taylor and Francis.

Scanlan, Padraic X. 2020. *Slave Empire: How Slavery Built Modern Britain*. Great Britain: Robinson.

Spencer, H. [1862a] 1967. *The Evolution of Society*. Edited by R. L. Carneiro. Chicago, IL: University of Chicago Press.

Spencer, H. [1862b] 1898. *First Principles*. New York: Appleton and Company. Accessed at https://www.biodiversitylibrary.org/item/60716#page/11/mode/1up

Spencer, H. [1873] 1896. *The Study of Sociology*. New York: Appleton. https://archive.org/details/studyofsociology12spenuoft/page/16/mode/2up

Tylor, Edward. [1871] 1903. *Primitive Culture: Researches into the Development of Mythology, Philosophy, Religion, Language, Art and Custom*. Fourth Edition. London: John Murray. Accessed at https://ia803009.us.archive.org/1/items/b31359668_0001/b31359668_0001.pdf

Weikart, Richard. 2004. *From Darwin to Hitler: Evolutionary Ethics, Eugenics and Racism in Germany*. New York: Palgrave McMillan.

Whewell, W. 1849. *Of Induction: With Especial Reference to Mr. J. Stuart Mill's System of Logic*. London: J.W. Parker. https://catalog.hathitrust.org/Record/011600793

Whewell, W. 1862. *Six Lectures on Political Economy, Delivered at Cambridge in Michaelmas Term, 1861*. Cambridge: University Press. https://catalog.hathitrust.org/Record/100870323

Winch, D. 2013. *Malthus. A Very Short Introduction*. Oxford: Oxford University Press.

3 Social Evolutionism and Political Economy after Darwin

Introduction

The latter half of the 19th century witnessed both an extension and intensification of the profound social, economic and political changes of the early 19th century, which were heavily dependent on the process of industrialization. In addition, the role of the nation state as a form of political organization became more solidified in Europe even as the nature of Imperialism changed from free-trade Imperialism to formal Imperialism. Capitalism itself underwent significant internal changes with the rise of large-scale firms, trusts and financialization. This process decisively shifted the balance of technological and organizational capacity to the core European states, which made the New Imperialism feasible. Though the process of industrialization was uneven, very few areas of the planet were unaffected by this process, even if that relationship was defined economically by primary commodity exports to industrializing areas. These processes brought European societies, and the U.S. into intensified contact with non-European societies on terms that favored the core European and American nation states. The processes at work in the late 19th century came to disaster with the onset of WWI.

Evolutionary social theory in the late 19th and early 20th century attempted to come to grips with the reality of this transformation. In doing so, some theorists were generally critical of invidious distinctions, and others less so, though none fully escaped the prisms of ethnocentrism and racism. As in previous eras, developments in the physical and natural sciences had ramifications for Philosophy of Science, which in turn impacted the social sciences. At the same time, social scientists influenced Philosophy of Science, and Philosophy of Science influenced the physical and natural sciences. The spread of evolutionary thinking in general was central to these developments: but not all, or even most, evolutionary thinking was necessarily Darwinian.

DOI: 10.4324/9781003170679-4

Darwin's Impact on Philosophy of Science

Overview

As argued in the previous chapter, though Darwin's work legitimized the idea of evolution as good science and had profound ramifications for both the Natural and Social Sciences, the view that the publication of *Origins* and *Descent* brought about a sudden shift in biology and the social sciences from pre-Darwinian to Darwinian thinking has little support. The term "Darwinism" was used to describe evolutionism in general, even though Lamarckian and Spencerian ideas continued to be prominent. Hence, though the idea of evolution gained widespread acceptance in the late 19th century, there continued to be significant debate over the meaning of the term as well as its mechanisms. In contrast to Darwin's approach, evolution was often conceived as a teleological and progressive process leading to higher levels of complexity and integration in both biology and society. In the social sciences, this was reflected in a general focus on the problems of industrial society, or in other cases, on the differences between industrial societies and non-industrial societies.

The emphasis on progressivism, coupled with the arrangement of civilizations hierarchically, interpreted through the prism of racialist ideas about evolution, and the confusion of social and technological progress, with biological progress, reinforced the general hardening of racial ideas in the late 19th and early 20th centuries. As the philosopher of science (and Darwin enthusiast) Michael Ruse (1989) has noted, evolutionary theory in the natural sciences in the late 19th and early 20th century was often a toxic stew of confused, inaccurate and socially repugnant ideas. Not surprisingly, these ideas were also prevalent in evolutionary social theory and in popular discourse. Yet the same misunderstandings could also be, and often were, employed in support of relatively progressive ideas.

German Idealism: Haeckel and Mach

Moreover, the spread of evolutionary ideas was interpreted through different prisms. In Germany, the influence of Kant and Hegel reinforced typological, progressivist and teleological thinking. But the actual expression of these concepts was both confused and confusing. This was especially due to the tendency of important working scientists to propose grandiose philosophical schemes, without necessarily taking the time to reflect on, or attempt to justify their philosophical foundations. In Biology, for example, Haeckel combined a rejection of dualism and spirituality with a teleological and progressivist view of evolution, while also rejecting final teleology (Mayr 1982, p. 517; Pojman 2020). Haeckel's views on embryonic development—that ontogeny recapitulates phylogeny (fetuses of more advanced organisms recapitulated the form of less advanced species)—stood in direct contrast to Darwin's views on evolution. Yet Haeckel came to be seen as the chief spokesperson for Darwinism in Germany. While many of Haeckel's conceptions and portrayal of evolution are universally recognized as erroneous, he nevertheless also made legitimate contributions to biology by sparking hypotheses in comparative embryology, early genetic research, as well as in ecology (Mayr 1982, pp. 534, 672).

Yet Haeckel's portrayal of evolutionary theory must be regarded on the whole as unfortunate. Haeckel also held to typological conceptions of race and argued for a separate evolutionary origin of races. His views about racial superiority are recognized today as both empirically and theoretically wrong as well as repugnant. The kind of romantic, teleological views held by Haeckel were later accepted in some fascist circles, and there are ways in which this kind of thinking can be put to use by fascism. But there is little evidence that Haeckel was ever held in significant esteem by the fascist movement a whole, or that he was a significant influence on the development of the fascist theory (reference on Haeckel). The combination of monism and teleology lends an air of general incoherence to Haeckel's theorizing.

Haeckel also exerted some influence on the development of Empirio-Criticism, primarily due to his monist view of the world, though there is no evidence that the Empirio-Critics were influenced by Haeckel's racialist views. It was the subject of extensive criticism by Lenin for its abandonment of materialism and a concept of objective reality. One need not accept Lenin's views on science in totality however to recognize the very large kernel of validity in Lenin's criticism. The two most prominent proponents of Empirio-Criticism were Avenarius and Mach. Avenarius's views were put forward in an odd and confusing fashion, while Mach's (1897, 1898) arguments were at least relatively clear. Consequently, my brief discussion herein focuses on Mach's arguments.

Empirio-Criticism was an effort to biologize knowledge by reducing knowledge to direct experience and sensory processing of the organism responding to its environment. Because Mach is strongly associated with physics, the idea that he sought to biologize knowledge at first seems counter-intuitive. However, Mach's views on Physics were in direct contrast to the realist position of Planck (Battan 2016). Planck's views on Physics were realist. In Planck's view there were universal constants underlying physical reality. Moreover, physical phenomena such as sound, heat, light etc. were taken as real independently and measurable independently of their impact on the observer. Similarly, Planck was realist about the existence of atoms. Many of these developments in Physics led to the erosion of Newtonian concepts of absolute space and time and set the stage for the development of the physics of relativity by Einstein. While Mach made multiple contributions to physics and had some influence on Einstein, Einstein rejected Mach's epistemological framework and embraced realism.

In contrast, as noted above, Mach sought to biologize physics. Mach began from the premise that the only thing we can actually know is what we experience from our own, direct sensations. These sensations are then processed and interpreted in the mind via their impact on the central nervous system. Since the mind is in the world and is part of the world, there is no real distinction between the mind and external reality. Empirio-critics such as Avenarius and Mach did not view themselves as denying the existence of the external world per se. Logically, sense experience implies that something is causing the sensation. Rather, their position was a reaction of the mind–body and mind–external reality duals. Since humans perceive physical phenomena differently depending on the circumstances, it is not possible to argue that such phenomena have an existence outside of our perception. Even the human concept of ego is misleading, as it is constantly, even if slowly, undergoing changes in response to the environment (Mach 1897, p. 11).

Yet Mach also incorporated teleological reasoning into his view. Science in Mach's view had developed as a means of humans adapting to the environment and encapsulating learned experience. This was also reflected in his argument that the human eye had developed for the purpose of viewing the world accurately (Mach 1898, pp. 66–98). This clearly implies the existence of an external world which provides the basis for sensory input. Consequently, I do not interpret Mach as saying that there really is no external world, but rather that our knowledge is limited to our sensory experiences and that we develop heuristic devices that are more or less reliable as a means to make sense of this experience.

With respect to theory, both Mach and Avenarius articulated a kind of evolutionary epistemology. In their view, theories are simply economical devices (the metaphor was deliberate) to simplify and explain the experience in the simplest terms possible. Over time, those theories which corresponded best with experience would survive. Mach took a curious view on the issue of atoms. Mach rejected the existence of atoms as real, though he recognized atomic theory as a useful heuristic device. But he was skeptical of the existence of atoms, as, at the time, they could not actually be seen. His argument that atoms may not be real however may have been a product of the available evidence of the time.

The other point that should be addressed is the controversy surrounding mechanisms of inheritance. Though the contributions of Mendel, Galton and Weisman genetics are accepted today, the available evidence in the 19th century was not clear. The concept of natural selection was widely accepted, but there was not a clear understanding of the differences between genetic evolution and cultural evolution or of the mechanisms of inheritance. Lamarckian ideas of inheritance competed with those of Galton and Weisman. In addition, there were questions about the amount of time in which evolution had taken place. The physical evidence of paleolithic humans and their ancestors was at best thin and what little there was, was often not well understood. In addition, the evidence also indicated, correctly, that more complex life forms arose after simpler forms and that modern humans came toward the end of the process.

The American Pragmatists

While evolutionary ideas in general exerted influence on Philosophy of Science, one area where specifically Darwinian understandings of evolution did have significant influence was on the development of American Pragmatism. The founder of Pragmatism, C. S. Peirce noted that Darwin's theory of evolution by natural selection was an application of the statistical method to biology. Peirce draws an interesting parallel between the development of theories about gases and Darwin's theory of evolution. Just as the theory of probability enabled predictions about the specific properties of gas molecules in the long run, so too had Darwin's theory been able to predict what the outcome would be under conditions of variation and selection (Peirce 1877, p. 2).

Though the implications of the above reference would appear to establish the credentials of Pragmatism as both realist and broadly Positivist, Pragmatism has been notoriously difficult to define. C. S. Peirce also used the term "Critical Common Sensism" but distinguished his position from that of Reid, by arriving at his views through straightening out of what he regarded as the confusing nature of Kant's categories. Peirce also referred to his Pragmatism as "Prope-Positivism". For Peirce this meant a kind of broad Positivism that acknowledged the importance of metaphysics, but only metaphysics conducted in a scientific spirit (Haack 2006, pp. 15–67: 2007). But as with Comte, Peirce rejected metaphysics of the kind that led to speculation or unverifiable propositions. Peirce is the originator of the verification theory of meaning.

As he noted:

> It appears, then, that the rule for attaining the third grade of clearness of apprehension is as follows: Consider what effects, that might conceivably have practical bearings, we conceive the object of our conception to have. Then, our conception of these effects is the whole of our conception of the object.
>
> (1878, p. 294)

It follows, therefore, that a statement that cannot be expressed in terms of practical bearings, is at best muddled. This is not, however, Peirce's theory of truth: it is a theory of meaning. If a statement has no clear meaning, it is not possible to evaluate its truth or falsity. Peirce's position points to a correspondence theory of truth, but in the end, that is not where Peirce went on the issue of truth. Firstly, in contrast to more naïve correspondence theories of truth Peirce argued that law tells us not just what happens on a specific occurrence, but what would happen if events were to occur. This position is perhaps best understood by Peirce's example (p. 9) that to say that a diamond is hard is to say that it would scratch another, softer surface: in other words, the diamond always has the potential to scratch other surfaces, but this potential is only activated under specific circumstances. In other words, in Peirce's view, laws and theories are not simply shorthand conveniences: they at least potentially describe real, actual entities and properties.

This leads us to the interesting issue of what truth means for Peirce, and why he thought that the method of scientific investigation would most likely, over the long haul lead to truth. Peirce's theory of truth is evolutionary in that we arrive at truth by eliminating false beliefs and establishing reliable beliefs. Unfortunately, Peirce's conception of truth is muddled. Peirce defines truth as the settled opinion, or final belief, that is arrived at by a community of inquirers who are genuinely committed to a process of truth-seeking inquiry. At the same time, Peirce embraced fallibilism which implies that even the best so best community of inquirers could be wrong. Furthermore, if the goal of inquiry is to eliminate doubt and arrive at a settled opinion that describes how things actually are, the final opinion of a community of inquirers might be truth indicative, but it is not truth.

With respect to what Peirce means as the scientific method of investigation, however, he is quite clear. In "The Fixation of Belief" (1877) Peirce compares four kinds of inquiry: tenacity, authority, a priori and the method of scientific investigation. In Peirce's view, the method of scientific investigation begins with genuine doubt and a genuine desire to know what the truth actually is. Peirce argues that the first three are likely to lead us to error. The latter is a continuous process, of abduction (formulation of hypotheses), deduction and induction. Peirce's use of these terms, however, requires at least some brief explanation.

In the "Fixation of Belief" Peirce takes the position that induction is generalization to a rule from the observation of specific cases (from the consequent to the antecedent of a syllogism) and that abduction is going from the subordinate clause to the antecedent. In later writings, Peirce defines abduction as the formation of hypothesis and induction as the method through which hypotheses are tested. The possible inconsistency however can be resolved by noting that if induction is a process of observation and generalization, then it is also consistent with the process of testing a hypothesis. Yet this does indicate that Peirce's understanding of the method of scientific investigation is one in which hypothesis formation is of critical importance. But the formulation of hypotheses in Peirce's view is not a process of wild conjecture and falsification of a prediction of novel results: hypotheses are formed on the basis of experience and subsequently verified, rejected, or revised in light of subsequent experience. Peirce is among the first to offer us an evolutionary view of epistemology in which an ongoing process of inquiry and our interaction with the environment and empirical evidence leads us to higher gradations of understanding of reality.

Another significant aspect of Peirce is the emphasis he places on coherence in scientific explanation (Haack 2006). On this point, Peirce is actually similar to the emphasis placed by Comte and others on the role of consilience. This is evidenced by Peirce's analogy of scientific explanation to a chain composed of multiple, interlocking links. Here again, we should note that the "fitness" of a theory is not confined just to the relationship of one theory to one set of data, but of the relationship of the theory to the data and to other theories.

Similarly, Peirce rejected dualism in favor of emphasizing continuity and connection. Peirce emphasized the ways in which categories blurred into each other at the edges. This rejection of dualism is reflected in the ways in which Peirce's writings defy easy classification of his positions on multiple traditional philosophical problems. He was an important contributor to formal Classical logic yet at the same time experimented with trivalent logic. His rejection of dualism was expressed in his embrace of what he termed an "ideal realism". On this latter point, however, Peirce's framework retains some aspects of Lamarckism, as opposed to Darwinism. Though there is some surface similarity with the Empirio-Critics on this point, he takes it in a very different direction. Peirce is asserting that there is at least potentially some ultimate ground of reality unfolding in the Universe, which he describes via the concepts of "agapeism" and "tychism". Thus, Peirce retains a teleology that is inconsistent with Darwinism, though the kind of teleology that Peirce appears to embrace is echoed by significant figures in evolutionary social theory such as Spencer, Sumner and Ward, though it was rejected by Veblen.

How much, or little, metaphysics and of what kind found its way into the thinking of Dewey, James and Mead, is an issue I address briefly below. I agree with Susan Haack (2006) that there is a significant continuity between Peirce and Dewey, but some daylight between his views and those of James and Mead. Nevertheless, all four can and should be viewed as advancing related understandings of a broad evolutionary epistemology with an emphasis on the importance of experimentalism as a means of arriving at reliable conclusions over the long haul of a process of genuine inquiry. Given space constraints, I will focus primarily on Dewey and then only briefly address James and Mead.

While Peirce's views on evolution, as noted above, to some extent reflected the influence of Lamarck, Dewey was clear about the influence of Darwin on American Pragmatism (1981, pp. 30–32). Dewey's position on the issue of realism is sometimes alleged to be ambivalent. In my view, this is a misunderstanding and confuses Dewey's anti-foundationalism with anti-realism. In multiple instances, Dewey articulated what has come to be known as the philosophic fallacy: the tendency of philosophers to assume that the conclusion of the end of inquiry could be known or assumed to exist prior to the process of inquiry. Similarly, Dewey was critical of the idea that only absolute knowledge counted as knowledge. He also drew a distinction between the multi-faceted aspect of experience and actual knowledge. For Dewey, the determination of what was and was not warranted as a claim to knowledge was an ongoing process of inquiry and experimentation constituted by consistently evaluating and re-evaluating hypotheses at each stage of inquiry. As with Peirce, Dewey views the problem of inquiry as addressed to a specific problem with the goal of arriving at a solution. Outside of the context of a specific problem, a claim to truth, or to warranted assertability, will make little sense. In more than one instance, Dewey stakes an explicit claim to realism (see, for example, Dewey 1910, pp. 115–121, 1981, p. 55; see also, Haack 2006).

Dewey's approach to epistemology is an extension of the Darwinian concept of adaptation as a continuous process of adjusting to the environment. Like Peirce, Dewey emphasized the role of experience and inquiry over the long haul as a means through which to distinguish warranted from unwarranted claims to knowledge and looked to the natural sciences as exemplifying this method. The importance of experience over the long haul as a means of justifying claims to warranted assertability is exemplified in his discussion of standard correspondence theories of truth as opposed to idealist views of truth. Correspondence theories of truth define truth as correspondence between a proposition and the object of that proposition at a point in time. Dewey's position is that taken in isolation, such statements are merely truth indicative. Truth, for Dewey, is when the practical implications of a statement result in the desired ends. Or in other words, we might say that the statement, "if I do X, then Y will occur", is true, or at least warranted in varying degrees by the extent to which doing X indeed produces results Y over the long haul (2010, pp. 175–185). Again, however, Dewey's argument implies Realism: In order for there to be a solution to a problem that we can take as reliable, the object of inquiry must have specific properties.

Dewey's emphasis on experimentalism was similarly reflected in his writings on the Social Sciences (for example, 1989). Dewey rejected utopian schemes, but he was a passionate advocate of social reforms. This is evident in his embrace of Democracy as a means of incrementally addressing and resolving pressing social problems. Dewey views Democracy as a means through which a society can instrumentally apply warranted claims to knowledge to solve pressing problems and improve the human condition. This of course suggests a theory of what is considered good, which for Dewey, as well as James and Mead, is the furtherance of those things that are truly desirable to promote the flourishing of the human organism. Though there is an aspect of hedonism as a foundation for morality, it goes well beyond the crassness of utilitarianism, which tended to look to the good as what is immediately pleasurable or desirable. But what is considered good or desirable is of course in part culturally dependent, which does at least point in the direction of cultural relativism. On the issue of race, Dewey rejected racist ideas and helped to found the NAACP along with W.E.B. Dubois.

The emphasis on the continuous adjustment of ends and means to the environment is similarly prevalent in the habit-instinct psychology embraced by Dewey, James and Mead (Haack 2006). In their view, humans possessed instincts, but that did not mean that humans acted blindly. Instincts expressed a proclivity to act in a certain way under certain conditions and their expression was shaped by social conditioning. Similarly, in their views on stimulus and response, they both stressed the continuity of the stimulus–response mechanism, the role of habit in forming a response and critically, the capacity of humans to create systems of valuation and meaning, communicated through linguistic signs. Thus, human action can be purposive and intentional and socially conditioned on the basis of genetic-based instincts. In that sense, a habit is a psychological propensity to act in a specific way under a given set of circumstances.

My point in the preceding discussion of the influence of Darwin on American Pragmatism has been to show the connection between the two, and the ways in which Pragmatism, as a general philosophical approach, conceived of science as a broad process of ongoing inquiry which could be applied to produce social improvement. As I will discuss below, in the case of Thorstein Veblen, Pragmatism, especially that of Dewey, James and Mead, exerted a direct and immediate influence on theorizing. This connection between Pragmatism and the development of American Institutionalist school, has been addressed by multiple authors (Poirot 2007, 2008; Tillman 1988; Webb 2002, 2007, 2012). Yet many Pragmatist concerns are reflected in much of late 19th and early 20th evolutionary social theory, even where that relationship was not explicitly acknowledged. Similarly, many of the concerns of Pragmatism reflected the general milieu of the late 19th and early 20th centuries, particularly with the ways in which social evolution might be viewed as an ongoing process of adaptation to the environment.

The More General Theory of Sociology

Overview

The idea of "Social Physics", or "Sociology", as a comprehensive and evolutionary science of society, as envisioned by Comte and Spencer, gained significant momentum in the late 19th century. Some of the writers who influenced Darwin, such as Spencer and others, continued to write well into the late 19th century. Yet the decades after Darwin also witnessed the rise of the second generation of Social Evolutionists. Though this new science was generally termed "Sociology", the boundaries between the several social sciences were permeable and fluid. Both Sociology and Anthropology envisioned themselves as comprehensive and the theoretical differences between the two are at least to some extent, artificial. That noted, Anthropology in the late 19th century began to chart an explicitly anti-evolutionary course. While Darwinian analogies were prevalent in Sociology, there was also significant attention given to the themes of increasing complexity, differentiation and integration between the component parts of society. Similarly, the idea that progress and improvement could be attained by the application of scientific knowledge to society was also prominent.

The emphasis on progress and improvement through the application of science however took two contrasting directions: that of "Social Darwinism" and "Reform Darwinism". However, given the predominant influence of Lamarck on the evolutionary thinking of the era, the terms "Social Lamarckism" and "Reform Lamarckism" are probably more appropriate. Social Darwinism was expressed most directly in the writings of Spenser and his chief disciple, William Graham Sumner (1883, 1885, 1906) whereas Reform Darwinism is prominent in the writings of Lester Frank Ward. Where the Social Darwinists emphasized progress as natural and were skeptical of the ability of the State to improve on social evolution, Reform Darwinists envisioned an improvement in society via state action, based on the application of scientific reasoning. But in spite of their ideological differences, both Sumner and Ward emphasized similar themes, and both subordinated the concerns of Political Economy to Sociology.

The Views of Sumner

Though Sumner was strongly influenced by Spencer, his writings provide further clarification and refinement of Spencerian Sociology. Like Spencer, Sumner's writings encompass seeming contradictions. Sumner is a methodological individualist, though he also emphasizes the role of folkways and mores as exerting a superorganic force on humans in the form of social pressure. Human beings in Sumner's view survive, or fail to survive, primarily through group selection (1906). Yet at the same time, they struggle against each other in society and achieve their status based on relative merit as individuals. He defines class primarily in terms of differential wealth and income, which he attributes to differences in the distribution of talent and thriftiness (Sumner 1883, pp. 8–9). The upper classes, Sumner tells us, owe nothing to the lower classes through the medium of the state, other than basic guarantees of social order. To do otherwise is to turn some men into slaves and lessen liberty. At the same, he acknowledges that wealth can be abused and lead to plutocracy. As later theorists were to do, Sumner places considerable importance on the maintenance of social equilibrium.

Sumner wrote extensively during this period, but many of his core ideas are articulated both in *What the Social Classes Owe Each Other* as well as in *Folkways*. The latter is more extensive and rigorous work, but it is generally consistent with the former. Sumner (1906) draws a distinction between Folkways, Mores and the conscious use of law as a means to regulate society. Folkways, according to Sumner, are social habits that emerge out of action undertaken to satisfy human needs and "take on the character of a social force". While they can be modified by purposive action, this is only possible to a limited extent. In addition, Sumner also describes a process of selection of folkways, in the larger context of "relations, conventions, and institutional undertakings". While they are not material, they are social and superorganic and consequently, "leading factors in the science of society". Mores in Sumner's view are "solidified folkways" that incorporate "a judgment that they are conducive to societal welfare". They "exert a coercion on the individual to conform to them though they are not coordinated by any authority" (all quotes p. iv).

Though laws may reflect folkways and mores, they are not the same. Law in Sumner's view reflects the conscious, rational design. While folkways and mores continue to exert influence in modern Industrial society, Sumner directly contrasts what in his view is the rational and contractual nature of modern Industrial society, with the emphasis on Primitive and Barbaric societies on custom, habit and tradition. Like Spencer, Sumner argues that social evolution is a process of increasing complexity in social organization and technology.

Sumner links Democracy, especially in the US, to the rise of modern Industrial society and the decline of feudal ranks and privileges. Under feudalism, as well as in barbarous societies, the upper classes engaged in predatory behavior and instituted this predatory behavior in the state. Sumner's view of the state is negative. Following Spenser, he emphasizes the role of militarism in creating consolidated states. Democracy emerged in Sumner's view as a means of people protecting themselves against the efforts of nobles and monarchs to seize their wealth. The challenge to the modern State is to protect the freedom of all, and guard against plutocracy, but also limit the ability of a Democracy to enact reforms to protect or advance one class over another.

Sumner views the purpose of the state as protecting liberty. But he also sees the state as a threat to liberty. Consequently, the state should confine itself to those areas in which it is most competent, primarily, the protection of order and liberty. State action in Sumner's view is unlikely to improve the evolutionary order, will have unforeseen actions and will impose costs on the "forgotten man". Sumner's defense of laissez faire and critique of the ability of the state to resolve social problems was also reflected in his critique of Imperialism. In Sumner's view, Imperialism would lead either to the incorporation of the conquered people into the existing polity, which in his view would represent corruption, or it would lead to the subjugation of the conquered people.

Ward's Social Reformism

While Lester Frank Ward's approach to Sociology (1903) was as systematic and comprehensive as that of Comte, Spencer and Sumner, in contrast to Spencer and Sumner he emphasized the ability of conscious, purposive design of social institutions to improve human well-being. Ward opposed both laissez faire as well as eugenics. Prior to turning to Sociology, Ward had been a paleontologist and his writings exhibit a command of the state of the science of his day, as exhibited in his discussion of the Weisman controversy (Ward 1891). Ward's views on biological evolution were a synthesis of Lamarckism, Darwinism and Weismanism. Ward did not disagree with Weisman's conclusion that heredity was transmitted through the germ plasm. Similarly, he accepted Darwin's emphasis on selection and adaptation as the primary mechanisms of evolution. However, he argued that over long periods of time, functional adaptations that were acquired during the lifetime of an organism could be transmitted to the germ plasm leading to changes in structure over time. Like Comte and Spencer, Ward's Sociology was an extension of the Natural Sciences. Similarly, his later comprehensive work (1903), *Pure Sociology*, exhibits extensive knowledge of the biology of his era.

Ward's views on the relationship between science and progress have similarities to the view of both Comte and Sumner and he articulates these ideas in multiple works. Though Ward identified as a Positivist, what he meant by Positivism clearly has a strong affinity with Pragmatism. Like Peirce he stresses the importance of empirical inquiry and also recognizes the importance of abstract theoretical generalizations for Science. His ontology is clearly realist. His view of scientific progress is that scientific progress is not uniform or linear, but rather uneven and ragged. He argues against reducing Sociology to mathematical formulation and criticizes economists for attempting to do so in economics.

Many of his ideas were articulated in a series of articles he wrote in *The American Journal of Sociology* between 1895 and 1897 which set out the relationship between Sociology and other areas. The idea of progress is central to Ward's thinking. Progress has come in Ward's view due to the realization that the Universe embodies rigid law. It is because the Universe is ordered in this fashion and is impersonal, that humans actually have the capacity to understand it. As he notes:

> Any conceivable fact or thing may therefore be regarded as a term in a series which is infinite in both directions. In science this is called the law of causation; in philosophy it is called the law of the sufficient reason.
>
> (Ward 1895a, p. 2)

There is another, interesting aspect that Ward shares with Peirce and that is the idea of a kind of telic or cosmic principle at work in the Universe. Ward writes of cosmic evolution in a sense that suggests an ultimate telic purpose to the Universe leading to progress, including, the rise of human beings as rational, intelligent, purposive and social. Similarly, the idea of improvement arising from greater integration is also present in his paper on the relationship of biology to sociology. Ward approvingly cites Spencer's views on evolution at length. Yet he argues that there is a homology between the body, which is directed by the mind, and the social organism, which is undirected. By consciously taking control of the social body, the mind, in the form of government, can direct the social organism to higher ends (1895a).

In addressing the relationship between Anthropology and Sociology, Ward did not draw a sharp distinction between Anthropology and Sociology. Anthropology in Ward's view is the study of humankind, and Sociology is the study of Society. Because Anthropology is focused on the human species in all its manifestations, Sociology in Ward's view is the more general science and incorporates Anthropology. Based on this argument, Ward could just as easily have argued that Anthropology incorporates Sociology (1895b).

But the foundational science for Sociology in Ward's view is Psychology. Here again, though Ward stresses the natural and step-by-step process of evolution, he also views evolution as having a purpose in leading to improvement in function. Hence the goal of humans is the satisfaction of wants and needs, which they realize through society. It is through psychology that we understand these wants and needs (1896). Ward divides Sociology into the followers of Spencer, which he labels the Static School and what he terms the Dynamic School. But his definition of Dynamic and Static differs from that of Comte. Dynamic Sociology by Ward's definition is the belief that it is possible to apply the knowledge of Sociology to the improvement of society, whereas Static Sociology is the belief that it cannot be applied to improve society. Ward also makes a further distinction, which is between pure and applied Sociology. It was the latter, which in Ward's view, was the ultimate purpose of Sociology (1896).

This idea that Sociology, or human action in general, has what Ward calls a telesis requires some clarification (1897a, 1897b, 1897c). Ward made a distinction between Genesis and Telesis. Social Genesis is not just about the origins of society, but about its becoming. Ward had a progressivist view of evolution, like Spencer and Sumner. He did not attribute progress in evolution to any kind of direction of the process and denied the relevance of theo-telesis. Hence one component of progress was due to natural evolution. In contrast to the kind of progress advocated by Spencer and Sumner based on natural evolution, Ward argued for what he termed anthropo-telesis. Anthropo-telesis is homology to development and is used by Ward to further his argument that society could ultimately be consciously and purposely improved.

Ward's views on human social evolution reflect the prevailing themes of the 19th century. In *Pure Sociology* (1903) he traces the rise of humans as a biological species to the rise of Civilization. Like many other 19th-century theorists, Ward argues that early human societies were gynocentric. Patriarchy arose in Ward's view due to a conscious, thought-out decision by men to assert power based on their superior physical size and power. In Ward's view, women are more moral than men in the sense that they are more focused on the needs of the group and social provisioning. The subjection of women in Ward's view is not warranted and is an example of the kind of social institution that can be reformed through an understanding of sociology.

Similarly, in *Pure Sociology* and elsewhere, Ward traces the origins of social inequality in general. Readers unfamiliar with the extensive influence of the concept of "race" on 19th-century natural and social sciences may find his discussion of "race struggle" to be initially disturbing. Yet Ward's discussion of it takes a critical turn. The origins of social distinctions such as caste and class in Ward's view arise due to the predation of some groups over others. Conquering races, once in power, create social ranks to enforce subordination. Ward is extremely critical of social inequality and notably argues that both Western and other civilizations have created similar systems of social inequality: the European feudal class system for example in Ward's view is the same as the Indian caste system.

Ward's view of social progress is neither strictly materialistic nor idealistic. In his discussion of Durkheim, whom I will discuss shortly, Ward praises Durkheim's theory of the division of labor enthusiastically. The Division of Labor, according to Ward, is a result of technological progress which leads to the elevation of human material prosperity and makes spiritual life possible. As Ward put it:

> I long ago defined material civilization as "the utilization of the materials and forces of nature." I always recognized, however, the immaterial or spiritual element in civilization as distinct from this, but not independent of it, and indeed as realizable only in a very slight degree without it. The spiritual life of man may be regarded as a function of his physical life, and only capable of a high development when the latter has reached a certain stage at which the higher psychic attributes are liberated and allowed to act. The division of labor, therefore, as a factor in civilization must depend upon the degree to which it contributes to the utilization by man of the materials and forces of nature. For my own part I look upon invention and labor as the chief factors, and the division of labor as simply the natural and necessary method spontaneously adopted for economizing the results of invention and labor. (1902c, p. 2)

But despite Ward's acknowledgment of the importance of material factors in the progress of civilization Ward also attributes significant importance to spirit and subjective factors in human social evolution and the role of purposiveness, or as he terms it, telesis, in human affairs. Ward's views on this are more sensible when he is placed in the context of Lamarckism. Ward denies that he is arguing for an ultimate teleology. Rather, he is attempting to thread a needle by suggesting that increasing complexity and the realization of rationality are ultimate, even if not necessarily pre-intended results of evolution in both the biological and social sense (1902c).

Ward was certainly not the only "reform Darwinist" of the late 19th and early 20th century. As I discuss below, there is some overlap between his views and those of Thorstein Veblen in Economics. But the idea that "Darwinism", or "evolutionism" was responsible for all the ills of the late 19th and early 20th century, which is often expressed by both the left and the right, has stuck. Some of this is undoubtedly owed to the views of Eric Hofstadter (1944), though Hofstadter did acknowledge the contributions of Ward and Veblen. Yet the problem that Hofstadter pointed to was not owed to Darwin, but rather to the biologization of social inequality. Nor was Hofstadter the only figure to blame "Darwinism".

Boas and Anthropology

Though the late 19th century might be considered the high watermark of Evolutionary Social Theory, anti-evolutionist currents were already present in Anthropology by the turn of the 20th century (I address the situation in Economics below.). In what came to be known as Cultural Anthropology, Franz Boas was the main opponent of Evolutionism (Carneiro 2003; Harris 1968). With respect to biology, Boas was a strong advocate of biological evolution. However, he drew a sharp distinction between human biological evolution and human social evolution. This provided, at least in part, the rationale for his further division of Anthropology into the four fields of Biological Anthropology, Archaeology, Cultural Anthropology and Linguistics. Cultural Anthropology was thus defined as the study of existing cultures, with an emphasis on pre-industrial, and often relatively isolated societies.

Boas' ideal for Anthropology was that theory should be built on a foundation of extensive, direct observation. To this end, Boas (1920) advocated that the proper method for Anthropology was a combination of cultural relativism and ethnographic fieldwork. Cultural relativism in Boas' view was primarily a tool with which to eliminate or reduce observer bias, not an ethical stance. Ethnographic fieldwork was based on direct, participant observation in which the observer immersed him or herself in the culture being studied. Boas was not necessarily rejecting the idea that cultures evolved or that there were different kinds of cultures. He rejected the view that cultural parallels could be explained in terms of similar evolutionary stages or by diffusion. In contrast, he emphasized the specific, unique, historical circumstances of each individual culture.

This raises a curious point. Early in his career, Boas was a Physicist and strongly influenced by Mach. Part of his goal was to put Anthropology on a sound, scientific footing. The general view of Boas is that he rejected Mach's views in formulating his approach to Anthropology. I am not so sure. Physics is generally thought of as a theory-heavy, top-down science. Mach did not reject the theory, but Mach's views on science as noted above were strongly inductivist and also idealist. Contemporary evolutionary anthropologists (cited above) writing on Boas have not surprisingly been mostly negative and noted his idealistic approach to culture. The idea that culture is an integrated whole, that it is primarily mental and that the observer should immerse oneself into the specific culture to understand it is at least not inconsistent with Mach's ideas. Consequently, I am not so quick to dismiss the influence of Mach on Boas and the direction he took in Cultural Anthropology.

I will return to Boas and the impact of his disciples in the following chapter but some additional points are in order at present. Boas was reacting to the speculative, and overgeneralized social evolutionism of his day as well as to racist ideas. Boas was a sharp critic of racism and of racialist ideas. Even if his anti-racism was limited to liberal anti-racism (Anderson 2019, chapters 1 and 2), his open opposition to racial categories and hierarchies amongst humans is still commendable, especially considering the era. The problem for the neo-evolutionists in the 20th century was how to maintain what was viable in the earlier evolutionary theories in the Anthropology of Tylor and Morgan and at the same time, jettison the ethnocentrism and racialist aspects of their theories. Having said this, it is not necessarily true that the historical particularism and purely idealistic understanding of culture advocated by Boas and his later disciples necessarily lead to a better understanding of the particularities of culture. As Wolf (1999, pp. 69–132) the analysis of the potlatch among the Kwakwaka'wakw (Kwakiutl) initiated by Boas and furthered by his student Ruth Benedict, missed important dimensions of both chiefly authority, ideology and the impact of commercialization and industrialization.

Sociology in Europe: Durkheim and Weber

Durkheim

While Lester Frank Ward made a substantial contribution to the creation of the modern discipline of Sociology in the US, the contributions of Emile Durkheim were to eventually gain greater recognition. Steiner (2011, footnote p. 11) briefly traces the evolution of Durkheim's Sociology. Steiner argues that eventually, he was to break it down into two components: the study of social structure and the study of social functions. Under the heading of social morphology, Durkheim included Political Economy, which in Durkheim's view should be re-integrated into the study of Sociology. To Steiner's categories, I would also add that Durkheim has a theory of social morphogenesis, even if he did not use that term. Hence it is a gross oversimplification to reduce Durkheim to narrow structural functionalism. Though there are other interesting aspects of Durkheim, my primary interest herein will be in his philosophical views as well as his treatment of economic activity. I will address the former first.

Durkheim's views on the Philosophy of the Social Sciences are explicitly addressed in his *Rules for Sociological Method* (1938), but they are also present both explicitly and implicitly in other writings as well. Durkheim's stated allegiance to Positivism places him in the Comtean tradition, but Durkheim develops Positivism in a distinctive fashion and was critical of aspects of Comte's system. Similarly, many of Durkheim's concerns echo those of the American Pragmatists, despite Durkheim's having been critical of Pragmatism. What Durkheim means by Positivism is the Natural and Social Sciences should make use of the same general approach, though clearly, in Durkheim's view, society was a phenomenon *suis generis*.

In spite of his professed adherence to Positivism, Durkheim was critical of what he regarded as Comte's overly abstract and speculative approach to Sociology. Durkheim's criticism of Comte was not a rejection of ontology, but of what he regarded as Comte's a priori approach to stage theory. Similarly, he was critical of abstract metaphysics with no connection to empirical reality. As will become clear as my discussion progresses, Durkheim's views of social morphology clearly imply at least a form or realism and an acknowledgment of emergent properties of social phenomena. For Durkheim, social facts are external to the individual and to the observer while the study of Sociology is independent of both biology and psychology: Society is a phenomenon *suis generis*. Durkheim also draws a distinction between "fact" and "value" and held that Sociology should not be guided by any particular social agenda. However, Durkheim clearly did not oppose the study of values and their role in society and clearly regarded values as real in the sense that they exerted an influence on society. There are also strong normative implications to Durkheim's views in general.

The object of Sociology in Durkheim's view is the study of "social facts" or "social things". These entities in Durkheim's view are not just useful creations of the Sociologist: they are actual entities with actual causal power. They are external to the individual or observer, are widely shared by society and exert a constraining influence on social action. Durkheim provides a clear, concise explanation of what he means by social things and his definition is notably very similar to Thorstein Veblen's definition of "institution".

> A social fact is every way of acting, fixed or not, capable of exercising on the individual an external constraint; or again, every way of acting that is general throughout a given society, while at the same time, existing in its own right, independent of its individual manifestations. (1938, p. 13)

These social facts, in Durkheim's view, are not isolated—rather, they exist in a set of functional relations to other ways of acting. Yet while "social facts" are observable, they exist as a shared set of mental rules amongst people in society. In stressing the shared "collective consciousness" of society, of course, Durkheim is not referring to an occultic property, but to the fact that such rules exist in people's minds, and that what is in people's minds regarding society's rules is not random or idiosyncratic. The naming and classification of social facts in Durkheim's view cannot be casual: it requires careful definition. Their grouping may contradict the normal societal use of such definitions. Durkheim approvingly quotes Bacon in arguing that Sociologists must break their "idols" in order to be good scientists. Though the social scientist may have biases, it is imperative that the social scientist be conscious of such biases and conduct inquiry in a way that recognizes and strives to limit such biases.

In setting forth his method of explanation, Durkheim draws a distinction between the social morphology of social facts and their function. The cause of social facts lies in the preceding form of social organization: social morphology arises from the constitution of society, or to use Durkheim's words: "the first origins of all social processes of any importance should be sought in the internal constitution of the social group" (p. 113). These consist of things and persons. Durkheim criticizes the asocial view of Hobbes and Locke, as well as the natural law view of Aristotle and the methodological individualism of Spencer and Sumner.

More importantly, he was particularly critical of the emerging focus of Political Economy on rational choice and methodological individualism, which in his view, detached economic analysis from any actual understanding of real economic phenomena. The reader may have noted an interesting and curious aspect of this facet of Durkheim's writings. While he consistently addresses many of the standard concerns of Political Economy such as the division of labor, the organization of production, the impact of technology and other similar issues, for Durkheim, Political Economy is subordinated to Sociological analysis. The social milieu is the factor that can explain change. Change does not come from either material or ideal factors—it comes from social action. Durkheim then states succinctly the task of the Sociologist is "to discover the different aspects of this milieu which can exert some influence on the course of such phenomena. Durkheim classifies these aspects as "the size of a society" and "its dynamic density" (p. 113).

While I have thus far emphasized the static and structural aspects of Durkheim's views, it is important to emphasize that he ties this to a theory of morphogenesis. Structure in Durkheim's view changes over time and types of societies differ in terms of their structures. Evolution in Durkheim's view is a product of the complex interaction of multiple factors such as population, technology and social structures (check on this in Rules). However, Durkheim's theory of agency is never fully developed. Though he is critical of the abstract and speculative excesses of Comte, Spencer, Sumner and Ward, he shares their view that social evolution leads to both greater complexity and greater integration.

In both *Rules of Sociological Method* as well as in *The Division of Labor,* Durkheim (1894) traces the evolution of civilization as well as the increasing division of labor. The origins of society lie in the gens or clan. Durkheim explicitly rejects the idea of society founded on a social contract as a contract implies the existence of contract law defined by society. As the population increases the division of labor also becomes more complex, leading to the combination of segments and the rise of Chiefdoms, to which Durkheim traces the origins of the State. The State, or Civilization, arises at a point in time in which there is a need for greater coordination to hold society together. He notes that France had gone from being an agrarian entity to an industrial entity but asserts that there was no actual change as France remained France. Durkheim's assertion here is both confusing and in my estimation contradictory. Had Durkheim traced the creation of France through the process of the transition from Roman domination, to feudal forms of political organization, to the creation of the French nation state, and changes in the structure of the French nation state, and tied that process to changes in the social structure, he would have strengthened his point.

The above also reflects the second weakness in Durkheim (and others), at least with respect to his argument in *The Division of Labor*: his tendency to bifurcate with respect to forms of social organization. This is reflected in his distinction between mechanical and organic solidarity. Mechanical solidarity is social solidarity based on the shared characteristics of the group. These shared characteristics require the subordination of the individual to the group. Organic solidarity is based on the increasing division of labor and heterogeneity and potentially provides the individual with a special sense of purpose and contribution to society. For Durkheim, the rise of early forms of despotism in societies characterized by mechanical solidarity was in fact an instance of an individual imposing his will on society and of the identification of society with that individual's will. Increasing heterogeneity and differentiation then provide for increasing levels of individuation and opportunities for increased integration. This is evidenced in Durkheim's view by the decreasing reliance of society on negative solidarity in the form of official, legal sanctions and the increase in positive solidarity with the rise of industrial society.

The above description may strike readers whose familiarity with Durkheim is shaped by surface familiarity with his concept of anomie as odd. Durkheim is often presented as arguing that Industrial Society automatically resulted in anomie. But this was not a necessary outcome in Durkheim's view. Durkheim did fear that Industrial society could develop an anomic division of labor. Here Durkheim was critical of the relationship between workers and capitalists in industrial production which by its nature could lead to a pathological division of labor. Similarly, the rise of modern industrial society also led to the danger of increasing breakdown of purpose and morality as people lost their sense of identity and belonging. Durkheim defines the "normal" as that which contributes to the well-being of society, and the pathological as the deviation from the normal which in turn undermines social society. Crime, in Durkheim's view, is necessary but also destructive, and thus requires a societal response in the form of a sanction. Yet while all crime may by definition be a form of deviance, and society tends to define deviance as crime, not all "normal' states are conducive to individual well-being and not all deviant states are of necessity "pathological". Part of the task of Sociology was to diagnose this condition and help develop conditions that would lead to integration into society.

My discussion of Durkheim has focused primarily on Durkheim's earlier writings, which are regarded by at least some Durkheim scholars to stress the mechanistic over the fluid aspects which emerged more strongly in his later work. Notably, the later Durkheim does present many of the same ideas as more fluid while also shifting to a detailed study of the role of religion. In this aspect of his work, there is some influence of Comte's negative view of the theological and metaphysical stages and Durkheim notes that early religions provided a basis for the later development of scientific thinking. While secular and scientific in his thinking, Durkheim viewed religion as real in the sense that people's beliefs and actions had a real impact on society by increasing social solidarity—a point that is not dissimilar to that of the American Pragmatist, Henry James.

Durkheim's influence on social theory in general has of course been extensive. His work was carried out further by his nephew, Marcel Maus, who also exerted significant influence on Anthropology. Maus' analysis of the differences in structural forms of exchange in different societies is clearly of relevance to evolutionary social theory and serves to highlight the peculiarities of exchange in a capitalist society. Maus was pivotal in the development of both French Sociology and Anthropology. Nevertheless, Durkheim's (and Maus's) effort to integrate the Static and Dynamic and Evolutionary and Structural aspects of social theory was largely lost by the tendency of both non-Marxist and Marxist Structuralism to pull social theory away from the analysis of change, and toward static analysis of structural forms.

Weber

Thus far, as we have seen, Social Evolutionism in the 19th century was generally associated with Positivistic approaches to the social sciences, in the sense that theories of social evolution rested on the premise that there were discoverable laws, or at least general principles, that could explain social evolution. Similarly, while there was significant emphasis on issues of concern to Political Economy, such as the division of labor, the rise of the State, the appropriateness of laissez faire vs. reform and other similar issues, Political Economy was subordinated to and incorporated under the umbrella of the new Sociology. Though Max Weber's contributions incorporated the above concerns, Weber rejected the Positivist view that there were specific causal laws that governed the process of social evolution in favor of his method of Verstehen. Social evolution, according to Weber, was the outcome of human social action which led to specific conjunctures of events. Social action and social evolution in Weber's view was understandable and explainable only in terms of the motivations and intentions of the actors: consequently, it could not be explained by the same methods as that of the natural sciences (Gerth and Mills 1958, pp. 55–65). Nevertheless, Weber did in actuality provide a theory of social change that was amenable to empirical inquiry.

Weber's emphasis on the meaning and intentionality of social action has often resulted in Weber being classified as a methodological individualist. Yet Weber's individual is not an isolated atom: Weber's individual is a socially conditioned individual. Nor do Weber's actors act independently of positions in society. Weber is clearly cognizant of the role of different kinds of social inequality in drawing a distinction between economic class, status and the ability to exercise power (see, for example, sections VI and VII in Gerth and Mills 1958). Though the three are interdependent and may be mutually reinforcing Weber notes that economic position may not be determinative. Nor does Weber define economic class exclusively in terms of relationship to means of production but rather in terms of one's economic position in society. There is no specific, historical subject or class in Weber's analysis that is imbued with the role of emancipatory action. Weber is also clearly cognizant of the importance of power and domination in society. Weber does not conceive of society as harmonious, but as conflictual. Thus clearly, social structures play an important role for Weber in influencing social action. Weber distinguishes between four different kinds of action: Instrumental rationality (consistency of means and ends), value rationality (consistency with values), traditional action (action based on authority or custom) and affective action (action based on emotion). Again, though all types of such actions are present throughout historical eras, contemporary Industrial society rewards and promotes instrumental rationality, at times to the exclusion of the other three (Collins 1980; Kalberg 1980).

Though Weber is critical of Positivism and its emphasis on the role of causal law in the social sciences, his method of Verstehen nevertheless leads to theorizing that is amenable to testability. Weber's ideal type is based on the actual characteristics of the entity being studied. This requires a degree of abstraction from some detail in order to permit logical analysis of the entity being studied. However, the formulation of the ideal type and logical analysis of its key features are then subjected to further revision in light of subsequent investigation. Weber's assertion that social theory should be "value free" is also reflective of some aspects of Positivism. But Weber's argument is not that values are irrelevant to social action or that social scientist should ignore the role of values in shaping social action. To the contrary: Weber's analysis consistently addresses the value orientation of the social actor. As with Durkheim, Weber argued for separating the analysis of society from specific social programs.

The idea that social evolution and increasing rationality and complexity do not necessarily lead to greater human freedom and well-being is expressed in Weber's Sociology, which also departs from the otherwise overwhelming Positivist emphasis of the late 19th and early 20th centuries. Where most 19th-century writers idealized science as liberating humans from superstition, religion and providing the basis for the improvement of society, Weber's stance toward science and rationality was ambiguous, and at times critical. Weber's partial skepticism of the emancipatory capacity of science and rationality was grounded in his view that industrial society and capitalism in the 19th century had brought with it the triumph of an overly narrow instrumental rationality. Weber clearly acknowledged that the application of instrumental reasoning had brought about gains in productive capacity and the overall efficiency of state-led bureaucratic action. At the same time, however, Weber stressed that this tended to subordinate all human action to this particular way of acting and feeling, thus in effect, trapping people in an "iron cage".

Weber's approach to social action is neither strictly idealist nor materialist. In Weber's view, there is a long, causal chain of development in European history that led to the rise of Capitalism. Though some elements of this chain were present in other societies, they were not all present. Hence it is not possible to isolate a single factor that led to the rise of Capitalism, or for that matter, to present a general theory of social change. Weber's initial theory of the development of modern capitalism rests on a specific conjuncture of historical events. In *The Protestant Ethic,* Weber (1905) emphasized the role of specific systems of belief, in this case, Protestantism as leading to greater discipline and rationalization of life as unintentionally conducive to the rise of Capitalism. Though Weber emphasized the role of Calvinism in this regard, he also extensively discussed the role of non-Calvinist sects. It should be stressed that Weber is not offering a history of Capitalism in terms of ideas per se, but rather, a history in terms of how ideas shaped behaviors and led to unintended consequences. In later work, Weber presents a more comprehensive theory of the rise of Capitalism.

Later writings of Weber provide a fuller explanation of the rise of Capitalism. In his multiple writings, Weber distinguishes between Capitalistic behavior, the spirit of Capitalism and the Capitalist form of business enterprise (Kalberg 1980; Kocka 2016; Tribe 2019). He develops this argument initially in *The Protestant Ethic* (1905, pp. 8–28) and then in multiple places throughout *Economy and Society* (1922). Capitalistic behavior is profit-seeking behavior. The Capitalist firm is organized on the basis of continuous seeking of profit and by rational, disciplined seeking of profit. It is this emphasis on discipline—constantly investing, reinvesting and saving—that distinguishes the spirit of Capitalism and Capitalism as a social system. Capitalist behavior in Weber's view is present even in Ancient Rome (Love 1986). Capitalism as a social system integrates value rational action and instrumentally rational action by elevating profit-seeking behavior to the ultimate valued and combining it with instrumental rationality. This system is characterized by industrial production for profit, predicated on the existence of integrated markets in land, labor and capital, and the organization of production by the Capitalist firm. In that sense, Weber's definition of Industrial Capitalism is similar to Marx's definition of Capitalism as a specific mode of production and historical epoch, premised on free wage labor in organized factories with industrial technology, and the continuous reinvestment of profits back into production.

Yet Capitalistic behavior and extensive markets, in Weber's view, are prevalent in multiple historical epochs and civilizations. However, the presence of non-rational, or irrational restrictions with respect to rules of trading and accumulation acted as a block to the development of Capitalism. What is unique in Western Europe in Weber's view is the rise of a rational, disciplined, mode of behavior, shaped initially by a specific religious ideal and reinforced further by ways of thinking that led to the triumph of instrumental rationality. This is the point of course in *The Protestant Ethic*. By identifying capitalistic elements present in multiple societies, including in the predatory or "booty capitalism" of the Roman Empire, Weber traces the gradual development of that aspect of behavior. Though one could argue that the eventual development of modern society is inevitable at some time and place in history, Weber does not posit any kind of teleological drive toward modern industrial society.

This brings us to an interesting question: does Weber's analysis point to the use of analogies of variation and selection? I think that it does, though Weber does not explicitly use such analogies. In explaining the importance of Calvinism to the rise of industrial capitalism, Weber does not argue that Protestantism causes Capitalism, or that Capitalism cannot co-exist with Catholicism or with other religions. Weber's argument is that modern industrial capitalism requires and rewards instrumental rationality, thrift and savings and that Calvinism specifically also requires and rewards these traits. Thus, there is an affinity between the "ideal type" of capitalistic behavior and the "ideal type" of the Calvinist (and other) Protestants. We should also note that Weber's method is comparative: Weber contrasts, perhaps wrongly, the cultural characteristics of traditional Chinese society as steeped in Confucianism with the cultural characteristics of an increasingly rational West. In Weber's view, the attributes of Confucianism blocked the application of instrumental rationality, thus blocking the development of industrial capitalism in China.

The End of Political Economy: Marx, Marshall and Veblen

Marx

At Marx's funeral, Marx's longtime friend and close collaborator, Frederick Engels is alleged to have said that just as Darwin discovered the laws of biological evolution, so too, Marx had discovered the laws of social evolution. Whether or not there are actual laws of social evolution and whether or not Marx discovered them are both arguable, as is the view that Marx attempted to predict the future on the basis of these laws. In addition, despite Marx's admiration for Darwin, Darwin had little to no impact on Marx, and Marx had no impact on Darwin. Furthermore, though aspects of Marx's and Engel's contributions were penned in the early 19th century, they did not reach mature expression until the 1870s. Consequently, Marx's and Engel's primary contributions to Political Economy and Evolutionary Social Theory are of more relevance to the late 19th century, than to the early 19th century.

Marx's theory of social evolution is expressed via Historical Materialism, of which Engels' contributions are also of considerable importance. Marx's Political Economy, while distinguishable from Historical Materialism, is both informed by and informs his Historical Materialism. Historical Materialism explains the origins and nature of the Capitalist Mode of Production and Political Economy explains the workings of the Capitalist Mode. Though Marx does not address the issue, it is logical to assume that one could also develop a Political Economy of the medieval era or other eras. Hence in my view, the two projects were intended to be complementary, not opposed. Though Marx argued that theory and praxis should be unified, it is possible to logically separate Marx's advocacy for Socialism from Historical Materialism and Political Economy, even if only for the purposes of analysis. In both cases, Marx's adaptation of Hegel's dialectic is central to the theory. This raises an interesting question as to what remains of Marx if the Hegelian mysticism is stripped away. I will address this issue below in my discussion of Veblen and return to it in Chapter 5.

Marx's views on Historical Materialism, as well as those of Engels, are articulated in several places. The basic schema as well as the method was set forth early on in *The Communist Manifesto* (1848). However, *The Manifesto* is only one source and not necessarily the most important as it was intended primarily as a political tract. Other, later sources are actually of more importance, including, but not necessarily limited to, *The Grundrisse,* the last third of Volume I of *Capital* (1867), Marx's correspondence with Vera Kasulich, *Origins of the Family, Private Property and the State* (Engels 1884) which was edited and published by Engels after the death of Marx, Marx's analysis of British Imperialism in India (1853), and *Socialism: Utopian and Scientific* (Engels 1882), also edited and published by Engels after Marx's death, as well as other writings.

As multiple other authors have noted, the term materialism is often misinterpreted as implying a crude economic determinism. But Marx provides a clear statement of what he does and does not mean by materialism in his preface to *A Critique of Political Economy* (1859). Materialism, as Marx defines it means in the first instance that it is people's social existence that shapes ways of thinking, or consciousness, rather than vice versa. Marx describes the "Mode of Production" in the preface as encompassing both relations of production and their levels of material development. Together, they "condition" the entire superstructure of society. Marx identifies the Asiatic, Ancient, Feudal and Bourgoise modes as defining a broad historical sequence of levels of development. Change occurs when the forces of production can no longer be contained within the boundaries of the existing mode. Changes in the economic base can be studied with the level of precision of the natural sciences, while changes in the superstructure are subject to some degree of indeterminacy.

In drawing on the above sources, it is possible to tease out a general schematic of how Marx and Engels viewed the progression of history. In each mode, the respective social classes, defined in terms of their relation to the productive process, are mutually antagonistic. Those who are engaged in the direct act of production are subordinate to and exploited by those who control the physical means of production. Exploitation in this sense means that the subordinate class produces more than is necessary for reproduction and subsistence as that level of subsistence is defined in a given historical epoch. This laboring class is compelled, prior to the rise of Capitalism, to hand over the surplus by direct force or threat of force, as is the case either with slavery or serfdom. In Capitalism, the laboring class is "freed" from any means of economic support and must thus sell its labor to the Capitalist Class in exchange for wages. The wages are less in value than the full value of the commodity produced.

It is possible to identify at least three possible mechanisms through which a society passes from one mode of production to a higher mode of production. This process cannot be understood independently of Marx's identification of dialectical processes. One mechanism is a contradiction between the development of new technologies within a given mode of production and the inability of the existing social structure to contain this new development. A second possibility is through the contradictions brought about by the social conflict between classes within a mode of production, including of course a conscious and deliberate revolution by one class against another. A third possibility is via the interaction of modes of production, including imperialism. On this last point, Marx's understanding of non-European societies was clearly lacking in that he attributed the potential for the development of Capitalism in India to be entirely due to British Imperialism.

In the last third of Volume I of *Capital* Marx provides a specific overview of the origins of the Capitalist Mode of Production. Amongst Marxist scholars, there is considerable disagreement as to whether Marx viewed the Capitalist Mode as arising directly out of the conflict between nobles and peasants, thus leading to "agrarian capitalism" before the rise of industrial capitalism, or whether the Capitalist Mode arose through a complex process of interaction between the internal conflict within the feudal mode and the circuits of commercial exchange (see, Aston and Philpins 1985; Hilton 1976). Both aspects are present in Marx's discussion of the process of Primitive accumulation in Capital. In some instances, Marx identifies the bourgeoisie of the medieval urban areas as the primary antagonists of the feudal nobility and Capitalism as arising out of the expansion of commerce and ultimately the world market. Yet he also places considerable emphasis on the role of primitive accumulation in rural areas and the tensions between noble and serf as the antagonism which leads to the ultimate creation of a propertyless class via the process of enclosure. Furthermore, in his discussion of British Imperialism in India, Marx (1853) identifies Imperialism as another mechanism through which a society can be transformed, though Marx's description of Indian society is subject to the same criticisms of ethnocentrism as other European writers.

Hence, in my view, in so far as one views adherence to the "correct" textual interpretation of Marx as the goal, the interactionist position is more consistent with Marx. If the goal is the correct interpretation of the historical record, my view is that Marx was at least heading in the right direction in identifying the evolution of Capitalism as arising from the interaction of the creation of a world market, urban development and conflicts between serfs and nobles. Similarly, Marx's analysis of the transition from slavery to serfdom also rests on the dynamics internal to the struggle between slave and master and the synthesis of the Ancient Mode with the free system of the Germanic mode.

Notably, there is some correspondence between Marx's historical schema and the four-stage theory of the Enlightenment. Marx's theory is generally viewed as a unilinear scheme with each stage necessary for subsequent development. Marx's schema, of history moving from the Ancient, or Slave Mode, to the Feudal Mode and to the Capitalist Mode provides a roughly accurate thumbnail sketch of Western European History. However, slavery existed prior to and outside of Ancient Rome. Serfdom, as it came to exist in Western Europe, reflected legal peculiarities of European society at the time, but it too was present in many societies. Moreover, the term "Feudalism" is tricky and has as much to do with the decentralized nature of political authority as it does with serfdom. Here again, many societies have gone through periods of centralization followed by decentralization. The argument that there is some kind of necessary, logical progression of societies through Slavery, Serfdom, and then to Capitalism cannot hold and certainly, the argument that Capitalism must give way to Socialism, based on the previous progression also cannot hold.

In my estimation, however, Marx was aware of and attempted to work out a theory of parallel development and interaction of modes of production in different civilizations. Whether or not the concept of an "Asiatic Mode of Production" was accepted by Marx can be disputed. Yet based on his analysis of Indian society, it is clear that Marx viewed the development of Asian civilization as distinctive from the development of Western Civilization and that he viewed this development as inhibiting Capitalist development. The passage to Capitalism in Asia in Marx's view could therefore only occur due to the breakdown of Asian society via European Imperialism. Marx's understanding of Asian society, in general, was clearly ethnocentric and ignored the negative impact of British Imperialism on Indian economic development. My point herein is to simply note that Marx did recognize that transformation could occur from outside a given society as well as from internal processes.

Marx's historical forms are general abstract, and even his discussion of European Feudalism leaves much to be desired as it does not address the problems of decentralization and the rise of nation states. However, *The Origins of the Family, Private Property and the State*, does partially address the evolution of specific political forms. The work was compiled, edited and published by Engels (1884), working on the basis of Marx's notes. Marx and Engels build on Morgan's analysis (previously discussed) to explain how the State (or Civilization) had arisen out of the process through which the gens (or kinship group) had been displaced and alienated from its hold over production to create mutually antagonistic classes, thus creating a social division of labor and necessitating the creation of a formal state to mediate this antagonistic relationship. Marx and Engels take this process a step further, postulating that under socialism with the disappearance of antagonistic classes both the social division of labor and the state must disappear. Similarly, Marx paid particular attention to detailed political analysis in his *18th Brumaire of Napoleon Bonaparte III* (1852). In that work, Marx analyzed in considerable detail the inherent conflicts within the French State and the contradictions arising out of the French Revolution. Marx takes this a step further in his analysis of the Paris Commune. On the whole, Marx was critical of the State and viewed all states as the product of and acting in the interest of, the dominant class. The State, therefore, would disappear with the abolition of social classes.

In evaluating Marx's development of Political Economy and Historical Materialism it is important in my view to note that both the use of the Hegelian dialectic as well as an ultimate teleology are critical aspects. Marx's choice of the industrial working class as the ultimate revolutionary subject of history can only be rendered sensible in light of his inverted Hegelianism. By beginning with a view of humanity as having a species being that is activated through creative labor to achieve freedom Marx arrives at his view of the working class as the bearer of the inevitable drive of history. Since the ultimate goal of humanity is to realize freedom through the free organization of work, Marx argues that the industrial working class under capitalism will be the vehicle through which an ultimate revolutionary breakthrough to socialism is achieved. In the *Communist Manifesto* Marx's model for this revolution was the mass insurrectionary traditions in Europe, as exemplified in the multiple uprisings of 1848. In interpreting Marx, Engels argued that by the end of the 19th century, this model was no longer applicable. This tension in the interpretation of Marx as arguing for insurrection or democratic transition to socialism of course hardened in the late 19th and early 20th centuries.

An important contribution of Marx's Historical Materialism is in the specific definition of Capitalism, or rather, the Capitalist Mode. The Capitalist Mode of Production, in its full mature form, is defined by Marx by the antagonistic relationship between the Capitalist Class (the owners of the factories) and the property less proletariat (the workers in the factories) who must sell their labor power to the Capitalist Class to survive. Marx makes the critical distinction between profit derived from mercantile exchange (M-C-M′) and profit derived from the process of Capitalist production (M-C-P-C′-M′). These features of Capitalism distinguish the Capitalist mode from all other modes. Though Marx locates its genesis in the 16th century, given Marx's definition, it does not come into full existence in Britain until the early 18th century and then somewhat later on the Continent. One can make an argument that it is not fully present until the late 19th century.

Political Economy for Marx is primarily an analysis of the laws of motion of the Capitalist Mode of Production. In his unfinished work "Critique of Political Economy" (1859) Marx defined the method of Political Economy in a fashion that is both similar to, and yet also distinctive from Ricardo. Like Ricardo, Marx relies on the abstract-deductive method. Both the *Critique* as well as *Capital*, especially Volume I, rely on an abstract presentation of categories of analysis. As Sweezy has argued however, Marx's use of abstraction is aimed at getting at the right level of abstraction: one abstracts sufficiently to get the actual and critical features of reality that one is attempting to explain (Sweezy 1942, pp. 11–21). While Volume I of Capital is the most general, Volumes II and III, which remained unfinished during Marx's life successively introduce qualifications. For Marx then, his treatment of the topics of Political Economy is a historically specific analysis of a specific era in human history, which Marx clearly believed was transitory.

A full discussion of Marx's Political Economy is beyond the scope of this study. My presentation herein relies in part on my own reading of Marx while also drawing loosely on Sweezy (1942) and to a lesser degree on Hunt (1979). Marx begins with the concept of a commodity and the division of labor as representing specific, historical forms and mediating relationships between people. What I take to be the critical components of Marx's analysis rests on his view, which he develops further from Smith and Ricardo, that the long-run inherent value of a commodity is defined by the amount of labor embodied in the commodity, which can be broken down into variable capital (labor costs), constant capital (fixed capital costs) and surplus value. The worker produces more in value than the worker is paid. After subtracting the amount required to cover the expenses of fixed capital from the value of the product, the Capitalist retains the surplus value. A defining feature of the operation of the Capitalist Mode is that at least a portion of this surplus value is continuously reinvested into the process of production, thus leading to continuous capital accumulation, or in other words, further development of the forces of production. The general tendency is for the rate of profit to fall over time as the capitalist must cover an increasing amount of capital costs. As the rate of profit falls and Capitalists pull back on capital expenditures, crisis ensues. While this is the general case, Marx clearly acknowledges that there could be exceptions and qualifications that might postpone the onset of crises.

In Marx's view, these crises would eventually reach a point at which the further development of the Capitalist Mode was blocked, and of necessity, the working class would seize the means of production and establish socialism. The achieval of Socialism could be hastened by the conscious, political organization of the working class into a revolutionary class for itself, which of course Marx advocated and worked to bring about. As is well known, how the Socialist Mode would operate is at best vague in Marx's writings. But his vision is clearly utopian as it would lead to an end to commodity production, wage labor, and even ultimately, specialization and division of labor. At the same time, Marx argued that the more conscious and deliberate coordination of the Socialist Mode would lead to more rapid and concerted development of the forces of production, thus providing a material base for the eventual establishment of Communism, at which point, and only at that point, as Marx emphasized in *Critique of the Gotha Program* could the slogan "from each according to his ability, to each according to his needs" be fully realized.

Alfred Marshall

Thus far we have noted several possible positions with respect to the relationship between Evolutionary Social Theory and Political Economy. While those who today are regarded as the founders of Sociology subordinated the study of economic processes to the study of the social structure, those regarded as the founders of Economics, including Marx, generally treated Political Economy as an abstract analysis of production and distribution, yet retained a strong connection between Political Economy and their theory of social evolution. In contrast, the direction advocated by Mill was to separate the study of Political Economy from the study of social evolution, while simultaneously acknowledging the validity of a broader theory. This latter path was also the one chosen by Alfred Marshall (1890). Hence, we cannot consider Marshall's Political Economy to have been evolutionary in any sense of the term in spite of the extensive influence of

Spencer on Marshall. However, in the broad sense of the term, Marshall was an evolutionist, albeit in a Spencerian, rather than Darwinian sense, though he made no original contributions to Evolutionary Social Theory.

In discussing Marshall, I will simply outline the nature of his arguments in his *Principles of Economics* (1890). As was the case with Mill, Marshall's approach to Political Economy stresses the cultural particularity of his analysis and the need to take account of the subtleties, qualifications and exceptions to what he terms as the "normal case". Marshall only limits the kinds of questions or issues economists should address to those boundaries where the scope and methods of economics no longer apply. Because the kinds of questions that economists address—those in which the acquisitive mode of behavior applies—permit more precise and exact analysis, economics, in comparison to other social sciences is more formal and exact. Hence economic analysis can make use of logical and mathematical reasoning as a means of helping to organize the analysis. In Marshall's view, induction is used to understand the specifics, deduction is used to reason out the consequences of the specifics and verification is used in relation to empirical evidence.

The concept of equilibrium is central to Marshall's analysis, though Marshall emphasizes the processes through which equilibrium is reached and the way in which equilibria can change. Equilibrium, in Marshall's view, is not a starting point nor a final resting point. Equilibrium is the state a market would reach if all the forces currently present in the market were to be allowed to work themselves out, ceterus paribus. Marshall does not argue that ceterae are, or will remain, paribae. For Marshall, the assumption of ceterus paribus functions as a means of conducting a thought experiment as to what would happen if certain conditions were met. The idea of continua is central to Marshall's analysis in general as in Marshall's view, commodities are continuously substitutable one for another. In addition, both consumers and firms are able to continuously adjust their behavior to continuous changes at the margin.

Marshall's motto, *natura non facit saltum,* is similarly reflected in those places where he does directly address the evolution of Industrial society as well as proposals for reform. In his appendix, Marshall traces the evolution of freedom and the progress of the Industrial Revolution. Yet though he rejects Spencer's argument for a unified social science approach, he follows Spencer in his views on both biological and social evolution. He attributes some of the initial misery surrounding the Industrial Revolution to a specific conjunction of circumstances at the time of the Industrial Revolution but views the Industrial Revolution as a whole presenting a meliorative trend that is reinforced by a drive toward increased complexity. In stressing the context and background in which markets adjust to equilibrium, Marshall acknowledges the cultural specificity of rational, maximizing behavior. Marshall does not reject the importance of habit, custom and cultural particularities. He acknowledges that the habits of the "city man" are characteristics of time, place and class, but which are also shared sufficiently with other classes in Industrial society. Marshall notes that biological species adapt and change over time. He argues that the idea of constant adaptation of a species to its environment applies better to invertebrates than to vertebrates. Modern Industrial society in Marshall's view is a particular species and a form of adaptation. Though it has changed in the past and could change in the future, its current form is fixed.

An economist in Marshall's view should have a knowledge of history and sociology. Mathematics, though helpful, is ultimately of value primarily as a check on one's reasoning. Marshall also argues that long deductive chains of reasoning in economics are unproductive and instead advocates the use of short chains of deductive reasoning that complement each other. Marshall's prescribed method for Political Economy is one that is informed by evolutionary analysis. But again, his Political Economy is not evolutionary. The cultural peculiarities of people in modern industrial society are taken as a given and their general characteristics are then used as the basis for postulates on which the analysis is based. On that basis, one then employs deductive reasoning to arrive at a conclusion that is taken to be close enough to a reliable conclusion.

The consequence of Marshall's approach is that it limits the kinds of questions that Political Economists can and should explore, in so far as they act in their capacity as Political Economists. But where Marshall stressed the qualifications, subtleties and exceptions to the general case, used his mathematics as a guide to reasoning, and held an understanding of history and culture in the background, the economics profession over the course of the 20th century increasingly embraced a much more formal and less qualified vision for economics, bereft of history and an understanding of cultural specificity.

Thorstein Veblen

Amongst the Evolutionary Social Theorists of the late 19th century, the contributions of Thorstein Veblen are unique for several reasons. There are both parallels as well as differences in his writings in comparison to Ward, Weber and Durkheim. But like them, he sociologized Political Economy, though he identified as an Economist. Veblen eschewed the abstract-deductive method and did not articulate a theory of value, prices and distribution of shares, was critical of both Marx and Marshall, all of which no doubt contributed to the unjustified accusation that he was a-theoretical. He is primarily remembered as a founder of what came to be known as the Original Institutionalist school in Economics. Yet his contributions are relevant to all the contemporary social sciences. With respect to the policy implications of his contributions, he was closest to Ward, yet there is no evidence of influence between the two in either direction. He was also influenced by Tylor, Spencer and Sumner and there are obvious echoes of all three in various places in his writings, but his views on class and power were nearly the direct opposite of those of Spencer and Sumner and he consistently rejected any kind of invidious distinction. He is quite obviously an evolutionist yet freely borrowed in his later writings from Boas. However, the chief characteristic that sets Veblen apart was his effort to fully incorporate the implications of Darwin for the social sciences. This was reinforced or perhaps owed at least in part to the clear influence of the American Pragmatists, especially Dewey, on Veblen. Nevertheless, while Darwinian analogies are prevalent in Veblen's writings, it is a mistake to view Veblen's writings as simply a generalization of Darwin's views on biological evolution.

In what is probably his most famous essay, "Why Economics is not an evolutionary science", Veblen (1919) explains what in his view and evolutionary science is not and why Marshallian economics was not evolutionary. As he put the matter:

> The Economists have accepted the hedonistic conceptions concerning human nature and human action, and the conception of the economic interest which a hedonistic psychology gives, does not afford material for a theory of the development of human nature. Under hedonism, the economic interest is not conceived in terms of action. It is therefore not readily apprehended or appreciated in terms of a growth of habits of thought, and does not provoke, even if it did lend itself to, treatment by the evolutionary method.
>
> (p. 78)

If one puts that passage into the larger context of the whole essay, Veblen's argument is clear. Marshall's theory of behavior, even if it was not meant as a universal description of human behavior, reduced human decision-making to responding to stimuli of pleasure and pain in an effort to reach an equilibrium. The emphasis on equilibrium as the end of economic action also lost sight of Darwin's focus on the process of continuous adaptation of a species to its environment. Marshall's failure to take this method into account in Veblen's view made Marshall's method outdated. In his essay "The Evolution of the Scientific Point of View", Veblen (1919) explained what it is that *does make a science evolutionary*. He wrote:

> This notion of process about which the researches of modern science cluster, is a notion of a sequence, or complex, of consecutive change in which the *nexus* of the sequence, that by virtue of which the change inquired into is consecutive, is the relation of cause and effect.
>
> (pp. 33–36)

Causation in Veblen's view was not synchronic. It was mechanical and took place over a period of time and it was also cumulative. In other words, the institutional structure of the economy today is a result of a long process of a chain of causation resulting in constant change.

In "The Economics of Karl Marx", Veblen (1919) extended this critique to Marx, and also to what is often today referred to as Classical Political Economy (i.e., the writings of Smith and Ricardo). In all three cases, Veblen was critical of what he characterized as the natural law view of science as expressed in their respective theories of value and distribution and their use of the abstract-deductive method. Furthermore, the idea that there is an inherent exchange value embedded in a commodity toward which the price of a commodity tends reflects a view of social and economic processes which assumes that there is a center of gravity in the system. It also reflects the continuation of animistic thinking in modern economics.

The relevant point herein is not whether or not Veblen got Marx and Smith right as my own view is that he misinterpreted them. The important point is that his critique of Marx reveals a lot about his attitude toward bad metaphysics. Notably, Veblen (1919) criticized Marx for his use of what he termed "the neo-Hegelian, romantic Marxian standpoint" which Veblen viewed as teleological. In contrast, "the Darwinian scheme of thought" was "controlled by nothing but the vis a tergo of brute causation and is essentially mechanical" (pp. 436 and 437). Hence it should be clear that Veblen rejected any kind of romantic metaphysics, vitalism, entelechy or final teleology as consistent with modern, Darwinian science. Veblen's rejection of animism, and his association of animism with pre-scientific reasoning that was especially characteristic of the stage of Barbarism, echoes similar points made by Comte. In criticizing metaphysics in this way, however, Veblen was not rejecting the role of Ontology per se for social theory—a point I will return to shortly.

The influence of Dewey, James and Mead on Veblen is strongest with respect to his incorporation of habit–instinct psychology. Whereas we generally think of instincts as fixed and genetically determined behaviors, Dewey, James and Mead all addressed the concept of instincts in humans as biologically given, but subject to social regulation. In addition, as Dewey emphasized, the response to a stimulus goes far beyond just a response to a specific stimulus but incorporates an entire reflex arc. This idea was also developed by Mead in stressing the active role of the self in socialization as well as the creation of meanings associated with actions. Veblen developed these ideas to argue that social habits arise over the course of history on the basis of underlying biological instincts, a point he developed in *The Theory of the Leisure Class* (1967, pp. 1–21) and in other places as well. On this point, in my estimation, Veblen actually veers toward Lamarckism when he argues that instincts evolve in specific stages of history and then set the parameters for the social evolution of specific civilizations.

At the same time, Veblen was also strongly influenced by the emerging concept of hard inheritance (1915, pp. 1–11), though again, as noted before in my discussion of Ward, it was not uncommon for people to attempt to combine the two and the general acceptance of Weisman over Lamarck did not come until late in Veblen's career. Veblen does draw a distinction between social evolution and biological evolution, though in some instances he appears to muddle the two. Social Evolution takes place in Veblen's views through a complex process of changes in instincts, technology and social institutions over time. Veblen's definition of technology is broad and is not confined just to the physical aspect of technology but also entails knowledge of technological processes and ways of thinking. In Veblen's view, technology changes faster than institutions, which tend to be resistant to change. For example, Veblen argues that the rise of machine technology requires people to engage in matter-of-fact reasoning. Matter-of-fact reasoning in turn will clearly lead to more technological innovation. In other words, change can be both cumulative and circular: social habits give rise to habits of thought and habits of thought feedback onto and shape social habits in a constant process of non-teleological change. It is these aspects of Veblen that are the most Darwinian in his view of social evolution.

As with all other social evolutionists of the 19th century, Veblen divided history into three stages: savagery, barbarism and civilization (1967). Veblen implies that tool using, or instrumental reasoning emerges in the savage state. In the savage state egalitarian relations, including between men and women predominate. Yet at the same time, this stage was also characterized by superstitious and animistic mythologies. In the barbarian stage, invidious distinctions and predatory behaviors arise as powerful chiefs engage in warfare and reinforce their power with ceremonial displays. Again, Veblen echoes the erroneous view, which as we have seen was prevalent from the Enlightenment on, that patriarchy emerged during this period. The status-reinforcing behavior of this era is in Veblen's view expressive of animistic traits of thinking. The final stage, that of civilization, emerges due to the more widespread application of instrumental reasoning and the application of scientific reasoning to pressing human problems. However, even in industrial society vested interests promoted and used the kinds of ways of thinking, feeling and acting that were prevalent in the stage of barbarism to further their interests. When Veblen appears to be engaging in satire about this kind of behavior, he is in fact making a serious, political point about what he views as the retrograde behavior of elites, the long-term persistence of institutions and specifically, the persistence of institutions characteristic of previous eras in contemporary society.

In spite of the Darwinian influences on Veblen, there are also obvious non-Darwinian aspects to this theorizing. Throughout Veblen's writings, there is an emphasis on multiple dichotomies such as matter of fact vs. animistic, the instinct of workmanship vs. predatory and pecuniary instincts. Though Veblen did not explicitly adopt the dichotomy of "ceremonial" vs.

"instrumental", the dichotomy is nevertheless in my estimation useful to understand the kinds of contrasts that were central to Veblen's theorizing. Firstly, the kind of dichotomous thinking that Veblen engages in is clearly not Darwinian, but instead, is ironically suggestive of a dialectic between scientific vs. animistic thinking. Secondly, in Veblen's view, some people in society could and did consciously and deliberately block necessary change to protect vested interests. In fact, the triumph of such institutions, reinforced by irrational ways of thinking, was in his view quite likely.

Veblen is obviously a conflict theorist and he directly addresses the problem of power in society. I agree with Hodgson that Veblen has a concept of emergence in which new properties emerge at the level of social organization (or other levels) and that the concepts of structure and agency are latent in his theorizing. Yet that serves to illustrate that Veblen did not simply view social evolution as a generalization from an ontological principle of variation and selection. In contrast, Veblen did put considerable emphasis on the ways in which social evolution differed from biological evolution.

A related issue is what Veblen thought about the role of progress in human history. Veblen obviously was aware that non-rational, and even irrational motives could predominate in a society (1915). But he viewed these as atavistic aspects that stood in the way of progress. Though Veblen does not use the term, his argument does in some respects parallel Nietzsche's dichotomy of Apollonian vs. Dionysian, save that in contrast to Nietzsche Veblen sees the Dionysian tendency as negative. This is clear in his criticism of the German militarism and patriotism that gave rise to WWI and would also clearly apply to the rise of Fascism in Europe or to many other social movements. Veblen traces the rise of German militarism back to German pre-history and emphasizes how institutional characteristics, rooted in the early ethno-genesis of the Germanic peoples, continued to exert an influence in the German of WWI, even as it made a transition to an industrial state.

Yet Veblen also recognized that groups of people could challenge invidious distinctions. The most likely path to challenge such thinking is through the application of scientific thinking. He clearly thought that progress had occurred, and much of his writing fits in with the general zeitgeist of the Progressive Era in American History with its stress on the ability of scientific thinking to solve pressing human problems when correctly applied. However, he also rejected the idea of teleology. In his argument for the Engineers to eventually have at least considerable control over production Veblen echoes the tendency of American Progressivism, also present in Ward, to turn society over to an elite, technocratic governance. But as noted above, continued progress in his view was not assured. Quite the contrary, Veblen was often pessimistic about the possibility of continued progress and noted that historically, what he termed "imbecilic" institutions often won out over more progressive alternatives.

Veblen is often accused of having focused overly on critique and offering no positive theory or program in its place and similarly of being "a theoretical". He is also at times viewed as engaging in criticism through the use of sarcasm. These are misunderstandings of Veblen. In contrast to the other Political Economists, from Smith through Marx and Marshall, Veblen does not provide any extensive discussion of the issues of value, relative price, profits, rent or wage determination, though, in his later work, he did offer some analysis of the Business Cycle. Veblen did not consider the concept of equilibrium values to be an interesting problem in economics. Like Weber and Durkheim and others, Veblen had a sociologized theory of economic processes. He obviously had a theory of how this process functioned. Furthermore, Veblen was strongly influenced by the view that the process of scientific inquiry should not be subordinated to a particular political program. Hence, he did not embrace any specific social-political program, though his rejection of invidious distinctions and his acknowledgment of the role that power differentials play in society, place him on the left of the political spectrum. Veblen's politics in that sense follow Dewey's: he is in favor of a step-by-step improvements in society via the application of instrumental reasoning (Tillman 1988).

Conclusion

The post-Darwinian emphasis on evolution as a central concept in social theory in the late 19th and early 20th centuries, with the exceptions noted in this chapter, was oddly, not necessarily strongly influenced by the Darwinian approach to evolution. For the most part, themes that had already been prevalent in the Enlightenment and which were further developed in the early 19th century, continued to be prevalent in the late 19th and early 20th centuries. Hence as we have seen multiple writers emphasized the themes of increasing complexity, greater social integration, the problems of industrial society and progress through the application of scientific reasoning. Darwin's influence was strongest in the writings of the American Pragmatists and Thorstein Veblen. Though the same themes are also present in Veblen's theorizing, Veblen did not view these trends as guaranteed and clearly saw them as potentially reversible. Marx and Veblen were the most critical of Capitalism, though Ward also made the case for Progressive Reform as did Durkheim. Weber was also critical of what he viewed as the overemphasis on rationality prevalent in Capitalism and there is much in Weber that is implicitly critical of Capitalism, though Weber does not make that critique explicit. Others, especially Sumner, were overtly apologetic for Capitalism. In Marx's case, the evolutionary aspect and the analysis of the operation of the laws of value that characterized the Capitalist Mode, were logically separable, but interdependent. In Marshall's case, the evolutionary theory was strongly separated from Political Economy. The general consensus in the social sciences that social theory should be evolutionary and interdisciplinary however was to be significantly challenged and weakened in the first half of the 20th century.

References

Andersen, Mark. 2019. *From Boas to Black Power: Racism, Liberation and American Anthropology.* Stanford, CA: Stanford University Press.

Aston, Trevor H. and C. H. E. Philpins. 1985. *The Brenner Debate: Agrarian Class Structure and Economic Development in Pre-Industrial Europe.* Cambridge: Cambridge University Press.

Batten, Alan H. 2016. "Comte, Mach, Planck, and Eddington: A Study of Influence Across Generations." *Journal of Astronomical History and Heritage* 19(1), pp. 51–60.

Boas, Franz. 1920. "The Methods of Ethnology." *American Anthropologist* 22(4), pp. 311–321. https://doi.org/10.1525/aa.1920.22.4.02a00020

Carneiro, Robert L. 2003. *Evolutionism in Cultural Anthropology.* Boulder, CO: West View Press.

Collins, Randall. 1980. "Weber's Last Theory of Capitalism: A Systematization." *American Sociological Review* 45(6), pp. 925–942. https://doi-org.proxy01.shawnee.edu/10.2307/2094910

Dewey, John. [1910] 2005. *How We Think.* With an Introduction by Gerald H. Gutek. New York: Barnes and Noble.

Dewey, John. 1981. *The Philosophy of John Dewey: Two Volumes in One.* Edited and with an Introduction by John McDermott. Paperback Edition. Chicago, IL: University of Chicago Press.

Dewey, John. 1989. *Freedom and Culture.* Amherst, NY: Prometheus Books.

Durkheim, Emile. [1938] 1964. *Rules of Sociological Method.* Translated by Sarah Solovoy and John Muelleran and edited by George E. Caitlin. First Free Press Paperback Edition. New York, London: The Free Press.

Durkheim, Emile. [1894] 2014. *The Division of Labor in Society.* Edited and With a New Introduction. Free Press Paperback Edition. New York, London: The Free Press.

Engels, Frederick. [1882] 1892. "Socialism: Utopian and Scientific." In Tucker, Robert C., ed. 1978. *The Marx-Engels Reader.* pp. 683-717. Second Edition. New York, London: W.W. Norton and Company.

Engels, Frederick. [1884] 2000. *Origins of the Family, Private Property and the State.* Online version, Marx-Engels Online Archive. https://www.marxists.org/archive/marx/works/1884/origin-family/index.htm

Gerth, Hans. H. and Charles. Wright Mills. 1958. "Introduction: The Man and His Work." Pp. 3–79 in *From Max Weber: Essays in Sociology.* Translated and Edited with an Introduction by Hans. H. Gerth and Charles Wright Mills, edited by Gerth, H. H. and C. Wright Mills. 1958. New York: Oxford University Press.

Haack, Susan. 2006. "Introduction: Pragmatism, Old and New." Pp. 15–65 in *Pragmatism Old and New: Selected Writings*, edited by Haack, Susan with Robert Lane, Associate ed. Amherst, NY: Prometheus Books.

Haack, Susan. 2007. "The Legitimacy of Metaphysics: Kant's Legacy to Peirce and Peirce's to Philosophy Today." *Polish Journal of Philosophy* 1, pp. 29–43

Harris, Marvin. 1968. *Rise of Anthropological Theory.* New York: Crowell.

Hilton, Rodney, ed. 1976. *The Transition from Feudalism to Capitalism.* London: Verso.

Hofstadter, Richard. [1944] 1992. *Social Darwinism in American Thought.* Boston, MA: Beacon Press.

Hunt, Emmanuel Kay. 1979. *A History of Economic Thought: A Critical Perspective.* Belmont, CA: Wadsworth Publishing Company.

Kalberg, Stephen. 1980. "Max Weber's Types of Rationality: Cornerstone for the Analysis of Rationalization Processes in History." *The American Journal of Sociology* 85(No. 5), pp. 1145–1179. http://www.jstor.org/stable/2778894?origin=JSTOR-pdf

Kocka, Jurgen. 2016. *Capitalism: A Short History.* Princeton, NJ: Princeton University Press.

Love, John. 1986. "Max Weber and the Theory of Ancient Capitalism." *History and Theory* 25(2), pp. 152–172.

Mach, Ernst. 1897. *Contribution to the Analysis of the Senses.* Translated by C. M. Williams. Chicago, IL: The Open Source Publishing Company.

Mach, Ernst. 1898. *Popular Scientific Lectures.* Translated by C. M. Williams. Chicago, IL: The Open Source Publishing Company.

Marshall, Alfred. [1890] 1920. *Principles of Economics.* Eighth Edition. London: McMillan and Company. https://www.econlib.org/library/Marshall/marP.html?chapter_num=1#book-reader

Marx, Karl. 1852. "The Eighteenth Brumaire of Louis Bonaparte." Pp. 594–617 in *The Marx-Engels Reader,* edited by Tucker, Robert C., 1978. Second Edition. New York, London: W.W. Norton and Company.

Marx, Karl. 1853. "On Imperialism in India." Pp. 653–664 in *The Marx-Engels Reader,* edited by Tucker, Robert C. 1978. Second Edition. New York, London: W.W. Norton and Company.

Marx, Karl. [1859] 1904. *A Contribution to the Critique of Political Economy.* Translated by M. L. Stone. Chicago, IL: Charles H. Kerr and Company. https://www.marxists.org/archive/marx/works/1859/critique-pol-economy/index.htm

Marx, Karl. [1867] 1887. *Capital,* Volume I. Translated by Samuel Moore and Edward Aveling. Ed. Frederick Engels. First English Edition. Moscow: Progress Publishers. https://www.marxists.org/archive/marx/works/download/pdf/Capital-Volume-I.pdf

Marx, Karl and Frederick Engels. 1848. "The Communist Manifesto." Pp. 665–675 in *The Marx-Engels Reader,* edited by Tucker, Robert C., ed. 1978. Second Edition, Pp. 469–500. New York, London: W.W. Norton and Company.

Mayr, Ernst. 1982. *The Growth of Biological Thought. Diversity, Evolution and Inheritance.* Cambridge, MA, London: Bellknap Press.

Peirce, Charles Saunders. 1877. "The Fixation of Belief." *Popular Science Monthly* 12(November), pp. 1–15. Accessed at http://www.peirce.org/writings.html

Peirce, Charles Saunders. 1878. "How to Make our Ideas Clear." *Popular Science Monthly* 12(January), pp. 286–302. Accessed at http://www.peirce.org/writings.html

Poirot, Clifford. 2007. "How Can Institutional Economics Be an Evolutionary Science." *Journal of Economic Issues* XLI(1), pp. 155–180.

Poirot, Clifford. 2008. "Is Pragmatism Good for Anything: Towards an Impractical Theory of Economics." *Forum for Social Economics* 37(1), pp. 61–76.

Pojman, Paul. 2020. "Ernst Mach." in *The Stanford Encyclopedia of Philosophy,* edited by Edward N. Zalta. Winter. 2020 Edition. URL = https://plato.stanford.edu/archives/win2020/entries/ernst-mach/

Ruse, Michael. 1989. *The Darwinian Paradigm.* London, New York: T. J. Press, Padstow Ltd.

Steiner, Phillipe. 2011. *Durkheim and the Birth of Economic Sociology.* Translated by Keith Tribe. Princeton, NJ: Princeton University Press.

Sumner, William Graham. [1883] 1974. *What Social Classes Owe to Each Other.* Caldwell, ID: Caxton Printers, Ltd.

Sumner, William Graham. 1885. *Collected Essays in Political and Social Science.* New York: Holt.

Sumner, William Graham. 1906. *Folk Ways. A Study of the Sociological Importance of Usages, Manners, Customs, Mores and Morals.* Boston, MA: Ginn and Company. https://www.gutenberg.org/files/24253/24253-h/24253-h.htm#Page_173

Sweezy, Paul. 1942. *The Theory of Capitalist Development.* Calcutta, New Delhi: K.G. Baggchi and Company. https://archive.org/details/in.ernet.dli.2015.461479/mode/2up?view=theater

Tillman, Rick. 1988. "Two Recent Critics of "Instrumental Social Science" in Defense of Veblen, Dewey, et alia." *International Journal of Politics, Culture and Society* 12(1), pp. 81–105.

Tribe, Keith. 2019. "Introduction to Max Weber's *Economy and Society*." In Weber, Max. [1922] 2019. *Economy and Society.* P. 1-73. Ed. and transl. by Keith Tribe. Cambridge, MA: Harvard University Press.

Veblen, Thorstein. 1915. *Imperial Germany and the Industrial Revolution.* New York, London: McMillan.

Veblen, Thorstein. 1919. *The Place of Science in Modern Civilization and Other Essays.* New York: B. W. Huebsch. Accessed at https://www.gutenberg.org/files/39949/39949-h/39949-h.htm

Veblen, Thorstein. 1967. *The Theory of the Leisure Class.* New York: Penguin Books.

Ward, Lester Frank. 1891. *Neo-Darwinism and Neo-Lamarckism.* Washington, DC: Gedney & Roberts Co. https://archive.org/details/neodarwinismand00washgoog/page/n2/mode/2up

Ward, Lester Frank. 1895a. "Contributions to Social Philosophy. II. Sociology and Cosmology." *American Journal of Sociology* 1(1), pp. 132–145.

Ward, Lester Frank. 1895b. "Contributions to Social Philosophy. IV. Sociology and Anthropology." *American Journal of Sociology* 1, pp. 426–433.

Ward, Lester Frank. 1896. "Contributions to Social Philosophy. V. Sociology and Psychology." *American Journal of Sociology* 1, pp. 618–632.

Ward, Lester Frank. 1897a. "Contributions to Social Philosophy. X. Social Genesis." *American Journal of Sociology* 2, pp. 532–546.

Ward, Lester Frank. 1897b. "Contributions to Social Philosophy. XI. Individual Telesis." *American Journal of Sociology* 2, pp. 699–717.

Ward, Lester Frank. 1897c. "Contributions to Social Philosophy. XII. Collective Telesis." *American Journal of Sociology* 2, pp. 801–822.

Webb, James. 2002. "Dewey; Back to the Future." *Journal of Economic Issues* 36, pp. 981–1004.

Webb, J. 2007. "Pragmatisms, Plural. Part I.: Classical Pragmatism and Some Implications for Empirical Inquiry." *Journal of Economic Issues* XL(4), pp. 1063–1086.

Webb, James. 2012. "Pragmatisms, Plural. Part II: From Classical Pragmatism to Neo-Pragmatism." XLVI(1), pp. 45–74.

Weber, Max. [1905] 2002. *The Protestant Ethic and the Spirit of Capitalism.* Ed. and transl. by Peter Baeher and Gordon C. Wells. London, England: Penguin.

Weber, Max. [1922] 2019. *Economy and Society.* Ed. and transl. by Keith Tribe. Cambridge, MA: Harvard University Press.

Wolf, Eric. 1999. *Envisioning Power. Ideologies of Dominance and Crisis.* Berkeley and Los Angeles, CA: Berkeley University Press.

4 The Dénouement of Evolutionary Social Theory

Introduction

The period from the end of World War I, through the 1970s was tumultuous in many respects. The economic and political imbalances that had led to the breakdown of the international order that resulted in World War I were not rectified in the interwar period. Consequently, the decades between the wars were characterized by a trend toward the dissolution of the international system. Revolutionary upheaval in the Russian Empire and the establishment of the world's first self-proclaimed socialist state later degenerated into Stalinist totalitarianism. The Great Depression of the 1930s helped to propel the Nazi Party into power in Germany but also led to breakthroughs in efforts to reform Capitalism and the growth of the administrative state. The end of WWII led to the creation of a dual world order—one order initially defined by embedded Liberalism and one defined by Stalinism. This order was complicated by the growing demands and eventual achieval of independence by the formerly colonized areas of Africa and Asia. The creation of new nation states also gave rise to extensive disputes, both within these newly independent countries and between these states and the Soviet Union and the U.S. over what kind of political economic system they would adopt. This conflict was also present in the previously established states of Latin America, Central America, the Caribbean and Mexico. The era was also characterized by a long boom following WWII until the early 1970s. As in previous eras, social scientists in multiple ways attempted to address the nature of these changes.

This era can also be viewed as an era in which the prestige and status of science increased. The period roughly from the beginning of the 20th century through the 1970s in the Sciences was decades of significant advances in scientific knowledge. Notably, there is a significant continuity between the developments in the sciences in the late 19th century and the early and mid-20th century. Work in mathematics and logic established the foundations for modern mathematics and logic and its multiple applications. The application of the new math proved fruitful both for theorizing as well as articulation of already established results. A significant number of

DOI: 10.4324/9781003170679-5

breakthroughs were a result of conceptual progress and the use of deduction and then verified through experimentation. For example, Einstein's Theory of General Relativity was published in 1915. The Bohr Theory of the atom was articulated in 1913. Work on the structure of what came to be known as DNA proceed throughout the period, culminating in our contemporary understanding in the 1950s. At the same time, statistical work in genetics set forth the criteria by which evolution in a population could be measured.

These developments reinforced each other and collectively gave rise to a world view that took knowledge in the Physical and Natural sciences to be the surest form of reliable knowledge, and formal, mathematical physics to be the archetype of scientific knowledge. Given the success of the natural and physical sciences, as in previous eras, social scientists sought to define how, if at all, the social sciences might replicate this success. The result, as I discuss below, was often both confused and confusing. Nevertheless, there were multiple theorists who retained both an evolutionary and empirically grounded perspective on the social sciences and linked their theorizing to the concerns of Political Economy, broadly defined.

Philosophy of Science in the Early and Mid-20th Century

Logical Positivists and Popper

The Vienna Circle and Logical Positivism

The term Positivism is generally used as a term of opprobrium. Yet the term itself is about as easy to define as other terms such as Political Economy or Pragmatism. As the last several chapters demonstrate, it is more useful to refer to Positivisms. Much of what is alleged about Positivism stems from the particular version that came to be known as Logical Positivism and then later Logical Empiricism advocated by members of the Vienna Circle. But much of how people often characterize this movement is at best a potted plant version and the views of the Logical Positivists are often run together with the distinctive position of Karl Popper. Amongst its other alleged sins, it is often blamed for the demise of Evolutionary Social Theory and the triumph of mathematical formalism in Economics. As I explain herein, there is a connection but it is weaker and more complex than is often understood. If one is searching for a villain, Popper is the more likely culprit but even then, it is not clear how much Popper actually influenced social scientists. The actual perpetrator, or more accurately, perpetrators were social scientists themselves whose views only fainted echoed those of either the Logical Positivists or of Popper. Understanding this point first requires a brief discussion of the actual position of both.

In the 1950s, the philosopher Willard Van Orman Quine (2004), presented an internal critique of Logical Positivism, or more specifically, of the position of Logical Positivist Rudolph Carnap. Quine characterized it as resting on two dogmas: the analytic synthetic distinction as a sharp dichotomy and the view that science could proceed sentence by sentence. I will address the ramifications of Quine's critique in more detail in the subsequent chapter. At this juncture, I wish to explain and expand on Quine's characterization. Though it is a simplification of a broad range of views held by the Logical Positivists, it is a useful simplification, albeit one that merits elaboration. Alas, it is not possible to provide the full story in this study.

Exactly who was a Logical Positivist is unclear. A narrow definition would confine its membership to only participants in the Vienna Circle, but then again, it would have to exclude Popper. The broader definition, which in my view is more useful, takes into account its multiple allies and fellow travelers such as Bertrand Russell and to a lesser degree, the early Wittgenstein. Initially, Logical Positivism was initially put forth as a scientific world conception, in opposition to idealist, conservative and religious conceptions of philosophy. The key points of this scientific conception of the world were initially set forth in a tract of the same title (Neurath et al. 1929). The manifesto was signed by a wide range of influential figures of the era, including luminaries such as Bertrand Russell and Albert Einstein. This scientific conception of the world had its roots in Mach's interpretation of Positivism and reflected Mach's effort to articulate a scientific view of the world (Richardson 2003). Fortunately, many of the signatories were not Machians and those who participated directly in The Circle did not adhere strictly to Mach. However, at least two core ideas taken from Mach were influential: the view that only direct, sensory experience really counted as knowledge and that theories were devices for gaining a handle on a complex reality.

The two strongest influences on the positions taken by multiple members of the Circle were Empiricism, though that was loosely defined, and the formal mathematics and logic of Hilbert, Russell and others. The Scientific view of the world was at the bottom in a class of protocol or observation statements and at the top in formal logic and mathematics. The method of science in their view was the application of logical analysis to empirical material. One alleged advantage of formal, logical analysis was that it provided a means by which to break free of the problems and constraints posed by natural language. In their view, natural language leads us to think in metaphysical terms and falsely leads to the acceptance of false problems such as realism vs. nominalism. Many of the traditional problems of Philosophy were viewed as pseudo-problems that would either disappear upon more stringent semantic analysis or could be turned over to the sciences to be solved as empirical problems.

One example of how this issue was addressed is provided by Rudolph Carnap, whose views actually evolved over time. In his famous 1936 article, "Testability and Meaning" Carnap made two critical points. One is his adaptation of Peirce's verification theory of meaning into the form that the meaning of a sentence is identical to our ability to determine its truth or falsehood and that a sentence is true if it corresponds to our actual observations. The second was his acceptance of what he termed "the thing language". Historically, Empiricism has been associated with nominalism. Yet in actuality, the language of science often uses language that implies that proper names and general laws refer to actual entities. The problem in Carnap's view was that the nature of language made it virtually impossible to not talk about actual general concepts. Carnap argued that a good empiricist could use the "thing" language with a clean conscience, much like a devout Protestant might be permitted a glass of wine on Saturday nights, provided of course, that one did not make the mistake of equating general concepts with real entities. The debate between realism and nominalism was therefore a pseudo-problem, albeit one which was settled more on the side of the nominalists, at least according to Carnap.

The Logical Positivists, mostly, not all, were verificationists. They were all fallibilists. Carnap in his above-referenced paper stressed that theories could only be confirmed by evidence—not decisively verified. Logical Positivists also drew a distinction between general laws that could always be regarded as true, theories that held true probabilistically and empirical generalizations. Their argument was not that correlation defined causality but that correlation of observations implied by observation sentences that followed from the general law or principle could be taken as evidence for or against a theory.

That the language of realism was often smuggled in through the back door is illustrated by the classic explanation of the covering law model of scientific explanation as later articulated by Hempel and Oppenheim. As is well known, covering laws have the same logical structure as the syllogism. But it is a misunderstanding to characterize this as axiomatic-deductive. The general principle had to be verified in either a universal sense or a probabilistic sense. The best explanation of this model of scientific explanation is provided by Hempel and Oppenheim (1948) who curiously cite Dewey, while trying to articulate a formal theory of confirmation. They then explain the cracking of a radiator in a car that is left out in the cold as an instance of the actual properties of water and metal, given certain conditions. The observation of a car radiator cracking under certain conditions can be taken as a confirming instance of the general law. Similarly, they explain the appearance of an oar bending in water as a case of the general properties of water to refract light. A sudden fall in the price of cotton is explained by a sudden release into the market of previously stored stocks. Interestingly, observable patterns of similarities and differences in language could also be explained as instances of linguistic evolution. Similarly, their explanation accepts the concept of emergent properties. Logical Positivism did not preclude evolutionary approaches to theorizing in the social sciences.

The picture I have provided of Logical Positivism is as noted earlier, vastly simplified. It can be viewed as a description, in general, of the positions of Rudolph Carnap and Carl Hempel. The movement had its coherentist wing represented by Otto Neurath and those who tended toward empirical realism. On the whole, they did hold to the view that normative statements were either meaningless or simply disguised empirical statements about people's beliefs and actions. But on the whole, they were proponents of the view that the application of science to human problems could lead to improvement. Nor can the Logical Positivist picture of theory confirmation really hold up. As the philosopher Susan Haack (2007a) has noted, whose views I will address in the next chapter, Logical Positivism only works, in so far as one adds in the more nourishing aspects of Critical Common Sensism into the formalist nail soup. One way to think about Logical Positivism is that it is rigidified and linguistified Pragmatism. A similar, but distinctive criticism was advanced by Larry Laudan, in his essay "Sins of the Fathers" (1996, pp. 3–25). By reducing issues of scientific explanation, or of philosophy in general to semantic analysis, the Logical Positivists contributed to the semantic, or linguistic shift, that in turn gave rise to many of the concerns of Post-Structuralists. In this sense, Positivism (at least in the form of Logical Positivism) is only apparently the polar opposite of Relativism. Logical Positivism requires that there be a formal logical criterion for theory verification and a class of incontrovertible, bluntly given empirical statements. But if it can be shown that neither is actually possible, all claims to the truth then can be claimed to simply be products of different languages or discourses, and ultimately, arbitrary. The argument rests on the fallacy that either we have completely secure knowledge or no knowledge at all.

Karl Popper

Popper originally articulated his position in 1934, in *The Logic of Scientific Discovery*. There are some similarities between his position and that of other members of the Vienna Circle, but there are also significant differences. Popper accepted the Logical Positivist view of scientific explanation as deductive, also rejected metaphysics as being outside of science, held to the rigid dichotomy of normative and positive statements and was a fallibilist. In some respects, his position bordered on skepticism. But he also rejected induction as valid logic and held that induction was unreliable. Also, like the Logical Positivists, he attempted to offer a clear criterion through which to distinguish science from metaphysics. But his criterion of demarcation differed significantly from that of the Logical Positivists.

Prediction in Popper's view is a logical consequence of the theory. Yet hypotheses are taken to be bold conjectures rather than provisional abductive generalizations. But even on this point, Popper is not necessarily consistent. Hypotheses may also be drawn in Popper's view from an existing theory or from systems of theories. But these hypotheses are not just tested in isolation—theories and hypotheses are also tested against each other. For example, let's say that theory x and theory y are genuine rivals: to date, they have both made reliable predictions, based on mutually exclusive premises, of observable phenomena. By formulating a decisive test we can determine which hypothesis to choose. If hypothesis X makes a successful prediction and hypothesis Y does not, we should then pick theory X. The similar argument that he later makes in his article "Conjectural Knowledge" (1979, pp. 1–31) is at least in part evolutionary: falsificationism acts as a stratagem that eliminates less "fit" theories. By proceeding in this fashion, science can accumulate theories that have a property of verisimilitude—they have a higher degree of probability of being closer to the truth.

The evolutionary component of Popper's epistemology is ironic, given what was at best an ambiguity in Popper about evolutionary theory in both the natural and social sciences. At least early on, Popper characterized natural selection as a metaphysical research program, since in his view, it was based on a tautology: whatever survives is by definition more fit. But Popper misunderstood the role of natural selection in evolutionary theory. The survival and passing on of traits that contribute to an organism's or species' survival, is not in and of itself a prediction, so much as a common sense kind of observation and assumption of evolutionary theory. Evolutionary theory predicts that the process of variation and selection will lead to speciation and that this process will take place step by step, rather than through qualitative leaps.

A second, and for the purposes of this study more important distinction between Popper and the Logical Positivists is with respect to whether or not the Social Sciences, and especially history, can and should, at least in principle, be studied in a scientific fashion. Popper had famously been sharply critical of what he regarded as the scientific pretensions of Marxism, and also of Adlerian Psychology. Popper's initial position that the social sciences, and especially history could not be scientific was later modified in "A Realist View of Logic, Physics and History" (1979, pp. 285–318) in which he conceded that eventually, history might be able to make some kinds of general, falsifiable statements about the past, though he did not think that History could become a predictive science. It might, however, he thought, become kind of science-like.

That noted, Popper's opposition to the concept of the social sciences as science was tied to his larger political vision and his overall theory of knowledge. While Popper is often viewed as a person who advocated for the objectivity of scientific knowledge, his views on what science could achieve were to some degree limited. In some respects, Popper borders on skepticism. It is this near skepticism, in my view, that lay behind Popper's rejection of the use of the social sciences as a means to improve human well-being—an epistemological and political view he shared with Frederick Hayek, whom I address briefly later in this chapter.

Like the Logical Positivists, Popper's system encounters significant contradictions and only works when the entire system is loosened up. To begin, it is not clear exactly what Popper is trying to demarcate. No Science, not even formal, mathematical physics, which is Popper's exemplar science, entirely meets the stringent criterion laid out by Popper. In a few instances, Physicists were able to construct decisive experiments but most advances in science have only come about as a result of multiple experiments and gradual modifications, including additions to theories. Outside of physics, the prediction of novel, unexpected observations is unlikely. In part, Popper is demarcating exact sciences from inexact sciences, and the physical and natural sciences from the social sciences. He is also in part demarcating political ideologies as manifested in the actions or statements of representatives of political parties and social movements, from the process of academic inquiry: or more to the point, when reframed in a less formal, common sense fashion, his criterion could be used to aid in that process. The argument that we should seek to test our theories against empirical evidence and revise our theories accordingly when the evidence goes against our theories is valid. The argument that we should not attempt to revise the theory but must instead throw the whole theory out when a theory fails a single time to predict a novel event, is not.

Having summarized the two most influential views on Philosophy of Science in the early and mid-20th century, we are now in a position to address to what degree these views actually exerted influence on the Social Sciences and to what extent they contributed to the relative decline of evolutionary approaches to social theory. Though their influence was not absent, few, if any social scientists followed, or attempted to follow the above strictures in any strict sense. Nevertheless, both approaches served in various ways to limit the kinds of research strategies that social scientists employed. Another factor was the influence of both on the growth of disciplinary specialization. Notably, however, even as evolutionary approaches were often pushed to the margins, they continued on in various forms and were in the process of revival by the end of this period. The remainder of this chapter provides a summary of these developments.

Evolutionary Social Theory: Marginalization and Reaction in the Social Sciences

Anthropology

Culture and Personality

In Anthropology, the decades in which the marginalization of evolutionary social theory was strongest were the 1920s through the 1950s. As noted in the previous chapter, Boas' rejection of evolutionism and the rise of historical particularism were already prominent prior to WWI his influence continued following the War (see, e.g., Boas 1920). Harris (1968, pp. 278–279) argues, convincingly in my view, that Boas himself underwent a shift from an emphasis on historical particularism to an emphasis on the relationship between culture and personality. This shift shaped the work of his two most famous students Margaret Mead (1930) and Ruth Benedict (1934) and gave rise to the culture and personality school. This work embodied a paradox: on the one hand, culture was envisioned as an all-encompassing force that gave rise to different personality structures yet simultaneously emphasized the inability to truly study culture scientifically. Many of these contradictions were embodied in the later work of others influenced by the Boasian milieu as well, reinforcing the trends toward entirely idealistic views of culture. This portrait is reinforced by Eric Wolf's (2001, pp. 23–37) essay "Kroeber Revisited" in which Wolf argues that Kroeber, one of the giants in Anthropology of the era in emphasizing an abstract idea of creativity instead of placing the interaction between creativity and culture in a contextual situation, had in effect returned to German idealism.

Yet at least with respect to Mead and Benedict, neither was anti-science, nor anti-evolution per se in so far as it was with respect to biological evolution. Rather, they posited a strong separation between culture and biology. This was evidence for example in Mead's famous *Coming of Age in Samoa* and in Ruth Benedict's six cultures project as well as her own study of the Kwakwaka'wakw (Kwakiutl) (see Wolf 1999, 69–132 for a critique and overview). The fieldwork of the era, of course, emphasized first-hand observation and in addition, there was a determined effort to find correlations between culture patterns and personality structures or to demonstrate the lack of correlation between biology and culture. Hence there was a definite Positivist influence, though not necessarily a Logical Positivist one.

The rejection of evolutionary approaches to anthropology should be placed in context. As we've noted, Evolutionary Social Theory in the 19th century was often speculative, sometimes engaged in biological reductionism, and in some versions incorporated racist, sexist and ethnocentric assumptions, and argued against social reforms, though notably, others challenged those assumptions. "Darwinism", as applied to society, was often held by figures on both the left and right to be responsible for biological determinism, eugenics, German militarism and aggression in WWI and of course later, the theories of racial superiority of the Nazi movement. As I have noted above, this portrayal is inaccurate for many reasons, but it was the interpretation that stuck in both the popular discourse as well as academic discourse. The collective contributions of Boas, Mead and Benedict did much to challenge theories of racial determinism, racial superiority and gender essentialism, even if their views were limited to liberal understandings. Having rejected the idea of biology as influencing behavior, social scientists instead could emphasize the role of education and socialization as well as social reform as ways of combating social ills. It fits into the Progressive milieu. Yet at the same time, they also rejected the totalitarianism of both Fascism and Stalinism. They both actively participated in supporting the U.S. Army's educational efforts in WWII. Mead (1951) also joined the Cold War and participated in and wrote a study focusing on the ways in which the Russian personality had created a need for a Stalin-like figure.

Structuralism and Structural Functionalism

Both Carneiro (2003, pp. 80–87), Harris (1968, 464–567) as well as Wolf (1982, pp. 1–23) also advance substantive criticisms of the spread of functionalism and structuralism into anthropology. Both functionalism as well as structuralism embraced theory and engaged in extensive generalizations. In the case of Structuralism, it had Positivist roots in Durkheim and the contributions of his most prominent student, Marcel Maus. The problem was that in both cases, an explanation was sought nearly exclusively in terms of the synchronic aspects of culture, and in the case of structuralism, in the linguistic structure of culture. Hence functionalists sought to identify nearly all cultural traits exclusively in terms of their contribution to the maintenance of the culture. Structuralists sought to identify those abstract, idealized forms that could define the basic building blocks or linguistic structures of the culture.

Nevertheless, I disagree with the entirely negative assessment of the contributions of structuralism of Carneiro and Harris. Marcel Maus' analysis of the role of mutual gift giving, or patterns of reciprocal exchange as a means of organizing kin-based societies provided a useful framework through which to understand non-market exchange. This emphasis on reciprocal exchange and ways of thinking, feeling and acting that do not conform with the neo-classical portrait of economic man was furthered by Marshall Sahlins (1972), who also contributed directly to the rise of neo-evolutionism. Based on his analysis of what he termed "stone age" societies, or more accurately, contemporary kin-based societies, he argued that such societies engaged in extensive leisure by limiting wants in adjustment to the environment. This laid the basis for the later rise of the Substantivist school in Economic Anthropology and its close connection to the Polanyi (1957) strand in Original Institutional Economics. Yet the nearly overwhelming emic focus of the school led to a denial of the usefulness of concepts such as surplus and exploitation, which are both admittedly etic terms. Similarly, the later Formalist–Substantivist debate that emerged as a consequence of this line of research, shed more heat than light on the issue (see, Wilk and Cliggett 2007, for a broad overview).

Revival: White, Steward and Childe

Yet by the late 1940s, evolutionary approaches were on a path to becoming respectable again. Carneiro dates the discipline's re-acceptance of cultural evolutionism to the centennial of the publication of *The Origin of Species*.

While the neo-evolutionism of this era did incorporate aspects of the 19th-century social evolutionism of Spencer, Sumner, Tylor and Morgan, it did so through a primarily Marxist and critical prism. Furthermore, it incorporated the distinction between cultural evolution and biological evolution of Boas and other prominent figures in Anthropology. At the same time, it allowed for extensive analysis of the interaction of humans with both the physical and biological domains. The collective contributions of Leslie White (1949), Julian Steward (1955) and Gordan V. Childe (1951) can in varying ways be characterized as "forces of production" Marxism. Their respective contributions were pivotal to the revival of Evolutionary Social Theory and laid the foundations for current directions that I will address in the subsequent chapter.

For the present, I want to emphasize what in my view were the important contributions to emerge during this era. Carneiro (2003, chapters 6 and 7) provides an excellent overview of their respective contributions, which I summarize here. Where Leslie White emphasized the ability of societies to capture energy from the environment, Steward emphasized the role of the ecosystem as both a limiting and enabling factor in cultural evolution. While White is often held to have maintained a unilinear stage theory, Steward emphasized the importance of a multi-linear stage theory. Childe's work in Archaeology focused on the role of technological innovation. Collectively, their work provided a better understanding of the complex origins of both settled agriculture and the state as well as the importance of major technological transitions in human history.

This is not to argue that their work provided the final word on these processes, and it was also less illuminating of processes that emerged and solidified from the 16th century onward. Yet it provided a useful framework for analysis. At present, I wish to focus on three important concepts that arose as a consequence of this line of research. The first was the concept of a socio-cultural system, divided into three general components: base, structure and superstructure. The concept of the base was expanded to incorporate all the features of human society–ecosystem interaction. The concept of the structure was expanded to incorporate both the class and the political structure, while the superstructure was viewed as the ideational or symbolic aspects of the system. The second useful aspect was the revision of types of societies into tribes, chiefdoms, city states and formal states, corresponding to changes in the material base. This latter point was a contribution of second-generation theorists such as Marshall Sahlins and Elman Service (1960). Similarly, they distinguished between general evolution (evolution from one kind of society to another) and specific evolution (evolution within a society). The third contribution was a shift toward multi-linear concepts of social evolution in which both similarities as well as different paths of development were recognized along with the interaction of different socio-cultural systems. Though imperfect as this research was, as I discuss in the following chapter, the second and third generations of researchers in this tradition have provided significant insight into the evolution of the modern world system.

Sociology

Parsons and C. Wright Mills

In Sociology, the contributions of Talcott Parsons (1950, 1951, 1971) defined the terms of debate by the 1950s. Though there is some basis for distinguishing between Parson's position, and that of his later interpreters, he played a rather uniquely negative role with respect to evolutionary approaches in both Sociology and Economics. Parsons was a Positivist in the very general sense of the term in that he advocated that Sociology could at least in principle be a science in the same sense as the natural sciences (1950). But he was not a Logical Positivist or a Popperian. His views on the philosophy of the social sciences were actually much closer to those of later writers such as Kuhn and Lakatos. Specifically, he drew a distinction between the general theory of a discipline, which in his view did not yet exist in Sociology, mid-level theories and applied research. With respect to the testing of individual theories, Parsons was a verificationist, not a falsificationist.

Parsons' (1950) goal was to formulate a general theory approach to Sociology and his general theory went through several modifications, though my primary emphasis herein is on his work in the early 1950s. In his view, the speculative systems of theorists such as Spencer, prior to Weber and Durkheim, were "proto-Sociology". Sociology began, according to Parsons, with Weber and Durkheim. In his 1950 ASA Presidential address, Parsons lamented the lack of a well-defined theory in Sociology that could integrate the contributions of empirical research and lead to cumulative progress in Sociology. Yet in his view, Sociology was not quite at the point of having such a general theory, rather, it had progressed to the point of a conceptual scheme. This scheme was based on three areas: culture, institutions and the contributions of Freud. The emphasis in Anthropology on Culture had shown the limits of biological explanations of behavior, the emphasis on Institutions had shown the limits of utilitarianism while Freud provided the basis for a theory of motivation.

In contrast to Boas, Parsons' argued specifically against the use of induction as a means through which to build a general theory. In Parsons' case, the conceptual scheme was built on his interpretation of the prior contributions of Weber, Durkheim and Freud, whose contributions were at least partially built on induction. This conceptual scheme in Parsons' view could be used to formulate hypotheses via deduction which could then be used to test the scheme via a strategy of verification. Parsons' own lifelong effort to construct a general theory drew on these three areas in an effort to integrate the interaction of Culture, Social Structure and Motivation into a general systems approach to Sociology.

This raises an interesting question, as to what kind of general theory Parson's general theory was? Parsons was prolific throughout his career, but the relevant work at present is *The Social System* (1951). The Sociologist C. Wright Mills (1959, pp. 25–49) labeled Parsons' approach in this volume as a "grand theory". Mills' philosophical criticism of Parsons' grand theory was that it was overly abstract and unnecessarily specialized, thus rendering it incapable of actually being applied concretely. For example, Mills criticized Parsons' concept of structure as positing a kind of a historical and non-specific concept of structure. Similarly, in Mills' view, Parsons' approach was one in which the concept referred to other concepts. Mills' drew a distinction between the syntactic nature of theories and the semantic aspects of theories. Mills' critique of Parsons in this respect was that Parsons' theory was overly syntactic and lacked concrete, semantic meaning.

Mills' Sociological objections to Parsons were similar and have been echoed by others as well. Parsons' system approach emphasized the system maintaining or equilibrating aspects of the system. Parsons' static theory was complemented by a more dynamic version that emphasized the process of social change. Of course, the problem of linking the theory of morphology to a theory of morphogenesis is one that many theorists have struggled with. According to Parsons' critics, he did so in an unsatisfactory fashion. Parsons later disavowed what came to be known as structural functionalism. But the structural-functionalist interpretation was the one that stuck and came to define Sociology. Some of Parson's foremost critics such as Mills and subsequently Marcuse and Habermas were radical critics of Capitalism, though arguably, Habermas is less radical than Marcuse. By comparison, Parsons was Conservative in the sense that he was strongly motivated by opposition to both Fascist and Stalinist Totalitarianism and to utopian schemes. Yet his Liberal Anti-Communism was one that emphasized the need for reform based on good social science. Ironically, Parsons himself was also falsely accused of being a Communist.

The contributions of C. Wright Mills (1956, 1959) notably merit some discussion in this context, though there is not sufficient space to do them justice. Mills was clearly an evolutionist, in the sense that his approach to Sociology was one that could explain change both within a system and from one kind of system to another, though Mills' *The Power Elite* was a study of social power in the U.S. Philosophically, Mills was a Pragmatist, in the sense that Dewey and Veblen were Pragmatists and the influence of both on Mills was directly acknowledged. This gave Mills' work a concrete, empirical quality. But Mills was not a theoretical. He was equally critical of what he termed "abstracted empiricism" (1959, pp. 50–75), which was the term he used to describe narrow, statistical-based studies shorn of context which were increasingly characteristic of Sociology. This same criticism notably could also be applied to the historical particularism of Boas and of his disciples.

In addition to Veblen and Dewey, Mills was influenced by Weber and Marx and synthesized aspects of both. Mills was among the first American social scientists to draw attention to and re-publish a sample of Weber's work in English. Parsons' also re-published a translation of Weber in English, but his translation emphasized the static and structural aspects of Weber. Mills argues that Parsons essentially kept two sets of books: one static and functional and one dynamic and processual and that Parsons never brought these two contrasting visions together. Though Parsons was eventually to partially recant his initial opposition to evolutionism, his later volume on social evolution (1971) is generally regarded as not having made a significant contribution to the revival of evolutionary social theory. Parsons emphasizes the growing role of specialization and differentiation and traces the development of modern American society. He was notably, the quintessential Liberal Cold Warrior.

In contrast, in *The Sociological Imagination* Mills argued that theory in Sociology imaginatively drew together biography (personal experience), history and structure to provide the participant with a sense of place in the world (1959, chapters 5 and 8). History for Mills was not just a dry collection of facts, but a weaving together of how structure had changed over time and his emphasis was on material factors. In other words, Mills' theory of Sociology was one that incorporated the concerns of Political Economy. In contrast to the structuralists, Mills argued that structures were found in the concrete, actual interaction of society's institutions. Though Mills provided many excellent examples, his characterization of Fascism provides a useful illustration of how he did theory. Fascism, in Mills' view arose due to the interlocking of elites in business, the military and politics to subordinate the workers and crush the Unions. This created a monopoly on both political power as well as a monopoly on the realm of ideas.

I have emphasized the role of Parsons in part due to his extensive influence in Sociology but also due to his influence on Economics. Though Parsons was influenced by Marshall's views on equilibrium, his emphasis on the role of socialization and Freudian psychology placed him at odds with the rational choice perspective of mainstream economics. But his opposition to inductive approaches led him to reject what he regarded as the a-theoretical nature of the American Institutionalists, while simultaneously remaining critical of neo-classical economics. As the story goes, the economist Joseph Schumpeter was instrumental in persuading Parsons of this point.

Economics

Schumpeter and the Mainstream

There is a clear irony in this in that Schumpeter (1919, 1943, 1954) must be regarded as one of the most important, as well as one of the most enigmatic contributors to evolutionary social theory. His contributions have played a prominent role in the revival of contemporary evolutionary approaches to economics. As Theofanis and Panayotis (2016) have pointed out, there are interesting parallels and differences between his approach and that of Veblen. But how then did Schumpeter contribute to the marginalization of evolutionary perspectives in Economics and what was the connection to Parsons? The answer requires some explanation.

Like Veblen, Schumpeter emphasized the importance of technological innovation and its disequilibrating impact on the economy, as is clear in his emphasis on creative destruction. Also, Schumpeter's (1919) view that the New Imperialism of the late 19th century was shaped by a combination of the persistence of non-capitalist social structures and cultural attitudes in combination with monopoly and finance capital, echoed Veblen's emphasis on the predatory nature of the leisure class which Veblen had seen as a persistence of instincts that had arisen during the stage of barbarism. The predominant influence on Schumpeter's views on social evolution however in my estimation was Max Weber, though there were certainly other influences as well. This influence is strongest in Schumpeter's stress on methodological individualism, the creative role of the entrepreneur and his criticism of bureaucracy. Like Weber, Schumpeter feared the overemphasis on rationalization of the production process and of society in general under Capitalism would lead to an end in which the Capitalist became a bureaucrat, thus laying the basis for the establishment of Socialism. This triumph of Socialism, which Schumpeter defined as State ownership and State control of production, was however to be mourned, not celebrated (Schumpeter 1943).

Schumpeter's evolutionism then clearly presents us with a puzzle. In my view, the link between Schumpeter and Parsons on this point is that both had a similar view of what theory means and both kept two sets of books. In Schumpeter's view, economics required a general theory that could tie the multiple aspects of Economics together (1954, p. 41). There was a strong connection between his concept of theory and his views on pre-analytic vision. Pre-analytic vision was not irrational or beyond refutation per se, but instead was defined by a general view of the kinds of questions or issues an economist might consider to be worthy of inquiry. The general theory, par excellence for Schumpeter, was Walrasian General Equilibrium Theory (Schumpeter 1954, pp. 14–20).

In setting forth the composition of the Profession, Schumpeter distinguished between Economic History (which included ethnology—or much of Cultural Anthropology), Economic Sociology, Theory, Political Economy and Applied Fields. The areas of Economic Sociology, Political Economy and Economic History, as conceived by Schumpeter clearly overlap, and describe, for all intents and purposes, what I have labeled as Evolutionary Social Theory. We can draw the line from Ricardo, through Mill, to Marshall and ultimately to Schumpeter of a definition of Economics, or at least of Economic Theory as distinct and separated from the study of social evolution and an emphasis on theory as purely syntactic and devoid of semantic meaning.

In contrast, the American Original Institutionalist school defined itself as evolutionary, though this self-characterization does require some clarification for the period from the 1920s through the 1950s. The accusation that the Original Institutionalist School of Economics, founded primarily by Veblen, and developed further by Clarence Ayres (1944) and others lacked theory is rendered understandable given the above. Yet its accuracy does not need to be accepted. What the Institutionalists did not develop was a theory of equilibrium determination of prices, value and distribution of income in the sense that either Marxists or mainstream Economists did. They did not do so because their goal was to develop a theory of economic provisioning as instituted process. In other words, their approach to Political Economy was similar to that of Durkheim, Weber and Comte who subordinated Political Economy to Economic Sociology and thought of Economic Sociology as incorporating both static and evolutionary analysis. The Institutionalists did not seek either a utility or labor theory of value, but rather a theory of social valuation and one in which both formal legal institutions, as well as informal institutions, defined the parameters of material provisioning.

One of the most influential figures in Original Institutional Economics was Clarence Ayres (1944). Yet even some members of the Original Institutionalist school have tended to view Clarence Ayres as a vulgarizer of the Veblenian tradition, and/or as breaking with social evolutionism. Neither in my view is a correct interpretation of Ayres, though this is not to argue that Ayres provided the final word on Veblen or Original Institutional Economics. Ayres in particular emphasized the process of institutional adjustment to technological change in the context of a dynamic, developing economy. While Ayres was not focused on fitting different kinds of societies into an evolutionary sequence, he did emphasize the unique problems and development of Industrial society. The other aspect of Ayres was his emphasis on the importance of policy applications as a means of instrumentally addressing pressing social problems.

Interpretations of Keynes

Early Cambridge Economics

In mainstream economics however the trend toward anti-evolutionism, as the appropriate method for Political Economy, or rather, Economics was triumphant. To understand how this process played out, it is useful to start with the early development of critiques of the mainstream, which began with Keynes' *The General Theory* (1936) as well as work by Michael Kalecki (1954), Joan Robinson (1942), Piero Sraffa (1960) and others (see, King 2002).

By the 1970s, collectively, the path they had charted in the 1930s is often referred to as Cambridge Economics, which includes both post-Keynesian and neo-Ricardians—terms which can be surprisingly contentious. These various strands are not necessarily fully consistent with each other. There is a vast literature that attempts to productively synthesize these strands, as well as a literature that argues against this effort. My concern at this juncture however is with the ways in which they were and remain potentially useful to Evolutionary Social Theory and how the mainstream charted a different course.

Keynes' argument in *The General Theory* that the normal, or more general, the outcome of an industrial-market economy was to settle at a level of output below full employment, due to a lack of effective demand, was primarily presented in the form of short-period analysis and depended strongly on the role of uncertainty (not risk). Though Keynes' emphasis on uncertainty undermines the Marshallian emphasis on equilibrium theorizing, Keynes' general approach was Marshallian and Keynes made extensive use of the concept of equilibrium. In contrast, Kalecki reached similar conclusions but did so by integrating concepts of aggregate demand on a foundation of imperfect competition coupled with Marxist concepts. Sraffa's analysis emphasized the long period analysis of supply while rejecting Marshallian foundations. Sraffa's analysis, which is best known for his much later 1960 work, represents a return to Classical Economics, in the tradition of Ricardo. This group, though in various ways, generally presented Political Economy as an abstract-deductive discipline. However, their method of abstraction was grounded in what they viewed as common sense understandings of day-to-day experience with economic processes. Work during this period and subsequently, especially by Joan Robinson and others on economic growth rejected equilibrium theorizing. Consequently, their collective contributions called attention to the specific institutional features of contemporary market economies. Contemporary evolutionary theorists who seek to explain and understand specifically how Capitalism functions at an abstract level, can find much in this tradition that is useful.

On the surface, the early post-Keynesian and neo-Ricardian models (or if one prefers "proto" post-Keynesian and neo-Ricardian) were couched in the same method as the mainstream in the sense that their arguments were articulated in the form of mathematical models, even if they were not necessarily as rigorously formal as some later mainstream models. That noted, Sraffa's analysis in *Production of Commodities by Means of Commodities* especially did not lack mathematical rigor. The issue was not whether or not to formalize, but how to formalize. Again, the issue was not about the role of abstraction per se—it was about the nature of abstraction. This is nicely illustrated by Joan Robinson's critique of the Labor Theory of Value as "metaphysical". Robinson was not rejecting metaphysics per se in my view. She was rejecting metaphysics that implied some kind of substance embodied in commodities apart from relationships between people. This does raise the question as to whether or not Robinson fairly interpreted Marx. But this kind of deflationary metaphysics was also expressed in Sraffa's reversion to a cost of production theory of value, rather than a labor theory of value. There is an interesting point in the source of philosophical influences in this. Keynes himself, as well as Keynes' circle were all associates and strongly influenced by fellow travelers of the Vienna Circle such as Bertrand Russell, G. E. Moore and the early Ludwig Wittgenstein. In some respects, they were better Positivists than their mainstream counterparts but drew on empirical, or one might argue, common sensist realism.

Formalization in Economics

The above represented one possible path forward from Keynes' *The General Theory.* But from the 1950s onward mainstream economics became yet more narrow. This was most strongly exemplified by the shift toward formal, mathematical analysis as the method of economics in the case of Debreu (1959) and other contributors to the development of neo-Walrasian General Equilibrium analysis and Paul Samuelson's (1947) aping of formal, top-down, mathematical physics. By the standards of logical positivism, Debreu's proof was a pure abomination, mixing the holy and unholy, and positing a purely analytical system as valid synthetic theory and defining terms with semantic meaning in ways that had little connection to their actual usage. Logical Positivism in contrast requires that theories be built on actual, observable, characteristics of entities under study and that the theory be translatable into observation statements, and that one then engages in confirmation via observation. Walrasian and neo-Walrasian General Equilibrium Theory does not meet these requirements. Despite the problems of Logical Positivism, the discipline would have had significantly more empirical contact with the economy had Logical Positivism been the actual defining method of Economics.

Samuelson's (1947) application of mathematics was only slightly more grounded. By drawing on formal mathematical physics as his exemplar science, Samuelson posited a distinction between static and dynamic analyses. However, by positing an analogy for this distinction in economics, based on the difference between Einstein and Newton, Samuelson in effect was arguing that his "Newtonian" economics was a close enough approximation to dynamic Einsteinian economics. Samuelson was both comfortable with getting close enough to the truth and at the same time, argued that what later came to be called the axiom of ergodicity (that the parameters of a system are constant) was necessary for science. In this sense, we might note, that Samuelson was not after truth per se. Rather, his objective was to formulate a theory that was true enough to be useful as a guide to policy. Samuelson's post-Keynesian critics, at least initially, did not quarrel with the formalization of economics, but rather with the formalization of economics on the basis of what they considered to be unrealistic critical assumptions that inappropriately biased the analysis as well as incoherent categories and measurement concepts.

Similarly, Milton Friedman's (1953) later vulgarization of instrumentalism did not actually rest on the argument that economics should actually present false assumptions. Friedman's statement to that effect in the beginning of his famous (or infamous) article was clearly intended as a rhetorical attention grabber. Friedman's view was that assumptions of models should be approximations of reality and capable of making accurate predictions. Here again, the controversy surrounding Friedman's position was not about the use of abstraction per se, but about the level and kind of abstraction. The matter was made worse by Friedman's assertion that assumptions should not be tested. The test of a model or theory in Friedman's view was its ability to make novel predictions. Friedman's defense of assumptions such as profit maximization by firms via vaguely Darwinian analogies that firms that did not maximize profits would be driven out of business begged the question. Friedman's method was important to his collaboration with Anna Schwartz on U.S. Monetary History (1963) which did address changes in the structure of banking but also put significant attention on lagging the M1 definition of the monetary aggregate with changes in the inflation rate.

Continuation of Evolutionism in Economics

But even as evolutionism as an explicit approach was marginalized in the economics profession, a de facto evolutionism continued to be prominent fields such as Economic History and Economic Development. A significant amount of the work in Economic History was influenced by Marxism, beginning with the extensive debate between the economists Paul Sweezy and Maurice Dobbs on the origins of Capitalism (Hilton 1976). Sweezy's work in Marxist Political Economy pointed to a synthesis of Keynes and Marx and he emphasized the interaction of the feudal, more accurately, manorial form of social organization which was predicated on serfdom, with the urban circuits of trade as important features of the transition. In contrast, Dobbs, arguing from a more orthodox perspective emphasized the internal contradictions within the feudal, or manorial system. This argument notably was later to morph into an extensive debate between more orthodox Marxists such as Robert Brenner (Aston 1985) and others.

Yet a third strand in Economic History was owed to the work of Polanyi (1957), referenced above. In my estimation, Polanyi's classic work *The Great Transformation* contained at least two flaws. It underestimated the presence of markets and market mechanisms prior to the 19th century and vastly overestimated the ability of the balance of power system to maintain peace in Europe. Yet his key points that the 19th century witnessed a social, cultural and economic transformation that required institutional coordination to make it work and that there are mechanisms of economic integration other than the market, were significant contributions to Evolutionary Social Theory and have ramifications well beyond economics. Yet another important point to emerge out of Polanyi's work (and that of the Substantivist school in general) was to emphasize the importance of custom and habit in maintaining lives and livelihoods. Hence Polanyi's work both influenced and was influenced by developments in Economic Anthropology, referenced above.

Similarly, work in Economic Development during this period, whether influenced by Marxism, by Modernization Theory, as in the case of Walt Whitman Rostow (1960), or by Institutionalists such as the extensive contributions of Gunnar Myrdal (1957) stressed the Institutional uniqueness of developing countries. Even though Myrdal's predictions about the future of Asian economic progress have turned out to have been erroneous, Myrdal's work was nevertheless important as it stressed the possibility of the persistence of underdevelopment due to path-dependent effects, economic dualism and circular and cumulative causation. Hence, Development was conceived by necessity as a transition from a pre-industrial to a fully industrial form of economic and social organization. There was a widespread recognition that Development was more than just an accumulation of machines, but rather required a comprehensive transformation of every aspect of society. The debate centered on what kind of transformation should take place.

Interestingly, Myrdal shared the Nobel Prize with Frederick Hayek. Hayek made multiple contributions to the economic debates of the 1930s and continued to write and influence economic debate in the 1980s. Original Institutionalist Economists and Hayekians (or Austrians and neo-Austrians in general) have tended to regard each other with mutual hostility and disdain. However, when ideology is put aside at least some aspects of Hayek do present an evolutionary approach to economics. Hayek's (e.g., 1945, 1988) views focused strongly throughout his many contributions on process and selection of institutions and the importance of the market as an information processing mechanism. On both, an epistemological and political level, Hayek and Popper shared a similar outlook. Hayek and other members of the Austrian school also have often viewed themselves as heirs to the tradition of the Scottish Enlightenment's stress on the emergence of markets and state, and in opposition to Social Contract Theory. In many respects, their argument for the inability of the State to improve on social evolution is built on the evolutionism of Spencer and Sumner.

Yet the de facto pluralism of the discipline was to change significantly by the 1960s and subsequently, the fields became increasingly defined by mainstream concepts and methods. Though there were, of course, multiple factors associated with this, at least with respect to economics I would emphasize two factors: one was the overformalization of the discipline and an overemphasis on the role of equilibrium theorizing. There is a remarkable correspondence between the kind of grand theory engaged in by Parsons, and that of mainstream economics. Nevertheless, the radical upsurge of the 1960s in society influenced the creation of professional associations that challenged the mainstream's dominance. Among all the social science disciplines, economics has been the least pluralistic and the least amenable to evolutionary analysis, though contemporary developments present a challenge to this otherwise dismal picture.

Political Science and International Relations

Nor did the fields of Political Science and International Relations fare much better. From the 1920s onward the emerging field of Political Science separated even further from economics. Perhaps the most influential person in Political Science over the next several decades was Charles Meriam (1931). Though Meriam had been trained in the older, more historically grounded tradition, he emphasized the importance of Political Science adopting formal techniques and focusing on the problems of achieving political order in the framework of Democracy. Like Ayres, he was instrumental in advocating reform and participated in the New Deal. He also envisioned a society run primarily by technocratic experts, guided by a new, positivistic and quantitative Political Science.

The older, historical method however did not vanish from Political Science in its entirety. For example, the contributions of Hans Morgenthau in International Relations were strongly historical and qualitative in the method. Yet Morgenthau (1948) separated the economic from the political and emphasized the challenge and importance of maintaining international order amongst nation states. As the prominent International Relations scholar Susan Strange (1970) was to note, International Relations scholars studiously avoided understanding economic processes and economists in International Trade and Finance, and studiously avoided politics. In addition, many International Relations theorists treated internal politics as a "black box", mostly irrelevant to International Relations while the field of Comparative Politics emphasized narrow, functionalist theories of politics.

Exceptions to this trend were exemplified by the kind of broad synthetic work by scholars whose work is difficult to classify. For example, Barrington Moore Jr.'s (1967) classic work *Social Origins of Dictatorship and Democracy* analyzed how different paths to Capitalist development led to variations in class constellations and ultimately to different forms political organization. Delayed development and the persistence of pre-capitalist class structures in Moore's view was more likely to result in political authoritarianism. That Moore's work was relevant to Political Science seems indisputable, though technically, Moore was considered a Sociologist.

Conclusion

In advancing my argument I have noted the presence of some very rough correlations between philosophies of science and approaches to social theory. Though Logical Positivism and Popper both tend to pull away from the kind of broad, synthetic theorizing required in Evolutionary Social Theory, despite their shortcomings, neither is quite the villain of the piece. Overly abstract views of theory, formally mathematical views of theory and naïve or abstracted empiricism in different ways pulled the social sciences away from evolutionary explanations. Ideology also played a significant role. In providing the above examples, I have sought to show that while the mainstreams of the several social sciences increasingly focused on the problem of equilibrium and narrowed the scope of inquiry, Evolutionism broadly defined, played a larger role than is often realized, even when Darwinian analogies or explanations for human behavior based in biology were eschewed. All areas of the social sciences had their critics who argued for more detailed historical, empirical and interdisciplinary grounding for the social sciences in general. Some of this theorizing was explicitly or implicitly evolutionary in its focus on the importance of qualitative change in forms of social organization and social action over time. Some of this was implicitly evolutionary. Some of these critics saw themselves as rebelling against Positivism. Others argued that they were in fact doing better science. If any significant connection stands out, it is the close relationship of Evolutionary approaches to a strategy of theory-guided empirical inquiry, and empirically guided theory.

References

Aston, Trevor H. and C. H. E. Philpins. 1985. *The Brenner Debate: Agrarian Class Structure and Economic Development in Pre-Industrial Europe.* Cambridge: Cambridge University Press.

Ayres, Clarence. [1944] 2021. *The Theory of Economic Progress. A Study of the Fundamentals of Economic Development and Cultural Change.* Fifth Edition. Association for Evolutionary Economics. https://afee.net/content/media/TEP-2021-10-18a.pdf

Benedict, Ruth. [1934] 2005. *Patterns of Culture.* Boston, NY: Houghton Mifflin.

Boas, Franz. 1920. "The Methods of Ethnology". *American Anthropologist* 22(4), pp. 311–321. https://doi.org/10.1525/aa.1920.22.4.02a00020

Carnap, Rudolph. 1936. "Testability and Meaning". *Philosophy of Science* 4(3), pp. 419–471. https://journals.openedition.org/philosophiascientiae/1615

Carneiro, Robert L. 2003. *Evolutionism in Cultural Anthropology.* Boulder, CO: West View Press.

Childe, Gordon V. 1951. *Social Evolution.* London: Watts.

Debreu, Gerard. 1959. *The Theory of Value: An Axiomatic Analysis of General Equilibrium.* New York: Wiley.

Friedman, Milton. 1953. "The Methodology of Positive Economics." Pp. 3–43 in *Essays in Positive Economics*, Chicago, IL: University of Chicago Press.

Friedman, Milton and Anna Schwartz. 1963. *A Monetary History of the U.S.* Princeton, NJ: Princeton University Press.

Haack, Susan. 2007a. *Defending Science within Reason: Between Scientism and Cynicism.* Amherst, NY: Prometheus Books.

Harris, Marvin. 1968. *Rise of Anthropological Theory.* New York: Crowell.

Hayek, Frederick. 1945. "The Use of Knowledge in Society." *American Economic Review* 35(4), pp. 519–530.

Hayek, Frederick. 1988. *The Fatal Conceit: The Errors of Socialism.* Princeton, NJ: Princeton University Press.

Hempel, Carl, & Oppenheim, Paul. 1948. Studies in the Logic of Explanation. *Philosophy of Science* 15(2), pp. 135–175. Retrieved May 12, 2021, from http://www.jstor.org/stable/185169

Hilton, Rodney (ed.) 1976. *The Transition from Feudalism to Capitalism.* London: Verso.

Kalecki, Michael. [1954] 2009. *Theory of Economic Dynamics.* London and New York: Routledge.

Keynes, John Maynard. [1936] 2008. *The General Theory of Employment, Money and Interest.* Hawthorne, CA: BN Publishing.

King, John. 2002. *A History of Post-Keynesian Economics since 1936.* Cheltenham: Edward Elgar.

Laudan, Larry. 1996. *Beyond Positivism and Relativism.* Boulder CO and Oxford: Westview Press.

Mead, Margaret. [1930] 2001. *Coming of Age in Samoa.* New York: Harper Collins.

Mead, Margaret. 1951. *Soviet Attitudes towards Authority.* Rand Corporation. https://archive.org/details/sovietattitudest009242mbp/page/n7/mode/2up

Meriam, Charles. 1931. *New Aspects of Politics.* Chicago, IL: The University of Chicago Press. https://archive.org/details/newaspectsofpoli00merr/page/n19/mode/2up

Mills, Wright C. [1956] 2000. *The Power Elite.* Oxford: Oxford University Press.

Mills, Wright C. [1959] 2000. *The Sociological Imagination.* Oxford: Oxford University Press.

Moore, Barrington Jr. 1967. *Social Origins of Dictatorship and Democracy.* Boston, MA: Beacon Press.

Morgenthau, Hans. 1948. *Politics among Nations.* New York: Alfred A. Knopf.

Myrdal, Gunnar. 1957. *Economic Theory and Underdeveloped Regions.* London: Duckworth.

Neurath, Otto et al. 1929. *The Scientific Conception of the World: The Vienna Circle.* Vienna: The Ernst Mach Society.

Parsons, Talcott. 1950. "The Prospects for Sociological Theory." *American Sociological Review* 15(1), pp. 3–16. https://www.asanet.org/sites/default/files/savvy/images/asa/docs/pdf/1949%20Presidential%20Address%20(Talcott%20Parsons).pdf

Parsons, Talcott. 1951. *The Social System.* Glencoe, IL: The Free Press.

Parsons, Talcott. 1971. *The System of Modern Societies.* Hoboken, NJ: Prentice Hall.

Polanyi, Karl. 1957. *The Great Transformation.* Boston, MA: Beacon Hill.

Popper, Karl. [1934] 1997. *The Logic of Scientific Discovery.* Translated by Freed and Freed. London: Routledge.

Popper, Karl. 1979. *Objective Knowledge.* Revised Edition. Oxford: Oxford University Press.

Quine. W.V. 2004. "Two Dogmas of Empiricism." Pp. 31–53 in *Quintessence: Basic Readings in the Philosophy of W.V. Quine*, edited by Roger F. Gibson Jr. Cambridge, MA: Belknap Press of Harvard University Press.

Richardson, Alan. 2003. "The Scientific World Conception: Logical Positivism." Pp. 391–400 in *The Cambridge History of Philosophy 1870–1945*, edited by T. Baldwin. Cambridge: Cambridge University Press. https://doi.org/10.1017/CHOL9780521591041.032

Robinson, Joan. 1942. *An Essay on Marxian Economics*. London: Ilian and Co. Ltd. https://archive.org/details/in.ernet.dli.2015.499589/page/n3/mode/2up

Rostow, Walter Whitman. 1960. *The Stages of Economic Growth: A Non-Communist Manifesto*. Cambridge: Cambridge University Press.

Sahlins, Marshall. 1972. *Stone Age Economics*. Hawthorne, NY: Aldine de Gruyter.

Sahlins, Marshall and Elman Service, eds. 1960. *Evolution and Culture*. Ann Arbor: University of Michigan Press.

Samuelson, Paul. 1947. *Foundations of Economic Analysis*. Bombay, Calcutta and Madras: Oxford University Press. https://archive.org/details/in.ernet.dli.2015.150369/page/n1/mode/2up

Schumpeter, Joseph. [1919] 1951. *Imperialism and Social Classes*. Cleveland, OH: Meridian Books.

Schumpeter, Joseph. [1943] 2003. *Capitalism, Socialism and Democracy*. London and New York: Routledge.

Schumpeter, Joseph. 1954. *History of Economic Analysis*. New York: Oxford University Press.

Sraffa, Piero. 1960. *Production of Commodities by Means of Commodities: Prelude to a Critique of Economic Theory*. Cambridge: Cambridge University Press.

Steward, Julian. 1955. *Theory of Culture Change*. Urbana, IL: Urbana University Press.

Strange, Susan. 1970. "International Economics and International Relations: A Strange Case of Mutual Neglect." *International Affairs* 46(2), pp. 304–315.

Theofanis, Papageorgiu, and Michaelides Panayotis. 2016. "Joseph Schumpeter and Thorstein Veblen on Technological Determinism and Institutions." *The European Journal of the History of Economic Thought* 23(1), pp. 1–30.

White, Leslie. 1949. *The Science of Culture*. New York: Grove Press.

Wilk, Richard R. and Lisa C. Cliggett. 2007. *Economies and Cultures: The Foundations of Economic Anthropology*. Boulder, CO: Westview Press.

Wolf, Eric. 1982. *Europe and the People without History*. Berkeley: University of California Press.

Wolf, Eric. 1999. *Envisioning Power. Ideologies of Dominance and Crisis*. Berkeley and Los Angeles, CA: Berkeley University Press.

Wolf, Eric. 2001. *Pathways of Power: Building an Anthropology of the Modern World*. Berkeley: University of California Press.

5 The Resurrection of Evolutionary Social Theory

Back to the Center?

Introduction

The late 20th century witnessed a global economic slowdown in the 1970s, followed by a shift toward neo-liberalism in the U.S. sphere of influence. By the mid-1970s, with a few exceptions, most formerly colonized countries achieved formal independence. However, in spite of proclamations of détente between the US and the Soviet Union, Cold War rivalry intensified in the form of proxy wars in Asia, Latin American and especially in Africa. By the mid-1980s, however, the Soviet Union began a process of reform that led to its demise. This gave rise to a dramatic increase in economic, political and social integration globally under U.S. leadership. Though the Communist Party retained political power in China, it too embraced market reforms. In the early 2000s, however, there were significant cracks in the edifice, of which the 2008 financial crisis was perhaps the most visible symbol. Over the course of the 2010s, tensions brought on by the process of globalization intensified. In February 2022, in response to a series of events, Russia invaded its neighbor, Ukraine. The most likely result of this invasion and the response to it by the US and the European Union is a reversal of global integration in the form of rival global power blocs, an accentuation of mercantilist strategies and a turn toward political authoritarianism. These changes were accompanied by a growing awareness of the problems brought on by ecological challenges such as human induced global climate change.

As in previous eras, social, economic and political changes gave rise to changes in the concerns of both Natural and Social Scientists. In the late 20th and early 21st centuries, there was a significant revival of evolutionary approaches to social theory. This was accompanied by challenges to the formalism of mainstream economics and the revival of broader approaches to Political Economy. The revival was in part a response to the extensive social, political and economic changes that occurred during this period and was facilitated by a shift in Philosophy of Science toward evolutionary conceptions of science as well as the increased prestige of Evolutionary Biology. The above trends gave rise to a perception that

DOI: 10.4324/9781003170679-6

concepts drawn from Evolutionary Biology Sciences could provide a better explanation of social change than models rooted in Physics and formal Mathematics. Three possible paths emerged for Evolutionary Social Theory: Sociobiology, Generalized Darwinism and Cultural Evolutionism. I argue that the latter path is likely to be the most fruitful.

Philosophy of Science: Neo-Positivism

Overview: The Problem

By the 1970s, the efforts of the Logical Positivists (Neurath et al. 1929) and their various offshoots, as well as of Popper (1934), to articulate formally logical criteria of theory confirmation or rejection, or to offer a clear basis for demarcating science from metaphysics were widely recognized as failures. This recognition set the stage for two different possible trajectories with respect to the philosophy of science:

1. A rejection of the possibility of objectivity for theory appraisal and of scientific approaches to the social sciences. At the extreme, some advocated a rejection of any objective standards of theory evaluation for the sciences at all and a turn to viewpoint theory;

2. Efforts to rescue the concepts of objectivity in theory appraisal, of science in general, and of the social sciences as science while taking account of the problems inherent in the prior efforts.

It should be noted that the view that these problems were unrecognized in the early 20th century is erroneous. As I argued in the previous section, Carnap, Hempel and Popper, for example, were all cognizant of the problems of linguistic reference with respect to theory appraisal. However, they were unable to provide an argument that could overcome the problems of the language game. Similarly, though not discussed in the previous section, the Logical Positivist movement also had a coherentist wing as represented by Pierre Duhem and Otto Neurath. Nevertheless, in the latter half of the 20th century, Philosophy of Science paid significantly more attention to the problems of theory confirmation and disconfirmation in the context of systems of theories. Quine's (2004) famous "Two Dogmas of Empiricism" essay, originally published in 1951, can be viewed as a watershed in the history of this shift.

As explained in the previous chapter, Quine's characterization of the "Two Dogmas" of modern empiricism as reductionism and a belief in the analytic-synthetic distinction as a strong dichotomy, though not necessarily true of all Empiricists, was an accurate description of the position of Rudolph Carnap. Quine staked his argument on a semantic analysis of the sentence "All unmarried males are bachelors". Quine's argument is that the term bachelor is not always substitutable for all meanings of the term "unmarried male". Therefore, we cannot have purely analytic sentences with semantic meaning. Whether or not there can be pure analyticity in formal math and logic is an issue that in my reading of Quine's writings, is unclear. In some interpretations, Quine can be interpreted as continuing in the tradition of Johnathan Stuart Mill and Bertrand Russell in taking the position that the truth of axioms of math and logic are contingent on their agreement with external reality and that they describe our most general experience. If such truths are contingent on our experience, then it is possible that they might be revised in the future. The implication is that no part of science is actually immune from disconfirmation. Quine's argument is anti-foundationalist: we cannot have any fully secure anchor for scientific knowledge.

Though some of Quine's other arguments have been put to use to support relativistic assertions, Quine was not a relativist. Quine was an Empiricist and his call was not to abandon Empiricism but to formulate a more thoroughgoing pragmatism. The problem of truth was a central concern of Quine (1990). But actually getting to Quine's position is tricky, given that he at times takes different positions even on the same page (Haack 2009, pp. 167–189). It is possible to interpret Quine as a realist in the sense that for Quine sets can describe actual natural kinds. Hence at least some of our categories potentially describe real entities with real causal powers. He can also be interpreted as a radical Empiricist, holding that the only thing we actually know is the experience of sensations on our skins.

What does this mean about theory confirmation and disconfirmation? In Quine's view, theories confront reality in much the same way that a spider web interacts with nature. An instance of potential disconfirmation might threaten all our beliefs, or it might just threaten some. We can rescue the theory "come what may" by making adjustments to the theory. But this does not address the problem of where we should make the adjustment. Elsewhere, Quine (1990, pp. 14–15) proposes a purely pragmatic maxim: that we reject the part of our theory that does the least damage to the system of theories. Yet even this maxim has ramifications for the larger "spider web" of theories that informs any individual test of a theory. Similarly, we might just be deceiving ourselves. Even minor repairs over time can ultimately lead to major revisions, not only in a specific system of theories, but to the entire structure of science itself, and ultimately, to all our beliefs. Hence science might rest on nothing more than pragmatic maxims. Yet Quine was an admirer of science. But for Quine, what ultimately justifies science is its demonstrated success.

Kuhn

Another way of viewing the problems of theory confirmation and disconfirmation is from an historical and sociological examination of theory changes in the history of science. Thomas Kuhn (1962) argued in his re-interpretation of the history of Science that the view that Science progresses by accumulating better theories and discoveries was at best misleading. *The Structure of Scientific Revolutions* was pivotal in shifting attention to the social context of scientific inquiry while raising questions about the actuality of progress. Kuhn argued that in the history of science inquiry was framed by paradigms. Paradigms shape the kinds of experiments scientists conduct both with respect to the questions they investigate and with respect to how the experiment is conducted and its results are interpreted. During periods of normal science, there is disciplinary consensus on what problems to investigate and how to do so. So far, so good. But if these background beliefs undergo periodic rapid shifts then there are times when science experiences crisis and revolution. Such crises are provoked by the accumulation of anomalies during the period of normal science. The Revolution leads to a new system of belief. But this new system in Kuhn's view is incommensurate with the previous system: basic terms, definitions, measurement concepts all acquire new meanings in the context of the new paradigm. There is no objective way to say that the new theory is better than the old. Though it is common to interpret Kuhn as a relativist, in my estimation, this is a misunderstanding. But that noted, Kuhn's position does lead to the conclusion that there is always a subjective and sociological aspect to theory confirmation and disconfirmation.

By its nature, the paradigm concept is fuzzy, though Kuhn does provide some examples—such as the shifts in Physics from Aristotle to Newton to Einstein—to illustrate what he means by the term. But Kuhn is not describing a set of clearly articulated axioms that guide inquiry. Kuhn provides us with a picture of scientific theories as matrices of multiple theories, concepts and background beliefs loosely drawn together. Kuhn does not distinguish between science and pseudo-science or between metaphysical and scientific statements. Rather, he distinguishes between immature science and mature science and between normal science and revolutionary periods in science. Immature science is marked by a lack of consensus on the core propositions of the discipline and competition amongst paradigms. Normal and mature science are marked by disciplinary consensus. Though the extent to which Kuhn allowed a role for subjectivity in his analysis is at times exaggerated, his approach makes it difficult to assess whether or not a given paradigm change constitutes progress.

Lakatos

In contrast, Lakatos' (1970, 1978) innovations on Popper's criterion of falsifiability points to the possibility of evaluating major shifts in accordance with more formal cognitively rational criteria. To this end, Lakatos distinguished between progressive SRPs (Scientific Research Programs) and degenerate SRPs. There is some correspondence between Lakatos' concept of an SRP and Kuhn's paradigm concept, except that Lakatos' concept of an SRP is more formal and deductive in structure: the hard core of the SRP can at least potentially be explained by recourse to a set of specific axioms. Propositions in the hard core are general and typically describe assumed properties of the entia under study: they are not directly and immediately testable. In that sense, they are metaphysical but metaphysical does not need to imply disconnected from the experience. But while they are not directly testable, they can be used in concert with auxiliary assumptions to formulate hypotheses. Such hypotheses can be tested and over time, confirmed or disconfirmed. But the hard core of the SRP is never directly tested: what gets tested is specific theories or hypotheses in the protective belt.

Like Popper, Lakatos emphasized the need for theories to be able to predict novel, as of yet unobserved phenomena. A progressive SRP is one that continues to predict novel facts without needing to resort to ad hoc restrictions on core theories. A degenerating SRP is one that requires the proliferation of ad hoc restrictions on axioms in the hard core. In and of itself, single instances of disconfirmation do not kill an SRP. Nor does the presence of ad hoc restrictions on a theory necessarily kill an SRP. The proliferation of ad hoc restrictions is however a sign of degeneracy. But even that does not necessarily kill an SRP. An SRP is only killed by a superior SRP. An SRP is progressive with respect to its rival if and only if it explains all the cases of the degenerate program and makes novel predictions. Hence a progressive SRP is clearly preferred to a degenerate SRP. But in Lakatos' view, it can be cognitively rational to continue to work with a degenerating SRP when no rival progressive alternative is available.

Though Lakatos is attempting to rescue science as a cognitively rational endeavor, his argument leads to some odd conclusions. He permits everything that Popper forbade—as long as there is no progressive alternative. We might cling come what may to any kind of theory that works at least some of the time, or even to a bad theory, provided there is no progressive alternative. Any effort to actually revise the theory is simply viewed as a degenerative shift. Substantive theory change is consequently an all-or-nothing affair—a problem that is also shared by Kuhn's approach.

Most of the exemplars of major Paradigm or SRP change provided by Kuhn and Lakatos are addressed to the history of Physics. They did not address their application to other sciences such as Biology and they did not directly apply their ideas to the Social Sciences. But one positive outcome of this has been the fuller realization of the importance of background assumptions to theory evaluation, and that theory evaluation takes place over the long haul. While the physical and natural sciences have tended to converge to disciplinary consensus on multiple, major theoretical and empirical issues, a disciplinary consensus has generally been lacking in the social sciences. Every social science has had some version of "paradigm wars". This has resulted in a proliferation of Paradigms, SRPs or

Research Traditions, and thus, varying degrees of disciplinary pluralism in the social sciences, with most disciplines having a dominant approach, surrounded by smaller dissenting schools. This has created disciplinary space for evolutionary perspectives in the social sciences.

On the other hand, it has also resulted in several negative and unproductive tendencies. One tendency has been to weaponize the concepts of Paradigms or SRPs. Adherents to the dominant approach in each discipline often allege that what their opponents are doing isn't "science", because it does not meet the disciplinary definition of science. The other tendency has been to charge that the dominant approach doesn't account for some feature of reality, or fails to solve some empirical problem and to thus allege that the Paradigm, or dominant Paradigm or SRP, is in crisis, or degenerate. At the same time, Paradigms or SRPs are often alleged to be more uniform than they actually are. The core postulates, or axioms of Paradigms and SRPs have at times been held to describe Ontological presuppositions (Dow 2005), a point I will return to below. But because Ontological statements are general, it is actually difficult to state categorically who has the correct Ontology. Perhaps no Ontological assumption captures all of reality. As I discuss below, there are ways of approaching the problem. One solution, proposed by Economist Sheila Dow is to argue that competing Paradigms or SRPs each describe a part of reality. Hence there is a case for structured pluralism.

Laudan

Another way to address the problem is that of Larry Laudan (1990, 1996), who has curiously received relatively scant attention in the Philosophy of the Social Sciences. Though I have included Laudan in the Neo-Positivist camp, there are notably Critical Common Sensist aspects of Laudan's approach. For example, Laudan (1996, pp. 3–25) is critical of both Positivism and Relativism. Laudan's goal was to articulate a path that is orthogonal to both Positivism and Relativism. Laudan criticizes Logical Positivism for its overemphasis on semantic analysis. The failure by the Logical Positivist to articulate a formal, semantic language that could avoid the pitfalls of natural language failed and gave rise to the emphasis of post-Modernism on linguistic relativism. In other words, post-Modernism has been visited upon us due to the "sins" of the "Positivist Fathers". Laudan also places considerable emphasis on the concept of warrant of belief.

Rather than trying to demarcate science from pseudo-science, Laudan argues we should focus on distinguishing between warranted and unwarranted claims of knowledge. But the issue of what makes a theory warranted or unwarranted is complicated. The concept of warrant and of degrees of warrant of belief plays a prominent role in Laudan's contributions to Philosophy of Science. Laudan points out that Kuhn and Lakatos forbid substantive theory change except in the case of major theory replacement. But at the same time, he acknowledges that inquiry takes place in the context of systems of belief. Laudan terms these systems Research Traditions. A Research Tradition is a complex, varied, interlocking system of background ontological premises about what kinds of entities exist or do not exist, theories that are testable, and an accepted range of specific methodological rules for testing theories. In addition, Research Traditions may be nested in wider Traditions, while adherents may hold to aspects of Research Traditions in varying degrees.

Progress in Laudan's view can be both conceptual and empirical. He offers an interesting way of decomposing the problem of assessing theories (1996, pp. 29–54). He agrees that even basic observations imply a set of background beliefs, including ontological assumptions about what kinds of entities exist and the properties they possess. As noted above, Ontological propositions are beyond direct and immediate falsification or verification due to the generality of such propositions. But this does not mean that they are never amenable to empirical evidence. Ontologies imply theories, and theories imply strategies for experiment and observation. Observations lead to theory confirmation or theory disconfirmation by degree. But even confirmation and falsification however are by degree: we can adopt multiple views on the matter based on the degree of warrant for accepting, rejecting, modifying or holding a theory with varying degrees of confidence. One single, or even multiple failures of a theory do not necessarily lead to a jettisoning of the entire structure of theories. The problem remains, however, that even a seemingly simple statement about direct, immediate reality is shaped by our Ontology: most of us will reject the sentence "Lo, a Unicorn" as suitable for fantasy and fiction, but not for Science.

Yet if we are intellectually honest, then a theory that consistently fails should lead to some revision of Ontological premises. Theories that succeed lead to increased warrant that the Ontological premise is valid. Where Lakatos views major revisions of an SRP as a sign of degeneracy, Laudan regards revisions of Research Traditions as potentially leading to progress. Progress can also take place by synthesis with other traditions. Judging progress may not always be formally logical. We may face gain and loss in the process of major theory revision or replacement of one tradition by another. Moreover, there may not always be a formally logical rationale through which to judge one tradition over another. However, we do not have to wait for a new progressive alternative to abandon and revise a faltering tradition. Yet the clear lesson of the late 20th-century Philosophy of Science is that scientific progress is a long-haul affair.

Laudan's approach can at least in principle resolve some of the problems raised by Kuhn and Lakatos. One interesting issue raised by Laudan is his recognition of the role of Ontology in theorizing. But a recognition of the role of ontology raises two further questions. Where do ontological assumptions come from and what kinds of ontological assumptions even make science possible? As I discuss below, both Critical Realism and Critical Common Sensism provide similar, yet ultimately distinctive approaches to this issue.

Ontology and Epistemology: Critical Realism and Critical Common Sensism

Origins of Critical Realism

As originally articulated by Roy Bhaskar (1989: Collier 1994), Critical Realism was intended as a metatheory to explain what makes science possible and as a guide to improving scientific practice. Ontology is a primary, perhaps the primary concern of Critical Realism. As such, it departs from the epistemological focus of the perspectives addressed above, though there is no inherent reason why the ontological emphasis of Critical Realism cannot be viewed as complementing those approaches. Critical Realism has significant implications for the conduct of science, whether in the natural or social sciences. Bhaskar's realism was also intended as a contribution to, and within Marxism, albeit as a contribution to Marxist Philosophy, rather than to Historical Materialism or Political Economy directly. Over time, Critical Realism has been integrated into social science research by both Marxists and non-Marxists. The two most prominent proponents of Critical Realism in the Social Sciences are Margaret Archer (1995, 1996, 2000) in Sociology and Tony Lawson (1996, 2003) in Economics, though Critical Realism has had its proponents across the Social Sciences. The contributions of Archer and Lawson clearly point in an evolutionary direction for the Social Sciences. In explaining the evolution and influence of Critical Realism, I will focus on three important concepts: depth realism, open systems theory and structure–agency theory. However, these issues may be more understandable placed into the context of the origins and development of Critical Realism out of its Althusserian roots.

Given that Bhaskar's Critical Realism was originally put forward as a contribution to Marxist Philosophy, a brief overview of this history will help to frame the nature of Critical Realist concerns. Marxist Philosophy has often been directly concerned with the nature of science, as at least traditionally, Marxists, going back to Marx and Engels, have sought to ground their positions in a scientific view of the world, albeit one that has often been distinguished the various forms of Positivism. This position traces back to Marx's distinction between Science that represented the interests of the working class and genuine emancipation, bourgeoisie but at times insightful efforts by theorists such as Smith and Ricardo, and crass apologetics for Capitalism. Yet Marxist Philosophy has incorporated a wide range of positions as to what science is and is not, not all of which are consistent with each other.

One particular effort to articulate philosophical foundations for Marxism was that of Louis Althusser (1969, 1970, 1972). But Althusser's approach also failed to provide an adequate of science. Its failure to do so contributed to the rise of post-structuralism (Boyle and Mcdonough 2015). Bhaskar's Critical Realism was a response to the failure of Althusser's contributions to Marxist Philosophy to provide for an adequate understanding of science and also to the problems of post-structuralism. It was also intended as a critique of an alternative to Positivist accounts of science. Consequently, a brief digression on Althusser will help to set the context for Bhaskar's arguments.

Althusser's account of science posited a strong distinction between ideology and science. For Althusser, ideology is the relationship between thought and practices that maintain the existing pattern of social relations. In contrast, Science illuminates the actual characteristics of reality. Following the French philosopher of science Bachelard, Althusser argued that the natural sciences stood in no need of further justification as their success justified their practices. In contrast, the social sciences, including most varieties of Marxism, had remained mired in a pre-history of ideology. In Althusser's view, Science progresses by creating novel theoretical constructs that are able to actually uncover the real characteristics of the entia under study.

Marx's accomplishment in Capital according to Althusser is to show how the labor theory of value illuminates the exploitative nature of Capitalist production. But Althusser's account is at odds with other Marxist accounts and was initially controversial amongst Marxists. One line of criticism, originally posited by both E.P. Thompson (1978) and Perry Anderson (1984), was that Althusser overemphasized the synchronic, structural and abstract-deductive aspects of Marx's Political Economy at the expense of Historical Materialism. Though I am sympathetic to Thompson's critique, I disagree with Thompson that Marx's goal was to destroy Political Economy and subsume it in its entirety to Historical Materialism. Rather, as I argued previously, Marx's goal was to unite the two. Anderson's critique of Althusser was less extreme and notably, later Marxist work, including contributions by Anderson himself (2013) acknowledged the usefulness of at least some Althusserian concepts.

The second point of controversy in Althusser is Marx's relation to Hegel. Marx is generally held to have stood Hegel on his head. As argued in a previous chapter, social evolution in Marx's view is due to the internal contradictions in a given mode of production with a strong emphasis on class struggle as the central contradiction, though other mechanisms are possible. Most interpretations of Marx also posit a dichotomous relationship between the economic base of society and the superstructure, in which in various ways, the superstructure is viewed as determined by the economic base. The breakthrough to a new mode of production occurs when the social relations of production can no longer contain the forces of production. In contrast, Althusser argued that it was not necessarily possible to identify that kind of direct causal relationship between base and superstructure. Althusser argued that the system is "overdetermined", by which he meant that the interaction and contingencies of the system determined every aspect of the system, with the economic base determinative only in the last instance. Althusser extended this argument in his critique of traditional Marxist interpretations of Marx having stood Hegel on his head, arguing instead that the contradictions emerged at the weakest points of the system.

Whether Althusser's account really resolves problems in Marxism or whether Althusser really had the secret decoder ring for understanding Capital can be debated, but that debate need not detain us here. What is relevant is that if structure is everywhere and every aspect of the structure determines every aspect of the structure, it makes evolutionary analysis of systems difficult, if not impossible. If the system entirely determines the person, then there is no possibility for an analysis of agency. In this sense, Althusser does not really improve significantly on Parsons. Althusser's "overdetermination" implies anti-humanism since "human nature" exists only as a direct product of the structure of a specific social formation. What criteria we should apply to determine the truth or falsehood of a theory is not specified in Althusser. Instead, Althusser emphasizes the link between Science and Praxis. Hence one might say that if a theory actually leads to a successful Proletarian revolution, that theory could be regarded as true. A consequence of Althusser's approach is that it does not provide a basis for connecting science with reality. Althusser does not actually provide a justification for science and does not clearly illuminate the difference between ideology and science. This sets the stage for post-structuralism (Boyle and Mcdonough 2015).

Post-structuralism itself is a vast cluster of positions and post-structuralists are often charged with relativism. Though this accusation might be disputed, there are strong currents, both within and outside of Marxist thought that reject post-structuralism due to its perceived relativistic implications. If post-structuralism is rejected, however, we do not necessarily default to Positivism. Bhaskar rejected both. Bhaskar's goal is to defend the usefulness of science by providing an explanation of what makes Science possible. Bhaskar argues that Positivism, which he treats as more or less synonymous with Empiricism, is characterized by a reductionist ontology in which phenomena are treated as discrete and subject to discrete effects, rather than being analyzed as part of a larger whole. Hence Empiricism, in Bhaskar's view must define causation as simply a constant conjunction of events, thus precluding analysis of the deeper structures that generate specific events. To this end, Bhaskar distinguishes between the empirical (observable events), actual (the relationships between events that may or may not be observable) and the real (the underlying structures that generate the actual, which are not necessarily observable). Empiricism in Bhaskar's view falsely equates knowledge with experience.

The task of science, in Bhaskar's view, is to go beyond the empirical and actual to a discovery of the real. Bhaskar argues that we can "find" these aspects of reality through the process of retroduction, or abduction: we ask what kinds of underlying structures are consistent with the observable aspects of reality. The knowledge which we generate however is fallible and this requires a stance of epistemological relativism. What Bhaskar and other Critical Realists mean by epistemological relativism however is somewhat unclear. One interpretation is that they simply mean fallibilism: a recognition that what we think we know today could later turn out to be false, and consequently, we should always be open to conceptual revision and new empirical evidence. Another interpretation is that Critical Realism as an ontological theory could be consistent with virtually any epistemological stance, including, the contributions of Kuhn, Lakatos and Laudan, or even with post-structuralist accounts. We might, for example, accept that there is in fact an external, objective reality, but that it is simply not possible for us to know it.

This gets us to the issue of openness. At least in my reading of Bhaskar, Bhaskar's position is not actually compatible with skeptical or relativistic accounts of epistemology. Because reality is stratified and exhibits emergent properties, it is never really possible to close off the analysis, though clearly, we may need to do so for the purposes of conducting a specific study. Bhaskar wants to understand what properties of the world have made experimentalism successful in science. Bhaskar does not reject experimentalism in the natural sciences per se, though he cautions that it may not always bring us definitive results and such results may not apply outside the laboratory. There are at least two problems with experimentalism from Bhaskar's view. One problem is that any experiment relies on the creation of artificially closed systems in a laboratory. A positive result or a failure to obtain a result thus may or may not fully account for the manner in which things interact outside the laboratory, so not all properties are necessarily actualized in a laboratory experiment. The second is the problem of induction. Induction is only reliable in so far as the same causes have the same effects and similarly, that the future will be like the present. Bhaskar rejects this latter claim, especially in the social sciences.

Bhaskar also draws a distinction between intransitive dimensions that are relatively unchanging and the transitive dimensions of our changing knowledge. Similarly, while even the physical world is open, social structures are continuously evolving. Since the physical and natural sciences deal primarily with intransitive structures, it is possible to have some degree of closure. However, since the social sciences address changing entia, closure is not possible in the social sciences. Bhaskar, like many others, is a proponent of emergence. Though the "higher" levels of reality such as the social sciences cannot break the laws of the "lower" levels (for example, humans cannot violate the laws of physics), nevertheless new properties emerge at each level that are not predicted by the properties observed at the lower level. Consequently, any kind of reductionism will face strict limits.

As noted at the beginning of this section, Bhaskar's approach is intended to clarify, not prescribe scientific practice. But Bhaskar's approach has clear ramifications for both the kind of theorizing engaged in by Social Scientists as well as the methods used by them. As such, Bhaskar's emphasis on Ontology does not preclude analysis of how general assumptions about the nature of reality guide actual empirical research. But Bhaskar is going a step further than this in that he is not just pointing out that Paradigms, Research Programs or Research Traditions either explicitly or implicitly rest on an Ontological framework, he is taking a stand on what kind of Ontological principles and methods for analyzing Ontological principles are warranted. Hence it is not surprising that Critical Realism has come to be regarded as a guiding philosophical system for social theory in general and that it is clearly conducive toward evolutionary theorizing. Two theorists, in particular, Margaret Archer in Sociology and Tony Lawson in Economics have been instrumental in this regard.

Critical Realism in the Social Sciences

Margaret Archer

Though Margaret Archer's (1995, 1996, 2000) work on structure–agency theory originated in Sociology, her perspective has permeated to multiple areas of the Social Sciences. Archer's work on structure–agency grows out of the earlier work of Sociologist Anthony Giddens (1982, pp. 1–17) on the theory of Structuration. Giddens begins with the dilemma posed by Parsonian Structural Functionalism in Sociology which in Gidden's view conceptualizes people as "cultural dopes", programmed by an all-powerful social structure. Yet an exclusive focus on agency ignored the way in which social structures exerted real causal efficacy on human action. But in trying to explain the complex relationship between structure and agency, Giddens emphasized the way in which the two were inextricably linked—there was no structure without agency and no agency without structure: in other words, Giddens conflated the two. Though Giddens did not consciously identify as a Critical Realist, many of his concerns clearly coincide with Critical Realism, in particular his anti-Positivist stance and his view that social scientists should search for hidden structures.

In contrast, Archer addresses the problem of structure and agency via the use of analytical dualism (see, for example, 1996, pp. xvi–xviii). In Archer's view, analytical dualism is justified because culture and agency, as well as structure and agency, are logically different entia, each with real causal properties and powers. Analytical dualism allows for an examination of the relationship between culture and agency and structure and agency. Archer criticizes the standard downward conflation of theories of structural determinism, the upward conflation of methodological individualism and the central conflation of Giddens, who collapses agency into structure. The advantage of this approach is that it allows us to distinguish the layers of social reality and thereby better analyze the interaction between the layers. Archer agrees that structures constrain and shape the behaviors and beliefs of agents and that the beliefs and actions of agents in turn shape and reshape the social structure. Both culture and agency and structure and structure and agency in Archer's view have actual, real causal powers.

Archer's work on culture and agency provides a good example of this method. Archer draws a distinction between the Socio-Cultural System (SC) and the Cultural System (CS). Where the Socio-Cultural System is the world of behaviors, the Cultural System, is roughly synonymous with the "Third World" of beliefs, ideas and values posited by Karl Popper. Archer criticizes what she terms the "myth" of the Cultural System as a uniform and all-embracing entity. Archer distinguishes between morphogenetic properties and morphostatic properties. Morphogenesis occurs when irresolvable contradictions arise between the structure and the actions of agents, thus leading to elaboration on both the social structure and culture, leading to change over time. Here again, we should take note of the emphasis on openness: neither structure nor culture are homogeneous, but are composed of different practices and beliefs, some of which are contradictory. Though Archer does not explicitly draw Darwinian analogies, it is but a short, logical step to an analogy of variation and selection.

Tony Lawson

In Economics, Tony Lawson (1997, 2003) has emerged as the most prominent representative of Critical Realism and structure–agency theory. Though he has more recently characterized his perspective as Social Ontology (Lawson and Morgan 2021a, 2021b), this is an elaboration on Critical Realism, not a departure from Critical Realist views. Consequently, I will focus on Lawson's exposition of Critical Realism.

Lawson criticizes mainstream economics for its reliance on what he terms "deductivism" as well as its reliance on what following Bhaskar, he calls Humean causation. By deductivism, Lawson means the reliance of the mainstream on *modus ponens* as a form of explanation. Lawson argues that mainstream economists seek explanation via the use of covering law models, which can only be confirmed by accepting Humean causation. By Humean causation, Lawson means reducing causation to a constant conjunction of events, an issue about which I have more to say below. Following Bhaskar, Lawson argues that this confines mainstream economics to the surface analysis of social reality while at the same time building implicitly or explicitly on closed systems analysis. Experimentalism cannot work in the social sciences in Lawson's view both because it wrongly isolates two or more variables from the rest of the system and because it ignores the changing nature of the parameters of a model. Econometric forecasting models falsely assume constant underlying parameters and attempt to predict the future, based on past and present probability distributions. Lawson's solution is to rebuild economics on the foundations of Critical Realism.

What would Political Economy built on the foundations of Critical Realism look like? Obviously, it would build on Bhaskar's views of abduction as the process through which one identifies causal laws that are relevant to the phenomena being studied. Perhaps a little less obviously, it might mean an end to economics as it is currently practiced. In Lawson's view, mainstream economics rests on a flawed ontology of a closed system which has led to the misapplication of formal mathematical methods to an area for which they are ill-suited. In order for modern Economics to be valid, the Economy would have to function as an entirely autonomous sub-system and the parameters of this subsystem would have to be stable. Both of these assumptions in Lawson's view are false.

> The social domain then, is an emergent realm that is dependent on human agency but irreducible to it. The structures of language, for example, have powers which facilitate speech acts but which are irreducible to human agency or these acts. Have we identified an emergent realm of specifically *economic* phenomena, necessitating relatively distinct methods for their analysis? Clearly not...In other words, there is no obvious basis for distinguishing economics according to the nature of its object, i.e. as a *separate* science.
>
> (Lawson 2003, p. 162). Emphasis in the original

What would Economics look like in Lawson's view if it were to be reoriented along the lines of Critical Realism. It would clearly look quite different. Lawson looks to the multiple forms of Heterodox Economics, such as Post-Keynesianism, Original Institutionalism, Feminism and other schools as exemplars. While Lawson is partially critical of these different schools for what he views as their inconsistency, they nevertheless are at least potentially consistent with Critical Realism in the sense that each of the above implicitly rests on a foundation of open systems (pp. 165–243).

For example, in his discussion of Veblen and the Original Institutionalist School (pp. 184–216), he interprets Veblen in the Critical Realist vein, arguing that Veblen's ontology is what defines his evolutionary method. This ontology is characterized by the selection algorithm. Darwinian analogies in Lawson's view are particularly useful to understand multiple problems in economics. This connection between Critical Realism, and the Generalized Darwinism of Geoffrey Hodgson and others is a point I will return to below.

This brings us to the issue of how Critical Realism might relate to the views of Kuhn, Lakatos and Laudan. Lawson has argued that the hard cores of Lakatosian SRPs are defined by what he terms "scientific ontologies", which presumably would be consistent with the concept of the "actual". I interpret Lawson to argue that there are implicit assumptions, which should be made explicit, of "real" ontological assumptions behind the Lakatosian hard cores. Hence these would be the true foundational axioms of different SRPs, a point that has also been echoed by Sheila Dow (2005). Again, as implied immediately above, heterodox economics in Lawson's view is by definition evolutionary as the foundational axiom of heterodox economics is open systems ontology while mainstream analyses rest on the foundational axiom of closed systems.

But are all heterodox economists truly Critical Realists now? More generally, must all Evolutionary Social Theorists embrace Critical Realism? Unless we wish to revert to no true Scotsman arguments this is not required. In the next section I address how Critical Common Sensism, or Neo-Classical Pragmatism provides another useful path to providing philosophical guidance to Evolutionary Social Theory in general and to heterodox economists specifically.

Critical Common Sensism, or Neo-Classical Pragmatism

In previous chapters, I noted the connection between Evolutionary Social Theory and Pragmatism, especially the Classical Pragmatism of Pierce and Dewey. Susan Haack is one of the foremost contemporary scholars and proponents of Pragmatism in this sense. While Haack's area of specialization in Philosophy is Epistemology she has also drawn the connection between Epistemology and Ontology and their ramifications for Philosophy of Science. Haack has described her position in multiple ways though she is probably best known as an advocate of Neo-Classical Pragmatism and the strong influence of Pierce on her thinking. Her use of the term "Critical Common Sensism" derives from Pierce's use of the same term and her work on the Philosophy of Science, *Defending Science, Within Reason* she uses the term to describe her views on Science. While the arguments in *Defending Science* stand alone, they are better understood in my view but relating them to her more general work in epistemology as well as ontology.

Haack's major work in epistemology (2009) is *Evidence and Inquiry.* In that work, she coined the term "foundherentism" to describe her approach to epistemology. Her coining of the term "foundherentism" is intended to articulate her synthesis of both foundationalism and coherentism, both of which Haack judges to be inadequate (pp. 1–117). Haack notes the obvious weaknesses in both empirical foundationalism and a priori foundationalism. Empirical foundationalism fails because it is not possible to have a purely empirical account of the world that is truly independent of our background beliefs. A priori foundationalism fails because it cannot offer any justification for the foundational axioms. Coherentism fails because it degenerates into purely circular argumentation and permits no input from the external world. But in Haack's view, the lack of a fixed point of reference on which to justify our beliefs does not imply we should give up the pursuit of truth (pp. 239–261). Furthermore, Haack argues that our beliefs are justified both to the extent that they are consistent with those background beliefs which we have a strong warrant to accept as true and to the extent that they conform to the empirical evidence (see, for example, pp. 126–139). Haack employs the analogy of a crossword puzzle to explain her position. She likens the consistency of an entry with the clue to empirical evidence and the other entries as our background beliefs. Thus, we test our entries both against our background beliefs and we also test our background beliefs against new entries. There is notably an affinity between Haack's "crossword puzzle" analogy and Quine's analogy of science to a spider web.

With respect to Ontology, Haack (2002) has described her position as "Innocent Realism". But she goes beyond what is sometimes termed "naïve realism" or simply "empirical realism". She has also described her views on Ontology as closely related to Bhaskar's realism. Following Pierce, Haack argues for the existence of "real generals". Haack explains this by reference to Quine's concept of "natural kinds". For Quine, sets are not necessarily arbitrary: at least some sets describe actual, real entities that belong together. Hence at least some of our general terms and concepts describe actual, real things. Quine's concept of a natural kind is that a real, actual entity with real actual properties is being described by the set. As was typical of Quine, this is somewhat minimalist, though my position is actually closer to Quine's. Haack is more explicit and stronger in her realism. Haack does not use the Bhaskarian triad, but she is clear that for her, realism means acceptance at least of properties akin to Bhaskar's concept of the real. As with Bhaskar, the goal of Science in Haack's view is to explain and understand these actual causal properties and mechanisms. Hence for Haack, theories in science are potentially more than just useful heuristic devices-they are at least potentially true. At the same time, Haack emphasizes the importance of metaphor, analogy and heuristic devices to explanation in science, as well as the role of logic.

This brings us back to the issue of the use of the term "Critical Common Sensism". On this point, the reader may recall the discussion in Chapters 1 and 3. Pierce used the term to describe his own views on the issue of realism and acknowledged Thomas Reid's use of the term. Yet Pierce did not follow Reid on this issue, but instead, sought to straighten out Kant's categories. Kant's position depends on the distinction between noumena and phenomena and multiple other categorical distinctions. Kant argues that we cannot access the noumena. Pierce, Haack and Bhaskar all disagree with Kant on this point. However, in arriving at their respective positions of transcendental realism, they all go through Kant, though Bhaskar also goes through Hegel. In the case of Bhaskar, this leads to a view that there are hidden structures and that reality is layered. In my own reading of Haack, I actually see potential for daylight between the two, but obviously, I will defer to Haack as the best source of interpretation of Haack.

While my own position is strongly influenced by Haack, I disagree with her and Bhaskar's position on Realism. My own views on Realism are more directly tied to Reid's (1788b) common sense realism which dispenses with the need for any positing of a noumenal realm or of "hidden" structures. Another point I noted about Reid was his discussion of "causation". Causation applies best to those instances where active powers are applied, resulting in change. The use of the word "causation" to describe the structure of nature or society can lend itself to confusion. We should at least clarify whether we are talking of efficient, material, formal and in cases that entail intentional human action, final cause. With respect to categories, here again, we can make us of Quine's views on natural kinds. Proper names, and at least potentially, theories in science, are more than just conveniences. Words such as "tree" describe an actual class that distinguish trees from other classifications of flora. This is not an arbitrary distinction. Gravity is an actual real force. But there is no further force behind gravity. In other words, to say that snow is white or that grass is green does not posit any property of whiteness or greenness: rather, in both cases, there is an actual way in which light is refracted, independently of our perception of the refraction of light and a way in which the human eye, in most cases, will perceive this refraction. The sentence "Opium has dormitive properties" is nonsense, unless by dormitive properties we mean the specific ways in which opioids attach to receptors, resulting in drowsiness on the part of the person who ingests opioids.

In the social sciences, terms such as "class", while subject to definitional dispute, describe groups of people who can be demarcated in actuality from other groups of people in non-arbitrary ways. Social structures describe actual, real sets of relationships between habitual and instituted ways of interacting in society. Hence even if one cannot directly and immediately observe an entire social structure, the patterns of relationship are clearly amenable to empirical inquiry. While discovering properties and causes requires extensive aids to inquiry and careful inquiry, I dispute that such things are "hidden" and unobservable in principle. I will return to what this might imply about the social sciences shortly.

With respect to epistemology and its implications for science, however, there are clear differences between Haack's views and those of the Critical Realists, and on that point, I am in complete agreement with Haack. Haack is a fallibilist, but not an epistemological relativist. Critical Realists find structures and causal properties via abduction. Haack argues that we find structures and causal properties through a process of empirical inquiry of abduction, deduction and induction. Inquiry begins in Haack's view when we are confronted with a situation that leads to genuine doubt about the way things are coupled with a desire to actually know how things are. The goal of inquiry is substantial truths. To say that a proposition is true in Haack's view is to say that things are in fact as the proposition describes. It is not sufficient to say in Haack's view that a theory is adequate or gives an accounting of the facts. Theories aim at substantial truths. In Haack's view, the discovery that "DNA is a double backbone, out molecule, etc." (p. 139) is the correct, or true model. Hack. Haack accepts the use of covering law models (Haack 2007a, p. 129) as one component, though not as the entirety of, scientific explanation.

In *Evidence and Inquiry*, Haack had already drawn the connection between this kind of everyday and common sense method of inquiry and the method of science. She expands on this in *Defending Science*. Like CR, CCS is an effort to defend the integrity of scientific inquiry from the extremes of post-Modernism, while simultaneously taking issue with Positivist, Neo-Positivist and scientistic accounts of science. Haack defines Scientism as the view that the natural sciences provide some kind of privileged, or unique method, that serves to make its claims stronger and more justified than other forms of inquiry and is often associated with excessive deference to all claims made in the name of Science. In contrast, Cynicism, drawing on a range of positions commonly identified as "Post Modern" is often critical of the claims of science and of scientists to be making warranted claims to knowledge. Indeed, taken at face value, post-Modernism denies our ability to stake claims to knowledge of the external world independently of our perspectives on the world. This position, associated with Rorty (as well as others) in Haack's view collapses into irrealism and/or, simply conventionalism. In contrast, Haack is arguing that when done well, inquiry in the natural sciences leads to strongly warranted, though potentially fallible claims to knowledge.

In defining what makes the natural sciences successful, Haack identifies the extent to which science incorporates standards of good evidence and good empirical inquiry (2007a, p. 23). Haacks' focus on science as continuous with the kind of good faith inquiry people of all walks engage in, is of course consistent with Pierce's focus on inquiry as guided by a circular process of abduction deduction and induction. Good science proceeds by informed conjecture consistent with our background beliefs and by judgments of the validity of the evidence for and against a theory.

Haack uses the term "scientific evidence" to refer to the evidence with respect to scientific claims. In contrast to the logical positivists and Popper, Haack argues that there is no class of basic statements or data that can strictly confirm or falsify theories. Instead, Haack's view of evidence encompasses both experience and reason. Haack argues that the nature of scientific evidence is ramifying in nature. Some theories may be strongly supported and thus well warranted. Other theories may be less well supported but strengthened due to their consistency with theories that are strongly warranted. A theory for which there is strong evidence may lead to a rethinking or even a reconfiguration of other theories previously regarded as true. Haack's view of evidence is thus one of degree: notably, it is not just the "amount" of evidence that matters, but also the quality of evidence. Haack's CCS is exactly that: a theory of *Critical* Common Sensism in that the claims of the sciences when done well are "more so" than that of our everyday inquiry in the sense that the sciences have refined inquiry: the scientific method is just "more so" than the techniques of our everyday inquiry.

While Haack does not use the term "Open Systems" or make direct reference to structure–agency theory, it is clear that with respect at least to the Social Sciences her approach is at least compatible with aspects of both. In comparison to the natural sciences, Haack defines the social sciences as "the same but different". They are the same in that the social sciences can at least potentially use the same standards of inquiry as the natural sciences. Similarly, at least some aspects of the social sciences can be explained in terms of the same explanatory structure of the natural sciences. They are different in that the study of social sciences must of necessity address the role of conscious, purposive agents. Haack is critical of strong reductionism that attempts to derive laws of the social sciences from the law of other sciences. Haack asserts that this effort at understanding can actually coincide with an effort at explanation.

To better understand Haack's theory of the social sciences it will be useful to reference a lesser-known article (2004) she wrote about the late economist Robert Heilbroner. Haack criticizes Heilbroner's argument that the social sciences, and particularly economics cannot be scientific because of the need to take values into account and the need to explain motivation in terms of purposive action. Haack notes that while there may be culturally specific explanation, explanation can still be put into the form of general principles. Why, she asks, for example, can we not derive statements about the relationship of the Fed Funds rate to levels of employment? Perhaps the clearest difference between Haack and Heilbroner however is her assertion of the possibility of separating analysis in the social sciences from statements of value. In other words, Haack accepts the is-ought distinction.

Where Haack clearly has an understanding of agency, her treatment of the concept of social structure is underdeveloped and my own discussion of it herein again confronts the issue of my objection to the concept of depth realism. The concept of "structure" in the social sciences has multiple, different connotations. Structuralists such as Giddens, and Critical Realists such as Archer, embrace a definition of structure in which there is an underlying or overarching structure that generates the observable patterns of behavior. This is of course consistent with the Critical Realist distinction between the real, actual and empirical. I have written elsewhere that Pragmatism, or Neo-Classical Pragmatism, is consistent with efforts to engage in systemic analysis beyond that of just immediate appearance. However, this kind of analysis also engages with directly observable and ongoing patterns of behavior.

Two Understandings of Critical Common Sensism

Here again, while Haack is the best authority on Haack's position, my own approach is to reject any concept of structures that structurate or that are "hidden". Rather, the position I take is that structures are located in the actual and observable habitual and path-dependent nature of what conscious, purposive agents do and the connections between the institutions that humans create. They are found through the process of empirical inquiry and can be used to then further guide our research, leading to degrees of confirmation or disconfirmation. But there is no structure above, beyond, to the side of, underneath of or anywhere else outside of actual, observable patterns of social behavior. Abduction alone is insufficient.

An example I have made elsewhere (Poirot 2008) may help with this point. Marx argued that an analysis based on freedom of contract ignored the deeper structure of capitalist society, rooted in the relationship between capitalist and worker. I agree with Marx that an analysis based on pure exchange, which ignores relationships between people in production or in society in general, is insufficient. But this relationship is only "hidden" in so far as social scientists elect to ignore it. It is also observable in the sense that we can observe the patterns of human behavior and the connections between these patterns of behavior. Again, we do not need to resort to statements about structures that structurate. Similarly, the reader may recall the previous discussion about C. Wright Mills' definition of structure and his criticism of "grand theory" as well as Veblen's rejection of metaphysical idealism.

This raises a second question about the meaning of the term open systems. The adaptation of Haack's Critical Common Sensism that I am putting forward herein has at least two points in common with Critical Realism. One is that phenomena cannot be fully understood by studying them in isolation. Second, once we allow that human action is conscious and purposive, predictability in the social sciences will always be at best strictly limited and by degrees of warrant or more and less, rather than in terms of stochastic processes and statistical error. Yet there are justifiable reasons as to what constitutes degrees of more or less about projections for the future. That noted, my approach allows for a considerable degree of path dependency and habitual social behavior so that some limited predictability is possible, once the institutional structure of a society is specified. Hence empirical generalizations will hold in varying degrees. If by predictability we mean that trying to develop time series forecasts of variables such as the rate of inflation or unemployment to a specified confidence interval, then I agree, that kind of predictability is unattainable. However, it is possible to have the predictability of what is likely to happen given conditions x or y, with varying degrees of warrant that some future events are more or less possible. That noted, the social sciences, for the most part, are retrodictive, not predictive sciences. My approach herein is somewhat stronger than Lawson's "demi-regs" yet much weaker than that of Samuelson's.

Haack's analysis assumes that inquirers share the same crossword puzzle and a commitment to good faith inquiry. Whether or not this is true of the physical and natural sciences is a complex question, but in the social sciences, it is clear that social scientists do not share the same crossword puzzle or the same understanding of how to conduct inquiry. The ontological premises of communities of inquirers on issues about the nature of reality itself and the kinds of properties and mechanisms that we deem worthy of investigation differ fundamentally both within and between disciplines. As I noted earlier in this chapter, these differences can be and clearly are, often exaggerated. Yet they are also real. Were social scientists to actually adopt the concept of social sciences as good faith empirical inquiry, we could no doubt make better progress. At present, however, it is clear that the social sciences must take into account the persistence of the ways in which fundamentally different background beliefs shape the process of inquiry. Simply put, though there may be areas where crossword puzzles overlap, it is clear that we are often not working on the same crossword puzzle.

To that end, my approach is to recognize the reality of competing Research Traditions in the Social Sciences, or alternatively, Research Strategies, but to minimize the boundaries between them. As noted in the first section of this chapter, a Research Tradition is a much looser concept than that of either a paradigm or SRP. Hence rather than attempting to delineate Research Strategies in terms of rigid lines or incommensurate Ontologies, I emphasize variation within the tradition as well as the potential for overlap between traditions. In other words, I am consciously borrowing and pushing Haack's analogy of the crossword puzzle, perhaps to its breaking point. I conceive of the Social Sciences as vast congeries of overlapping and sometimes contrasting crossword puzzles. The goal is not to determine which tradition is "best" per se, but rather, to discern what theories are warranted and to what degree, and to attempt to unite those theories for which we have strong warrant into a coherent whole. But coherence in this sense, again, to borrow an apt analogy from Haack, is conceived more in terms of general consistency, rather than consistency in terms of deductive logic from foundational axioms.

This raises an interesting point about how to view the "orthodox-heterodox" split in contemporary Economics. In the previous chapter, I noted that in the late 20th century mainstream economics adopted either a purely formal mathematical approach or sought to ape mathematical physics. Empirical testing was carried out via the use of Econometrics and this was increasingly reflected in mainstream economics even into the 21st century. Here again, the term "deductivism" may be correct in that this kind of Economics takes a few postulates about rationality, scarcity and methodological individualism with an emphasis on equilibrium and other similar characteristics and uses them to formulate rigorous mathematical models. That noted, 21st-century mainstream economics has allegedly taken an "empirical turn". Similarly, there have always been prominent economists who achieved professional recognition and status whose work challenged one or more mainstream propositions or expressed their arguments in natural language. Yet the portrait of the mainstream I have painted here is one that in my estimation remains largely accurate in the sense of describing an ideal type of profession. Lawson's argument again is that these ways of thinking represent closed systems ways of conceiving social processes.

As noted as well in my discussion of Lawson, there has also been a revival of heterodox thinking in Economics, of which Lawson and Hodgson are widely recognized participants. What then characterizes heterodoxy? There is no clear, unifying principle or method that can unite Feminist Economics (a category that includes multiple strands), Marxian or Radical Economics, Original Institutional Economics, Post Keynesianism and Neo-Ricardianism. Whether Austrians and Neo-Austrians should be grouped amongst the heterodox, is a point of contention. Nevertheless, it is fair to say that heterodox begins exactly where the mainstream ends and declares the question as out of bounds. All the above, with the possible exception of the Austrians, do seek to make the connection between the more narrowly conceived definition of economics and the broader societal forces. Many explicitly seek to explain the origins and evolution of these processes (see, for example, Dugger and Sherman 2000). The difference is Political Economy is broadly conceived, and Economics is narrowly envisioned. Nevertheless, rather than viewing schools of thought as deriving from specific axioms, perhaps ensconced in more general axioms, we would be better served by thinking of Economists and all Social Scientists as varying populations inhabiting a common ecosystem, sometimes giving rise to sterile offspring and sometimes to fertile offspring.

Contemporary Evolutionary Biology: An Overview

The mid and late 20th and the early 21st century have been marked by considerable success in Biology in general and Evolutionary Biology specifically (Mayr 1982, pp. 477–829, 2001; Futuyma 2017). Evolutionary biology has come to be considered the glue that holds the discipline of biology together. In addition, the extensive literature on Philosophy of Biology has served to highlight the ways in which Biology is unique amongst the natural sciences as well its potential ramifications for the social sciences. In this section, I briefly highlight some of the significant developments as a means both of better understanding the problems of significant theory change and also in laying the foundations for analyzing the relationship between Evolutionary Biology and Evolutionary Social Theory. In (Poirot 2007) I provided a more extensive review. My own views are thus closer to

Cordes (2007) and while I cite a significant amount of the literature outside of Economics, there is some precedent for a general systems approach to Evolutionary Social Theory in Economics in the work of Boulding (1974).

At the beginning of the 20th century, Biology was still in many respects a disorganized field and Evolutionary Biology, in particular, was particularly vulnerable to speculative excess and interpretation in ways that supported invidious distinctions, though again, I emphasize that it was interpreted to support more egalitarian visions as well. Over the course of the 21st-century Biology has made the transition to a well-organized and empirically grounded discipline and its use of support for invidious distinctions has lessened considerably. Rather than providing us with an example of a paradigm revolution, however, progress in Biology has been cumulative and synthetic. Furthermore, advances in Evolutionary Biology have been substantially aided by advances in functional biology, especially with respect to the progress in molecular biology.

Since functional biology addresses "how questions" it lends itself more readily to reductionist strategies. The utility of reductionist strategies in biology is exemplified by the extensive advances in molecular biology, which were aided by the progress in biochemistry. The discovery of the molecular structure of DNA would not have been possible without an understanding of the differences in amino acids, proteins and peptides, and their respective properties. The ability to explain the replication process of DNA in turn played a decisive role in disproving Lamarckian and quasi-Lamarckian concepts of inheritance. While the contributions of Watson and Crick were decisive on this latter point, this work built on earlier advances in the understanding of what had been referred to as the germ plasm. Progress in understanding the role of genes in the inheritance and selection of traits was then reinforced by the work of Dobzhansky in isolating the genetic components of inheritance in fruit flies significantly advanced our understanding of inheritance. In concert with the development application of statistical methods to population genetics, this led to a workable model of how populations of varying characteristics adapt to the environment over time and to quantitative measures of fitness and evolution.

The Neo-Darwinian synthesis is a combination of population genetics and the concept of natural selection. Before addressing the issue of selection, however, a brief digression about the nature of inheritance is in order. Recent work has demonstrated that the basic model in which DNA codes for RNA and RNA in turn codes for proteins, which build structures is a simplification of a more complex process. Consequently, more emphasis is now placed on the interaction of genes in the genome and the developmental process and how that leads to variation in the phenotype. Some have argued that it is possible for environmental factors in the developmental process to lead to changes in the genome in the gametes, thus perhaps partially justifying a limited Neo-Lamarckian counter-revolution. This does illustrate however how developments in different areas of biology have ramifications in other areas of biology and how theory change is not always unilinear. Yet these criticisms hinge on how the synthesis is understood. Criticisms of the synthesis that posit biology is on the cusp of a new Kuhnian revolution, often rest on overly rigid views of the synthesis. The debate on what is known as the Extended Evolutionary Synthesis recently made its way into the public discussion via an article published in *The Guardian* (Buryani 2022). The evolutionary biologist, Jerry Coyne (2022) provided a useful critique and references to the extensive literature on the topic of the misunderstandings of the modern synthesis and the significance of the Extended Evolutionary Synthesis presented in the article.

This brings us to the issue of selection. Natural selection is often described as a force. However, describing natural selection as a "force" in the physical sense of the term oversimplifies the processual nature of natural selection. Regardless of what is being selected and at what level, differential survival is a result of the interaction of the organism with its entire environment. Those characteristics, at least in the modern Neo-Darwinian synthesis are a product of a complex process of recombination of DNA in the sex cells and the interaction of the organism with the environment with respect to the developmental process. Hence, the structure of an organism, the genetic and phenotypic variation within a species, and the variation of other species are a result of a process of hereditable variation and selection. These terms are clearly a shorthand mechanism for describing a complex, interactive process that leads to variation over time. While contemporary evolutionary biology addresses multiple mechanisms of selection such as sexual selection, peripatetic selection and other similar mechanisms, these are logically special cases of the more general concept of natural selection.

This does however lead to the issue of levels of selection. The original emphasis in Darwin's writings was on selection both within the species as well as between species. In other words, group selection was at least a possibility in Darwin's original formulation. The molecular revolution led in turn to an understanding of how selection act at the molecular level. This gave rise to some controversy, especially given the popularization of reductionist views of selection as articulated by people such as Richard Dawkins (1999, 2016). Yet even Dawkins' emphasis on reductionism as a strategy was qualified by his assertion that a focus on selection at the genetic level was just one way of looking at the issue of selection and that the metaphor of "selfish genes", was just that: a metaphor. Hence there is widespread recognition that selection takes place at multiple levels.

Explanation in contemporary evolutionary biology is consequently in terms of a step-by-step process of continuous change. The debate between Steven Gould's (1991; see also Barnes 1979) emphasis on punctuated equilibrium, randomness and sub-optimal adaptations is often contrasted with the strong adaptationist program of others such as Richard

Dawkins. But rather than seeing these as competing or rival theories, I would stress the complementary nature as well as the semantic nature of these differences. Contemporary evolutionary biology is non-teleological and mechanical in its explanatory structure. In looking back over the history of evolution, it is possible to see the development of increasingly complex structures. Yet simultaneously, relatively simple structures survive and evolution takes place via a branching pattern leading to a multiplication of species. This pattern makes the application of concepts such as a drive to perfection or progressivity in evolution, difficult to apply at best. This view of evolutionary processes however emerged over nearly two centuries of theorizing and empirical inquiry into the nature of evolutionary processes and is still in some details in flux. In other words, evolutionary biology is a general concept and general principle science, not a general law science.

The emergence of this contemporary understanding of biological evolution represents a fundamental shift in world views, both in terms of pre-Enlightenment understandings but also in terms of concepts that were central to Enlightenment thought itself. But the emergence of our contemporary understanding was not a sudden, one-time event, but a continuous process. The displacement of the argument to design from the natural sciences did not lead to a sudden acceptance of Darwin's views on evolution. Similarly, Darwin's contributions built on and incorporated concepts from naturalism, while altering the meaning of other concepts and introducing new concepts. As we noted, Darwin's views on natural selection were in some respects clearly rival to Lamarckian and other views on evolution, yet not necessarily rival to Lamarckian views on inheritance. In contrast, Mendelian, and further developments in genetics based on the concept of hard inheritance were clearly rivals to Lamarckian concepts of inheritance based on acquired characteristics. By the early 20th century, this latter view had become the dominant theory of heredity and at times viewed as a rival to the Darwinian program.

The core of the modern evolutionary theory, with a few specific exceptions, rests on the concepts of natural selection and hereditable variation based on "hard inheritance", leading to a branching pattern of speciation over time. This part of the theory does make extensive use of reductionist approaches to science. However, contemporary evolutionary theory also pushes us toward understanding evolution as a complex process by which individual organisms and entire species interact with each other and the environment. This emphasis on interactive processes leads to a focus on the interdependent nature of all living organisms in entire ecosystems and that ecosystems have emergent properties. In other words, contemporary evolutionary theory pushes us toward system thinking and an emphasis on complex, dynamic interactive processes.

How, and whether, this is generalizable to the Social Sciences is the question to which I now turn.

Biology and Evolutionary Social Theory

Sociobiology and its Discontents

If we begin from the established premise that differences in DNA lead to variations in phenotypic appearance and that the interaction of the phenotype is what determines whether an organism survives and reproduces, then it follows that at least some animal behaviors are dependent on the existence of specific genes or sets of genes. The idea, for example, that different species of wasps have genes for constructing different kinds of nests, is not particularly controversial nor disconcerting. Yet the idea that there are genes for human behaviors is contentious. But unless one is developing a special pleading for humans, then there must be genes for at least some general human behaviors even though there are no genes in humans for constructing certain types of houses. If humans have genes for language acquisition, they do not have genes for learning French, English or Chinese. To say that there are "genes for" a specific behavior means that in the absence of those genes, the behavior would not occur. Controversy with respect to the allied research programs of Sociobiology and Evolutionary Psychology arises as both respectively, to some degree, attribute at least some significant human behaviors to genetic endowments.

Like all research traditions, Sociobiology (Wilson 1975a, 1975b, 1998) and Evolutionary Psychology (Pinker 2003; Tooby and Cosmides 2000) are not uniform. The underlying premise, however, is grounded in the strong adaptationist interpretation of the neo-Darwinian synthesis discussed above (Dawkins 1983; Dennet 1995). Sociobiology explains broad patterns of human behavior in terms of the ability of that behavior to enable reproduction. Though some interpret Sociobiology as viewing people as innately selfish and violent it is also possible to conclude that evolution has endowed human beings with the potential to cooperate, or both (DeWaal 1996). Similarly, Evolutionary Psychology focuses on the brain as an adaptation that was cobbled together step by step via the process of natural selection. The argument is in part theory-driven in that the Neo-Darwinian tradition takes the construction of organisms step by step as a well-established principles.

However, in seeking to explain human behaviors as rooted in genetics, Sociobiology challenges the traditional assumption of the social sciences of social structures and culture as phenomena suis generis. Not surprisingly, the initial appearance of E. O. Wilson's *Sociobiology* set off a long and acrimonious debate, based in part on arguments over what the program did and did not entail. Misunderstandings and recriminations on both sides of the divide were immediate and often vitriolic (Allen et al. 1975; Barnes 1979; Gould et. al. 1975; Gould 1996). Opponents of these programs charged that Evolutionary Psychology and Sociobiology were resurrecting Social Darwinism and genetic determinism. Proponents of these programs countered that they were trying to explain general human behaviors, not cultural or racial differences, as an outcome of biological evolutionary processes (Wilson 1975b). Nor were matters helped by the use of sloppy metaphors such as "selfish genes" and reductionist approaches to science (Dawkins 2016). Jared Diamond's (1997) work on global biological and social evolution presented a geographical determinist account of social evolution, neglected the role of institutions in history and failed to address decades of scholarship on global history that was directly relevant to his arguments.

The rejection of any role for biology whatsoever in the study of social evolution and a general suspicion of the use of any strong biological analogies between biological and social evolution has a long and venerable pedigree in the social sciences. Gould and Lewontin (1979) regarded what they viewed as a near-exclusive focus on natural selection advanced by many advocates of the neo-Darwinian synthesis as a misunderstanding of Darwin and drew a sharp line between the social and biological realms. Not surprisingly, Gould and Lewontin, who were themselves strongly influenced by Marxism, enjoyed considerable influence amongst many social scientists who maintained allegiance to the concept of culture as autonomous from biology. This emphasis on the centrality of cultural emergence to the social sciences was also prevalent in the arguments of many social evolutionists in the mid and late 20th centuries. Some Original Institutional Economists (Dugger and Peach 2009) and Marxists (Brenner 1976; Meiksins Woods 2017; see also Aston and Philpin 1985) have gone so far as to reject any role of ecology as a limiting or explanatory factor in social change.

But critics of the emerging programs of Evolutionary Psychology and Sociobiology often attacked straw-person versions of those programs and were not always on as strong a scientific ground as they claimed (Segerstrale 2000). By the mid-2000s however, the potential for a truce between the warring factions was discernible in the work of several people. For example, Sarah Blaffer Hrdy (1981, 1999) emphasized the importance of female choice in reproduction, thus countering earlier theories of female passivity in evolution. Others have emphasized the importance of cooperation as well as competition as part of the process of evolution (DeWaal 1996). And work by Richerson and Boyd (2001, 2005) has stressed the role of evolution in giving rise to the capacity of the human brain to store and process complex information and thus laying the foundation for culture. In contrast, the rise of gene-culture co-evolution theory assigns an important role in culture. Initially, E. O. Wilson had argued that genes held culture on a string thus implying that the causation was from the cultural string to the genetic kite. Boyd and Richardson however argued for a less strong relationship in arguing that humans have two endowments: genetic and cultural. Culture in their view is information stored in the human brain. In their view, culture can act as a force for selection so that the cultural string can move the genetic kite. The cultural string can also exhibit substantial degrees of freedom though it can never be entirely untethered.

If the programs of Sociobiology and Evolutionary Psychology are not quite as rigid and reactionary as some of their critics have charged, that does not necessarily mean however that we are all Sociobiologists now, at least not to the extent that genetic factors are used to explain socio-cultural evolution. At most these programs can only explain generally shared human capacities for language, cognition and general behaviors. If people have instincts to be selfish and aggressive, they also have instincts for cooperation and peaceableness. What Sociobiology and Evolutionary Psychology cannot explain is the broad pattern of cultural variation and how and why these patterns undergo change. If humans have instincts in some instances, for example, not to eat rotten meat, we should also note that foods that evoke gag reflexes and foods that appear appetizing vary across cultures. This points to building on the habit-instinct psychology of American Pragmatism and Veblen's views of human behavior with an emphasis on how all these underlying instincts emerged in the Paleolithic, rather than at points in time following that era. If our goal is to explain changes in a given system, or the transition from one system to another, Sociobiology is not particularly insightful. Biology will not tell us what the marginal tax rate should be or whether the future of humanity is best served by Capitalism or Socialism.

Generalized Darwinism

As noted in the introduction to this study, the Neo-Darwinian synthesis provides a level of rigor and precision that is absent in more general definitions of evolution. It also provides a conceptual glue that holds contemporary biology together. Its' explanatory ability has led to multiple efforts to generalize beyond the domain of biology. The original usage of the term is owed to the position of Dawkins and Dennett, who emphasized the ability of the basic Neo-Darwinian algorithm of variation and selection to provide an explanation for virtually everything from genes to memes. Similarly, Boyd and Richerson (1985, 1992) and Richerson and Boyd (2001, 2005) also argued for envisioning the social sciences as Generalized Darwinism. In Economics, Geoffrey Hodgson has emerged as one of the most prominent advocates of "Generalized Darwinism", and clearly, the most prominent amongst economists. Though Hodgson's position stresses emergence over reductionism, he views the basic mechanism of variation and selection as the glue that can hold Evolutionary Social Theory together. While Hodgson has been prominent amongst Original Institutional Economists and he draws extensively on Veblen, his overall direction is one that aims to integrate multiple strands in contemporary Evolutionary Economics, which is potentially synonymous with Evolutionary Social Theory, or, it might be viewed as a subfield within it, or as a specific subfield within Economics.

This brings us to another issue about directions within Evolutionary Economics. As the reader has no doubt inferred, most Economists, or Political Economists, who have addressed the issue of Evolution have done so outside of the framework of Neo-Classical Economics. Notably, Veblen specifically critiqued Marshall's approach as not evolutionary. Yet in the late 20th century, there was a significant growth in the literature applying Marshallian, and closely related concepts to the study of economic change and the role of institutions in that process. In addition, their method has tended to be Marshallian, in that they employ natural language. For example, Nelson and Winter have used game theory, a method normally associated with mainstream economics, to show how institutions can evolve in a dynamic sense. Neo-Schumpeterians, of which one might consider Nelson and Winter to be, have interpreted Schumpeter's dynamic views of evolution, competition and monopoly to be useful for constructing an evolutionary economics. As noted, Schumpeter's views on economic theory were entirely mainstream. In addition, others have sought to incorporate Austrian, or Neo-Austrian (Hayek 1945, 1988) perspectives into this corpus which raises a conceptual problem given the historical opposition of Austrians to equilibrium theorizing and their emphasis on the purposiveness of agents, as opposed to their narrow rationality (see Arena and Palermo 2007, pp. 198–210; Hodgson 2007; Nelson 2018, pp. 1–34; Pyka and Nelson 2008, pp. 104–128).

Though initially, most of the adherents in the New Institutionalist camp sought to distinguish their views from the Original Institutionalists, over time, there has been some effort to initiate a dialogue between the two. But reconciling the "New" Institutional Economics with the Old is, to say the least, a difficult, if not impossible conceptual process. This is not to say however that some have not tried. Nelson and Winter, for example, have acknowledged the earlier contributions of Veblen. Hence what has emerged as a kind of vague consensus is a new field of Evolutionary Economics, which attempts to draw together both strands. Hodgson has been particularly influential in this regard while seeking reconciliation clearly more on the side of the Original, rather than the New. Generalized Darwinism thus potentially provides the glue with which to draw these disparate camps together. The term itself originates with the view of Richard Dawkins (1983) and Daniel Dennett (1995).

Initially, in the sense used by Dawkins and Dennett, it was associated with Sociobiology and put forward as a universal model. Hodgson and Knudsen however proposed it as a general model and dissociated their view of it from Sociobiological interpretations (2006). Hodgson's view is that Darwinian evolution applies to any entity which is ontologically similar to that of biological species. The two necessary components are hereditable variation and selection. Hodgson notes that the mechanism of inheritance in social institutions does not necessarily follow Mendelian rules and that culture is an emergent phenomenon. But this does not mean in Hodgson's view that the core Darwinian ideas are inapplicable to the study of social evolution. Therefore, the analogy between social and biological evolution holds in a strong sense. In actuality, Hodgson is arguing for more than analogy: he is arguing that social systems and biological systems share the same ontological characteristics. The task of social theory therefore, is to apply these principles to specific institutional and historical contexts (Hodgson 2004, 2010; Hodgson and Knudson 2006). Since there is no significant differences between the interpretation of the modern, synthetic theory of evolution outlined above and Hodgson's treatment, there is little sense in repeating that summary again.

In drawing on Veblen, Hodgson (2007, 2010) interprets Veblen in the context of both structure–agency theory and Generalized Darwinism. Hodgson is not arguing that every aspect of Veblen's writings reflects a generalization of Darwinism, but rather that those aspects were present in Veblen's work and are the most promising for constructing or reconstructing Evolutionary Economics. Notably, Hodgson also sees a proto structure–agency theory embedded in Veblen. As noted in the previous section, Veblen viewed human agents as purposive, yet conditioned by their social environment, leading to habitual behaviors in the form of Institutions, yet simultaneously elaborating on those socially inherited habitual behaviors, thus leading to social change over time. Hence there is both upward causation (the actions of purposive agents cause the social structure), downward causation (the social structure causes the actions of purposive agents) and cumulative causation (outcomes are a consequence of human action taken over time, leading to step by step changes in social structure). Hodgson explains the emergence, persistence and change of institutions in terms of the fitness of institutions to the overall social environment. The social environment is explained as a product of human action, which itself is shaped by the overall social environment.

With respect to Critical Realism and structure–agency theory which Hodgson draws on, Lawson has provided both potential support as well as some caveats (2015a, 2015b). Lawson characterizes the application of the variation-selection algorithm to Economics and the Social Sciences in general as a metaphor. Metaphors make direct comparisons between dissimilar entities. Hence for the metaphor of variation and selection to work in the Social Sciences, there needs to be a strong similarity between the two domains. Lawson argues that what is needed for the metaphor to hold is the presence of a Population (P), Variation (V), Replication (R) Selection (S), or PVRS, leading to transformational change and in the Neo-Darwinian model, to a branching pattern with no determined direction. Lawson thus poses the Ontological question: does the domain of the Social Sciences actually lend itself to this metaphor?

In answering this question, Lawson argues that the metaphor is limited. It is limited because variation amongst and between human societies occurs due to agency of human beings and also because social evolution can be usefully thought of as in part Lamarckian with respect to the inheritance of cultural characteristics. Cultural characteristics are acquired during socialization and agents may vary these characteristics and pass them on to succeeding generations. In my view, Lawson's point on this is well taken, though it should be noted that Hodgson has argued that this does not contradict Darwinism per se, as the Darwinian selection algorithm applies even with Lamarckian inheritance.

Though as noted, I disagree with Lawson on some other points, I agree that with respect to social evolution the emergent nature of social evolution presents obstacles to the full application of analogies and metaphors of variation and selection. Social evolution does appear, over the long haul to lead to increasing complexity and integration. Secondly, social institutions can emerge by conscious design, people may deliberately block innovations on social institutions and may deliberately seek to alter social institutions. Unlike biological species, social institutions can merge with each other. Again, there is a place for such analogies and metaphors, but they cannot be taken as the whole story. My approach sees biological and social arenas as continuous in that the human capacity to create social systems is a product of evolution. However, I emphasize the importance of emergence. Secondly, I envision the two realms as interactive: Human social systems are based on biological systems.

Though Hodgson's work has been relatively well received among his fellow Original Institutional Economists, it has also been subject to some criticisms. In my own contribution to the discussion, I focused on three potential objections to Hodgson's Generalized Darwinism. One, the difference is in the area of philosophical foundations: Hodgson draws heavily on Critical Realism while I draw on Critical Common Sensism (Haack 2006, 2007a, 2007b). Secondly, I disagree that the biological and social domains are as similar as Hodgson assumes (Cordes 2007). Three, Hodgson's discussion of sources on which to build an evolutionary social science is relatively limited, even within the scope of Original Institutional Economics. In contrast, I argue for a broad synthesis of a diverse range of theorists across multiple disciplines whose work is of relevance to social evolution and which incorporates the traditional concerns of Political Economy. It is to that issue that I now turn.

Toward the Neo-Evolutionary Synthesis

Evolutionism in Anthropology and Sociology

In the previous chapter, I addressed the contributions of Childe, White and Steward as figures whose work was pivotal in the maintenance and subsequent revival of Evolutionary Social Theory. Despite differences on substantive points, all three shared the following premises: the human capacity for culture was a product of biological evolution, and at some point in human history, culture had replaced biological adaptation as the primary means through which humans adapted to new environments, and that the emergence of culture created new rules which could not be reduced to generalizations from concepts in biology. However, they also shared the premise that the social sciences could be scientific in the sense that the natural sciences are scientific. Again, as emphasized previously, there was a strong Marxist or Marxian influence on their respective contributions, and their position can be fairly characterized as "forces of production" Marxism. In this section, I will address how their contributions were further developed from roughly the 1970s on.

Steward's emphasis on culture as an adaptation to the environment gave rise to the tradition of Cultural Materialism, of which the late Anthropologist Marvin Harris is generally considered as its founder (1968, 1977, 1999). In contrast to the emic emphasis of theorists such as Marshall Sahlins (1972, 1976). Harris' approach stressed the importance of etic analysis. Cultural Materialism can be viewed as a variant of Marxism. Like Althusser, Harris rejected Hegelianism as a foundation for social theory, but otherwise, the two have opposing theories. Harris' views on Philosophy of Science, which were articulated throughout his writings were strongly shaped by the Neo-Positivist approach of Kuhn and Lakatos. Harris' goal was to articulate empirically verifiable causal and nomothetic statements about cultural variation and evolution. Harris also posited a causal or at least functional relationship between the relationship of the material base (or infrastructure) and the structure and superstructure of Socio-Cultural Systems. As with Steward, it is easy to interpret Harris in a mechanistic and deterministic fashion as Harris' style of writing often lends itself to that interpretation. Notably, however, Harris disavowed such interpretations on multiple occasions. Cultural Materialists after Harris have denied that that is the appropriate interpretation of Harris' concept of infrastructural determinism (see for example Murphy and Margolis 1995). In Harris' view, the principle of infrastructural determinism was a research strategy that shaped priorities for researchers. The other difference between Harris and Althusser of course was that Harris was interested in the process of social evolution, rather than the synchronic aspects of culture.

This brings us to an interesting issue as to whether Cultural Materialism is a "closed systems" or "open systems" theory. Answering this question requires us to first understand what Cultural Materialists mean by the term "Socio-Cultural System", or SCS. Whether one accepts other aspects of Cultural Materialism or not, the concept is useful as a means of developing a coherent taxonomy of societies. An SCS is composed of the Infrastructure, Structure and Superstructure. The Infrastructure includes the ways in which a given SCS interacts with the ecosystem and patterns of demographic reproduction. The Structure incorporates the behavioral and institutional aspects of a society, including the family structure, the class structure and the political structure. The Superstructure is the ideational aspect of a System. It is useful to think of the direction of causation of arrows going both from the Base up and from the Superstructure down, with the arrows going up as the stronger causative forces. In principle, the Structure and Superstructure will not depart too far from the material needs of the Base, or, if they do, this will lead over the long toward disruption and change in the entire system. As a general rule, however, Cultural Materialists prioritize changes in the Material Base as the primary forces that drive changes both within a given SCS and which also lead to the creation of a new SCS.

There are of course any number of ways to classify Socio-Cultural Systems, as well as other similar schemas. One question of course however is whether or not it is useful to classify. Classification is useful in my view in that it allows us to identify differences and parallels in both historical epochs as well as cross-culturally. Thus, we can illuminate how one kind of system is transformed into another as well as how systems interact. The problem with stage theories however has always been whether or not all societies must pass through the same series of stages. As a developmental process, the likelihood, for example, that industrial technology would develop spontaneously in a hunter-gatherer society is unlikely. Hence settled agriculture is a necessary precursor in world history to industrialization. However, once a transition to one form of social organization has occurred in one area of the world, diffusion and conquest can lead to transformations. In addition, historically, there have been multiple cases of tribal confederations overtaking more centralized states. Provided that careful definition and analysis is conducted and the appropriate distinctions are made, typologies of societies can serve a useful purpose. However, the application of the concept of progress can only be applied when the criteria are specified. There is no moral distinction to be made between more complex and less complex social systems. But the trend in human history, from the point of humans living in small, decentralized bands to modern, industrial states, has clearly been a story of increasing complexity and integration (Carneiro 2003, 2012). In Harris' view, social evolution takes place through the intensification of production.

As Anthropologists, Cultural Materialists were generally more concerned with the evolution within non-industrial societies and the interaction of non-industrial societies with modern, industrial states. Yet Cultural Materialism can also be usefully applied to modern societies. Race and gender were both central to Harris, who was especially critical of the way in which Race was defined and racial boundaries were enforced via state coercion. He was also sharply critical of efforts to biologize social inequality (Andersen 2019; Harris 1999). By integrating reproduction and the family directly into his schema, Harris places gender and gender relations in the context of broader patterns of social relations. Harris also extended his analysis to analyze the forces which led to the breakdown of the Soviet Union. Though the challenge for Cultural Materialism is to avoid lapsing into a narrow functionalism in which all superstructural features of society are explained in terms of their functional-adaptive relationship to the base it is more flexible than has often been realized. That said, when the mismatch between the Base, Structure and Superstructure becomes manifest, social crises and major transformations are likely to occur.

In Sociology, the work of Gerhard Lenski (Nolan and Lenski 2004) has to some degree paralleled that of Harris. However, Lenski's work remains mired in a view of agents as rational and self-interested, rather than as sometimes self-interested and sometimes cooperative. The Sociologist Frank Elwell (2006, pp. 103–136) has provided an interesting comparison of Lenski and Harris and argues that Lenski assigns relatively more importance to the Social Structure and the Super Structure, than does Harris. But given the strong similarities between Lenski and Harris, there is little to be gained herein by extending the comparison. Instead, I will address the further development of the neo-evolutionary perspective and its close relationship to Political Economy.

A distinctive, though nevertheless clearly materialist approach was exhibited in the work of Immanuel Wallerstein (1974). Wallerstein's World Systems approach has strong parallels and is closely related to other work in Dependency Theory, an approach that cuts across multiple disciplinary lines. Wallerstein's approach has been labeled as "historical sociology" and as such presents a significant challenge to mainstream Sociology. Though Wallerstein was clearly influenced by Marx, there is also a strong Weberian as well as Braudelian (1979) aspect to his work. Weber emphasized the nature of Capitalism primarily in behavioral terms-in other words, as profit-seeking behavior. Hence, to the extent that Weber is the reference point, Wallerstein's definition of Capitalism is defensible. In addition, in borrowing from Braudel, like other similar writers such as Arrighi (1994), Wallerstein distinguishes between Capitalism primarily as Monopoly that is insulated from competition, and market exchange that takes place between actors dependent on smaller units of production, which are subject to competition. Wallerstein also incorporates Braudel's emphasis on Social Structures persisting over longue durees.

That is not to say that Wallerstein's model is static. Like Arrighi, Wallerstein places considerable emphasis on the evolving nature of the state and the rise of the Nation State system as co-evolutionary with Capitalism. It is the failure of any one Nation State to create a world political Empire that allowed for the rise of a World Economy. Wallerstein distinguishes between Core States (states with strongly developed state apparatuses and high levels of economic development), Peripheral States (states with relatively weak states and low levels of economic development) and Semi-Peripheral States. The status of any given State is not fixed: States can descend from Core to Semi-Periphery, ascend from Periphery to Semi-Periphery and in a few cases, ascend from Semi-Periphery to Core. Nation States struggle for hegemony over the world system. What is never made clear in Wallerstein's analysis however is what the mechanisms are exactly that allows for this to happen. In my estimation, Wallerstein is guilty of overemphasizing Structure and underemphasizing Agency.

Where Cultural Materialism and World Systems Theory were weak on the issue of agency and overemphasized the consistency of Structural Behaviors and ideational aspects of a Socio-Cultural System, the Political Economy approach of Eric Wolf (1982, pp. 1–23) in Economic Anthropology opened the door for considerably more agency. Wolf's use of the term Political Economy corresponds with what I have termed "Evolutionary Social Theory". For Wolf, Political Economy means the unification of analysis across disciplines. However, in developing his analysis he makes extensive use of Marxist economic theory drawing both on Marxist and quasi-Marxist work on long cycles as well as World Systems Theory and Dependency Theory (pp. 296–309). Though Wolf's earlier work had drawn on his own ethnographic studies, his later publications emphasized broad, comparative ethnology and the use of historical and comparative data against which to test theory.

For the most part, Wolf's emphasis was on class agency and conflict, defined in terms of relationship to Modes of Production (2002). Wolf significantly broadened Marx's use of the concept through his categories of Kin based, Tribute based and Capitalist Modes of Production. Following Marx, Wolf classifies societies by how they mobilize labor. Wolf then further developed this taxonomy by classifying Bands, Tribes and Simple Chiefdoms as Kin based, Complex Chiefdoms and Agrarian States as Tributary Modes and Modern Capitalist Economies as based on surplus extraction via the mechanism of wage labor. There is a correspondence between the growing intensification of production, complexity in society, coercive authority and surplus extraction by a class of takers. Wolf also extends this schema to analyze the interaction of differing modes of production in the world following the rise of European mercantilism and then later of a World Capitalist System.

Wolf is very specific about his definition of the Capitalist Mode in asserting that Capitalism does not come into existence until Capital enters directly into the sphere of production and is continuously reinvested. This contrasts with the definition proferred by Wallerstein and others in defining the World System as Capitalist since the start of the 16th century based on systems of coerced cash crop labor. In contrast, Wolf defines the system of the 16th century as one of a Commercial System, in which nascent European nation states vied with each other and non-European Empires for dominance over what was still primarily a Tributary structure. Capitalism, in Wolf's view, comes into existence with the Industrial Revolution.

By reference to Wallerstein, who defined the unit of analysis as the World System with a global division of labor knit together by profit-seeking, market exchange, Wolf emphasized the role of local, regional and global interaction in creating the world system. Wolf's model emphasizes the different interests of actors, whether they are elites, participants in kin-based networks, peasants, or workers in responding to and creating changes at both the local and global levels. In analyzing developments from the rise of Capitalism proper, Wolf draws this together by building both on Marx's theory of capital accumulation of falling rates of profit and Kondratieff cycles to address the modes of integration of areas into the global system, thus producing differential outcomes.

Later work by Wolf (1999) put a stronger emphasis on the role of what Archer has termed "cultural elaboration", though Wolf does not cite Archer nor use that specific term. Yet in emphasizing the mechanisms through which elites and non-elites deployed cultural symbols as a means of advancing differential interests, Wolf clearly acknowledges cultural variation, the relationship of culture to the social structure and behavior, as well as upward and downward causation in determining outcomes. As a Marxist however, Wolf ties this to conflicting class interests. As referenced earlier, Wolf's analysis of the Potlatch amongst the Pacific Northwest Kwakiutl-speaking peoples leads to a different conclusion than that of Boas which stressed the purely irrational behavior of the destruction and giving of wealth. In contrast, Wolf tied this directly to the integration of the Kwakwaka'wakw into the Canadian nation state and the emergence of Industrial fishing and canning of fish. Wolf extends this analysis to the pre-Spanish Conquest use of human sacrifice by the Nahuatl elite as well as the use and deployment of cultural symbols by the German Nazi movement. All of these are explained as a cultural backlash or reaction by elites to maintain power in the face of threats and cultural change. While seemingly "irrational" cultural practices are understandable in light of Political Economic analysis Wolf emphasizes how as these trends emerge, there is a kind of a runaway effect leading to both an irrational, emotive emphasis and a reinforcement of the position of the dominant elite against challengers.

Neo-Evolutionism and Global Politics

The turn to Political Economy as a comprehensive evolutionary understanding of society has also had strong parallels in Political Science, especially in the areas of Comparative Politics and International Relations. As discussed in the previous chapter, historically, International Relations have been theory-heavy and ignored the "black box" of domestic politics. Comparative Politics has at times gotten lost in the minutia of differing political processes. In addition, Comparative Economics and International Economics have tended to ignore Politics. Fortunately, over the last 40 years, there has been significant attention to bringing these aspects together into a dynamic framework that also incorporates the concerns of the social sciences more broadly. I focus below on the seminal contributions of two contributors: Ronald Chilcote (1994) and Susan Strange (1970,

1996, 2015). Whereas Chilcote wrote primarily in Comparative Politics, Susan Strange was considered primarily an International Relations Theorist, though her PhD was in Economics.

Much of Chilcote's emphasis is on comparing Marxist and Mainstream, or as Chilcote termed it, "Bourgeois" views of Comparative Politics. While Chilcote's review of both general approaches is exhaustive, the dominant influence on Chilcote as a Marxist was clearly dependency theory. Since I have addressed many of the issues surrounding Dependency Theory and World Systems Theory above, I will not repeat that discussion herein. Instead, I will focus on Chilcote's critique of the mainstream and his very interesting adaptation of dialectical materialism to the study of Global Political Economy. Chilcote critiques the method and focus of mainstream Comparative Politics for leading to a functionalist and narrow view of Comparative Politics. He notes that this has been exhibited over the last several decades by a tendency of Political Scientists to focus on narrow issues related to Political Culture or issues of electoral politics and mechanisms of government. Here again, as in Economics, the trend was toward focusing on issues of stability and political equilibrium. Chilcote attributes this to the widespread presence of Positivism, which he interprets narrowly, and overt hostility to Marxism.

In contrast, Chilcote advocates a method that he terms "dialectical". His interpretation and application of this however are marked by flexibility and attention to empirical detail, rather than dogma. The dialectical method in Chilcote's view is one that looks at components of Political Economic Systems holistically in terms of the relation of the parts to the whole. Secondly, this method is historical—it examines how these systems have evolved and changed over time. Thirdly, it emphasizes the need to look at the points of contradiction or social conflict in the system. Perhaps most importantly Chilcote stresses the need for the empirical inquiry to verify theories. Chilcote interprets dialectics as a flexible paradigm intended to glue the study of Comparative Politics and International Relations together. Despite his explicit reliance on Kuhn, however, Chilcote's approach is closer to Laudan's concept of a research tradition. The task is to unite the study of the issues related to Class and State, which are the concerns of Comparative Politics, and the study of Imperialism, which is the study of International Political Economy. Chilcote ties this together with a theory of accumulation on a global scale.

In contrast to the above theorists, the work of Susan Strange in International Relations was not explicitly or avowedly Marxist. Yet her work reflects a keen awareness of the importance of the different dimensions of power and the different levels at which it is exercised. Nor was Strange particularly interested in placing societies in a sequential process. She was also very much aware of the potential instability brought on by financialization. This is not to argue that history was unimportant to Strange, quite the contrary. Strange dealt extensively with historical change. But her work was oriented primarily toward the controversies arising as a result of globalization in the late 20th century. Strange near single-rspb. royalsociet handedly invented a new discipline: that of International (or Global) Political Economy, or IPE. IPE today is both a subject area within Political Science and International Relations as well as an approach that cuts across all the social sciences.

At the time that Susan Strange published her seminal article (1970) on the mutual neglect of International Relations and International Economics, International Relations as a discipline was primarily focused on the narrow issues of maintenance of international stability and great power conflict, with little attention to Economic issues. International Economics in turn notoriously entirely ignored International Politics. Strange's goal was to bring the two together. Hence Strange defined International Politics primarily as the realm of the exercise of state power and Economics as the arena of markets and the power of firms.

Strange's (2016) analysis of International Finance was originally published in 1986 but she was already addressing the problems brought about by excessive financialization. Her views on the rise of speculative finance had a clear Keynesian favor and in multiple ways were consistent with the Post Keynesian emphasis of theorists such as Hyman Minsky (1982) on financial fragility and financial instability. Strange was clearly cognizant of the changing structure of the Global Political Economy and the importance of the institutional framework to coordinating economic activity, for good or bad.

Structure and power were both central aspects of Strange's perspective, but there was also explicit recognition of agency at multiple levels. Strange (2015) divided structures into four interactive areas: the Security Structure, the Trade Structure, the Finance Structure and the Technology Structure. Strange's analysis in many respects was State centric. Though she had earlier written about the *Retreat of the* State (1996) and changing definitions of Sovereignty, she was sharply critical of the trend in the late 1990s to emphasize the triumph of liberal institutions over the State and instead emphasized that Nation States continued to play a critical role in creating multi-lateral institutions. With respect to Nation States she strongly emphasized the creation and evolution of Nation States as products of historical action by conscious, purposive agents and the role of human design in general in creating social institutions. Her views of interlocking and interactive Structures were complemented by her emphasis on action and actors at multiple levels: Individual, Class, Firm and Nation State. Obviously, Strange's analysis takes into account both upward and downward causation.

In summarizing the above trends, I have not necessarily sought to propose a grand synthesis. Such syntheses require extensive conceptual and empirical work. My argument has simply been to illustrate how both explicit evolutionism and implicit evolutionism have operated as forms of empirical inquiry and gone beyond the variation-selection metaphor.

Conclusion

In this chapter, I have addressed the resurrection of Social Evolutionary Theory in the late 20th and early 21st centuries, across several disciplines of the Social Sciences. I argued that the movement toward broader understandings of the nature of scientific inquiry played an important role in the revival of Evolutionary Social Theory, along with multiple other factors. I have also argued that Evolutionary Social Theory in the late 20th and 21st centuries was better grounded than in earlier centuries. In my discussion of the philosophy of science I noted the inadequacies of Neo-Positivist views to provide a coherent account of Science and then turned to two related, but distinctive approaches: Critical Realism and Critical Common Sensism. I then turned toward addressing more concretely what it means for a theory to be evolutionary, starting with the way in which biologists understand the evolutionary theory and then addressing how evolutionary theory has influenced seminal work in the social sciences that addresses the problems of change both within and from one social system to the other. I noted that Generalized Darwinism encounters difficulties in that multiple aspects of Social Evolution do not fit the biological pattern of social evolution and then turned toward examining an alternative path for Social Evolutionism. Notably, that path reincorporates Political Economy into Social Evolutionism as a broad study of social processes.

References

Allen, Elizabeth, Barbara Beckwith, Jon Beckwith, Steven Chorover, and David Culver, et al. 1975. "Against Sociobiology." *New York Review of Books*. November 13. https://www.nybooks.com/articles/1975/11/13/against-sociobiology/. Accessed on 6/7/2020.

Althusser, Louis. 1969. *For Marx*. Translated by Ben Brewster. Allen Lane: Penguin Press. https://www.marxists.org/reference/archive/althusser/1965/index.htm

Althusser, Louis. 1970. *Reading Capital*. Translated by Ben Brewster. London: New Left Books.

Althusser, Louis. 1972. *Politics and History: Montesquieu, Rousseau, Hegel and Marx*. Translated by Ben Brewster. London: New Left Books.

Andersen, Mark. 2019. *From Boas to Black Power: Racism, Liberation and American Anthropology*. Stanford, CA: Stanford University Press.

Anderson, Perry. 1984. *In the Tracks of Historical Materialism*. Chicago, IL and London: University of Chicago Press. https://archive.org/details/AndersonInTheTracksOfHistoricalMaterialism/page/n21/mode/2up

Anderson, Perry. 2013. *Lineages of the Absolutist State*. London: Verso Press.

Archer, Margaret. 1995. *Realist Social Theory: The Morphogenetic Approach*. Cambridge: Cambridge University Press.

Archer, Margaret. 1996. *Culture and Agency: The Place of Culture in Social Theory*. Revised Edition. Cambridge : Cambridge University Press.

Archer, Margaret. 2000. *Being Human: The Problem of Agency*. Cambridge: Cambridge University Press.

Arrighi, Giovanni. 1994. *The Long Twentieth Century: Money, Power and the Origins of our Times.* London and New York: Verso.

Arena, Richard and Sandye Gloria-Palermo. 2007. "Evolutionary Themes in the Austrian Tradition: Menger, Von Wieser and Schumpeter on Institutions and Rationality." Pp. 199–210 in *The Evolution of Economic Institutions: A Critical Reader,* edited by Geoffrey Hodgson. Cheltenham: Edward Elgar.

Aston, Trevor H. and C. H. E. Philpins. 1985. *The Brenner Debate: Agrarian Class Structure and Economic Development in Pre-Industrial Europe.* Cambridge: Cambridge University Press.

Barnes, M. Elizabeth. 1979. "The Spandrels of San Marco and the Panglossian Paradigm: A Critique of the Adaptationist Programme." in *Embryo Project Encyclopedia (2014-11-14),* edited by Stephen J. Gould and Richard C. Lewontin. ISSN: 1940–5030. http://embryo.asu.edu/handle/10776/8239

Bhaskar, Roy. 1989. *The Possibility of Naturalism.* Second Edition. Hemel, Hempstead: Harvester, Wheatsheaf.

Boulding, Kenneth. 1974. *Toward a General Social Science.* Boulder: University of Colorado Press.

Boyd, Robert and Peter J. Richerson. 1985. *Culture and the Evolutionary Process.* Chicago, IL: University of Chicago Press.

Boyd, Robert and Peter J. Richerson. 1992. "How Microevolutionary Approaches Gave Rise to History." Pp. 179–209 in *History and Evolution,* edited by Nitecki, Matthew and Doris V. Nitecki. Albany: State University of New York Press.

Boyle, Brian and Mcdonough, Terrence. 2015. "Critical Realism and the Althusserian Legacy". *Journal for the Theory of Social Behaviour* 46(2), pp. 143–164. https://doi.org/10.1111/jtsb.12092

Braudel, Fernand. 1979. *The Mediterranean World in the Age of Phillipp II.* Translated by Sian Reynolds, Abridged, Richard Ollards. Great Britain: Harper Collins.

Brenner, Robert. 1976. "Agrarian Class Structure and Economic Development in Pre-Industrial Europe." *Past and Present,* 70 (1), pp. 30–75.

Buryani, Stephen. 2022. "Do We need a New Theory of Evolution." *The Guardian.* Originally published June 28, updated July 4. https://www.theguardian.com/science/2022/jun/28/do-we-need-a-new-theory-of-evolution

Carneiro, Robert L. 2003. *Evolutionism in Cultural Anthropology.* Boulder, CO: West View Press.

Carneiro, Robert. L. 2012. "The Circumscription Theory: A Clarification, Amplification and Reformation." *Social Evolution and History* 11(2), pp. 5–30.

Chilcote, Ronald H. 1994. *Theories of Comparative Politics: The Search for a Paradigm Reconsidered.* Second Edition. Boulder, CO and Oxford: Westview Press.

Collier, Andrew. 1994. *Critical Realism: An Introduction to Roy Bhaskar's Philosophy.* London and New York: Verso.

Cordes, Christian. 2007. "Turning Evolution into an Evolutionary Science: Veblen, the Selection Metaphor, and Analytical Thinking." *Journal of Economic Issues* XLI(4), pp. 135–154.

Coyne, Jerry. 2022. "Once Again: A Misguided Article on Why the Theory of Evolution Is Obsolete." *Evolution Is True.* June 29. https://whyevolutionistrue.com/2022/06/29/once-again-a-misguided-article-on-why-the-theory-of-evolution-is-obsolete/

Dawkins, Richard. 1983. "Universal Darwinism." Pp. 403–425 in *Evolution from Molecules to Man,* edited by Derek S. Bendall. Cambridge: Cambridge University Press.

Dawkins, Richard. 1999. *The Extended Phenotype*. Oxford and New York: Oxford University Press.
Dawkins, Richard. 2016. *The Selfish Gene*. Fourth Edition. Oxford: Oxford University Press.
Dennet, Daniel C. 1995. *Darwin's Dangerous Idea. Evolution and the Meaning of Life.* New York: Simon and Schuster.
Dewaal, Franz. 1996. *Good Natured. The Origins of Right and Wrong in Human Animals.* Cambridge, MA, London: Cambridge University Press.
Diamond, Jared. 1997. *Guns, Germs and Steel. The Fates of Human Societies.* New York: W. W. Norton.
Dow, Sheila. 2005. "Axioms and Babylonian Thought: A Reply." *Journal of Post Keynesian Economics* 27(3), pp. 385–391.
Dugger, William and James T. Peach. 2009. *Economic Abundance: An Introduction.* Armonk, NY: M.E. Sharpe.
Dugger, William J. and Howard J. Sherman. 2000. *Reclaiming Evolution*. New York: Routledge.
Elwell, Frank. 2016. *Macrosociology: Four Modern Theorists*. New York: Routledge.
Futuyma, Douglas. 2017. *Evolution*. Oxford: Oxford University Press.
Giddens, Anthony. 1982. *Profiles and Critiques in Social Theory.* Berkeley and Los Angeles: University of California Press.
Gould, Steven J. 1991. *Bully for Brontosaurus. Reflections in Natural History.* New York: W.W. Norton.
Gould, Steven J. 1996. *Full House: The Spread of Excellence from Plato to Darwin.* New York: Three Rivers Press.
Gould, Stephen J. and Richard C. Lewontin. 1979. "The Spandrels of San Marco and the Panglossian Paradigm: A Critique of the Adaptationist Programme." *Proceedings of the Royal Society of London* 2055, pp. 88–98. http://rspb.royalsocietypublishing.org/content/205/1161/581. Abstract Accessed on 6/7/2020.
Gould, Steven J. et al. 1975. "Letter from Sociobiology Group." *New York Review of Books.* 22(18) November 13. https://www.nybooks.com/articles/1975/11/13/against-sociobiology/. Accessed on 6/7/2020.
Haack, Susan. 2002. "Realisms and Their Rivals: Recovering Our Innocence." *Facta Philosophica* 4, pp. 67–88.
Haack, Susan. 2004. "Science, Economics, Vision." *Social Research* 71(2 Summer), pp. 223–233.
Haack, Susan. 2006. "Introduction: Pragmatism, Old and New". Pp. 15–65 in *Pragmatism Old and New: Selected Writings,* edited by Haack, Susan with Robert Lane, Associate ed. Amherst, NY: Prometheus Books.
Haack, Susan. 2007a. *Defending Science within Reason: Between Scientism and Cynicism*. Amherst, NY: Prometheus Books.
Haack, Susan. 2007b. "The Legitimacy of Metaphysics: Kant's Legacy to Peirce and Peirce's to Philosophy Today." *Polish Journal of Philosophy* 1, pp. 29–43.
Haack, Susan. 2009. *Evidence and Inquiry: A Pragmatist Reconstruction of Epistemology.* Second Expanded Edition with a New Preface by the Author. Amherst, NY: Prometheus Books.
Harris, Marvin. 1968. *Rise of Anthropological Theory*. New York: Crowell.
Harris, Marvin. 1977. *Cultural Materialism*. New York: Random House.
Harris, Marvin. 1999. *Theories of Culture in Postmodern Times.* Walnut Creek, CA: Altamira Press.

Hayek, Frederick. 1945. "The Use of Knowledge in Society." *American Economic Review* 35(4), pp. 519–530.

Hayek, Frederick. 1988. *The Fatal Conceit: The Errors of Socialism.* Princeton, NJ: Princeton University Press.

Hodgson, Geoffrey. 2004. *The Evolution of Institutional Economics: Agency, Structure and Darwinism in American Institutionalism.* New York and London: Routledge.

Hodgson, Geoffrey. 2007. "Introduction." Pp. 1–18 in *The Evolution of Economic Institutions: A Critical Reader,* edited by Hodgson, Geoffrey. Cheltenham: Edward Elgar.

Hodgson, Geoffrey. 2010. *Darwin's Conjecture. The Search for General Principles of Social and Economic Evolution.* Chicago, IL and London: University of Chicago Press.

Hodgson, Geoffrey and Thorbjorn, Knudson. 2006. "Why We Need a Generalized Darwinism and Why a Generalized Darwinism Is Not enough." *Journal of Economic Behavior and Organization* 62(1), pp. 1–19.

Hrdy, Sarah Blaffer. 1981. *The Woman That Never Evolved.* Revised Edition. Cambridge, MA and London: Harvard University Press.

Hrdy, Sarah Blaffer. 1999. *Mother Nature. A History of Mothers, Infants and Natural Selection.* New York: Pantheon Books.

Kuhn, Thomas. 1962. *The Structure of Scientific Revolutions.* Chicago, IL: University of Chicago Press.

Lakatos, Imre. 1970. "Falsification and the Methodology of Scientific Research Programs". Pp. 91–195 in *Criticism and the Growth of Knowledge,* edited by Imre Lakatos and Alan Musgrave. Cambridge: Cambridge University Press, 1978.

Lakatos, Imre. 1978. *The Methodology of Scientific Research Programs.* in edited by John Worrel and Gregory Currie. Cambridge, MA: Press Syndicate of the University of Cambridge.

Laudan, Larry. 1990. *Science and Relativism: Some Key Controversies in the Philosophy of Science.* Chicago, IL: University of Chicago Press.

Laudan, Larry. 1996. *Beyond Positivism and Relativism.* Boulder, CO and Oxford: Westview Press.

Lawson, Tony. 1997. *Economics and Reality.* London and New York: Routledge.

Lawson, Tony. 2003. *Reorienting Economics.* London and New York: Routledge.

Lawson, Tony. 2015a. "A Conception of Social Ontology." in Pp. 19–52 *Social Ontology and Modern Economics,* edited by Pratten, Stephen. New York: Routledge.

Lawson, Tony. 2015b. "An Evolutionary Economics: On Borrowing from Evolutionary Biology." Pp. 162–169 in *Social Ontology and Modern Economics,* edited by Pratten, Stephen. New York: Routledge.

Lawson, Tony and Jamie Morgan. 2021a. "Cambridge Social Ontology, the Philosophical Critique of Modern Economics and Social Positioning Theory: An Interview with Tony Lawson" part 1, *Journal of Critical Realism* 20(1), pp. 72–97. https://doi.org/10.1080/14767430.2020.1846009

Lawson, Tony and Jamie Morgan. 2021b. "Cambridge Social Ontology, the Philosophical Critique of Modern Economics and Social Positioning Theory: An Interview with Tony Lawson, part 2." *Journal of Critical Realism* 20(2), pp. 201–237. https://doi.org/10.1080/14767430.2021.1914904

Mayr, Ernst. 1982. *The Growth of Biological Thought. Diversity,* Evolution *and Inheritance.* Cambridge, MA and London: Bellknap Press.

Mayr, Ernst. 2001. *What Evolution Is.* New York: Basic Books.

Meiksins-Wood, Ellen. 2017. *The Origin of Capitalism: A Longer View.* London and New York: Verso.

Minsky, Hyman. 1982. *Can "It" Happen Again? Essays in Instability and Finance.* Amherst, NY: M.E. Sharpe.

Murphy, Martin F. and Maxine L. Margolis, eds. 1995. *Science, Materialism and the Study of Culture.* Gainesville: University Press of Florida.

Nelson, Richard R. 2018. "Evolutionary Economics from a Modern Perspective." Pp. 1–34 in *Modern Evolutionary Economics: An Overview,* edited by Nelson, Richard. Cambridge: Cambridge University Press.

Neurath, Otto et al. 1929. *The Scientific Conception of the World: The Vienna Circle.* Vienna: The Ernst Mach Society.

Nolan, Patrick and Gerhard Lenski. 2004. *Human Societies. An Introduction to Macrosociology.* Eleventh Edition, Revised and Updated. Boulder, CO: Paradigm Publishers.

Pinker, Steven. 2003. *The Blank Slate: The Modern Denial of Human Nature.* New York: Penguin Books.

Poirot, Clifford. 2007. "How Can Institutional Economics be an Evolutionary Science." *Journal of Economic Issues.* XLI (1), pp. 155–180.

Poirot, Clifford. 2008. "Is Pragmatism Good for Anything: Towards an Impractical Theory of Economics." *Forum for Social Economics* 37(1), pp. 61–76.

Popper, Karl. [1934] 1997. *The Logic of Scientific Discovery.* Translated by Freed and Freed. London: Routledge.

Pyka, Andreas and Richard R. Nelson. 2008. "Schumpeterian Competition and Industrial Dynamics." Pp. 104–128 in *Modern Evolutionary Economics: An Overview,* edited by Nelson, Richard. Cambridge, MA: Cambridge University Press.

Quine, W. V. 1990. *The Pursuit of Truth.* Cambridge, MA: President and Fellows of Harvard College.

Quine, W. V. 2004. "Two Dogmas of Empiricism." Pp. 31–53 in *Quintessence: Basic Readings in the Philosophy of W.V.* Quine, edited by Roger F. Gibson Jr. Cambridge, MA: Belknap Press of Harvard University Press.

Richerson, Peter J. and Robert Boyd. 2001. "Built for Speed and Not for Comfort. Darwinian Theory and Human Culture." *History and Philosophy of the Life Sciences* 23, pp. 423–463.

Richerson, Peter J. and Robert Boyd. 2005. *How Culture Transformed Human Evolution: Not by Genes Alone.* Chicago, IL and London; University of Chicago Press.

Sahlins, Marshall. 1972. *Stone Age Economics.* Hawthorne, New York: Aldine de Gruyter.

Sahlins, Marshall. 1976. *The Use and Abuse of Biology.* Ann Arbor: University of Michigan Press.

Segerstrale, Ulica. 2000. *Defenders of the Truth: The Battle for Science in the Sociobiology Debate and Beyond.* Oxford and New York: Oxford University Press.

Strange, Susan. 1970. "International Economics and International Relations: A Strange Case of Mutual Neglect." *International Affairs* 46(2), pp. 304–315.

Strange, Susan [1986] 2016. *Casino Capitalism.* Manchester: Manchester University Press.

Strange, Susan. 1996. *Retreat of the State. The Diffusion of Power in the World Economy.* Cambridge: Cambridge University Press.

Strange, Susan. 2015. *States and Markets.* London and New York: Bloomsbury Academic.

Thompson, Edward Palmer. 1978. "The Poverty of Theory: An Orrery of Errors". Pp. 1–210 in *The Poverty of Theory and Other Essays*, edited by Edward Palmer Thompson.New York: Monthly Review Press.

Tooby, John and Lena Cosmides. 2000. "The Psychological Foundations of Culture." Pp. 19–136 in *the Adapted Mind*, edited by J. Barkow, L. Cosmides and J. Tooby. Oxford and New York: Oxford University Press.

Wallerstein, Immanuel. 1974. *The Modern World System: Capitalist Agriculture and the Origins of the Modern World System*. Four Volumes. New York: Academic Press.

Wilson, E.O. 1975a. *Sociobiology and the New Synthesis*. Cambridge; Cambridge University Press.

Wilson, E.O. 1975b. "For Sociobiology." *New York Review of Books*. December 11. https://www.nybooks.com/articles/1975/12/11/for-sociobiology/. Accessed on 6/7/2020.

Wilson, Edward Osborne. 1998. *Consilience: The Unity of Knowledge*. New York: Alfred Knopf.

Wolf, Eric. 1982. *Europe and the People without History*. Berkeley: University of California Press.

Wolf, Eric. 1999. *Envisioning Power. Ideologies of Dominance and Crisis*. Berkeley and Los Angeles, CA: Berkeley University Press.

Wolf, Eric. 2001. *Pathways of Power: Building an Anthropology of the Modern World*.

Woods, Ellen Meiksens. 2017. *The Origin of Capitalism: A Longer View*. London and Brooklyn, NY: Verso.

6 Conclusion

At the beginning of this book, I argued that a broad definition of Evolutionary Social Theory would allow for consideration of a range of approaches to the study of social evolution, including both Darwinian as well as pre- and non-Darwinian views of social evolution. I set as my goal to explain the rise, consolidation, marginalization and revival of Evolutionary Social Theory and how this process was related to differing conceptions of Philosophy of Science and Political Economy. This study does point to some tentative conclusions about what kinds of connections have led in the past to useful theorizing about social evolutionary processes and consequently points to what might prove useful in the future.

In the beginning, Social Contract Theory was challenged by Philosophical History. Though Social Contract Theorists, with the exception of Kant, were strongly influenced by Empiricism it offered little insight into the far-reaching nature of changes in the social order of the era. Instead, it rested on a non-empirical, mythological view of the problem of social order. In other words, it had little empirical content. Nor was it particularly illuminating with respect to the problems of Political Economy. In contrast, though there were shortcomings in the various formulations of Philosophical History it was capable of providing significant analysis of the concrete challenges of the time. Though the focus of Philosophical History was empirical, it was influenced as much by the "Common Sensist" approach of Reid and others, as by pure Empiricism. It also, as we saw, provided a foundation for the rise of Political Economy. Political Economy in this era was defined as the study of the causes of wealth and the distribution of that wealth in concern with the problem of how the state could best enact policies to create wealth. Smith and Turgot married the concrete, empirical and historical, analysis with abstract and deductive analysis.

Evolutionary Social Theory has followed this trajectory, albeit with zigs and zags, over the approximately two and a half centuries since the initial publication of Adam Smith's *The Wealth of Nations*. While Science was dominated by Newtonian Physics in the late 17th and 18th centuries, biology increasingly came into its own over the course of the 19th century.

DOI: 10.4324/9781003170679-7

Hence it is not surprising, that with the exception of Spencer, theories of social evolution built on the shaky foundations of early 19th-century evolutionary theory in biology which was dominated by Lamarckian and quasi-Lamarckian ideas. Much of 19th-century Evolutionary Social Theory was speculative and emphasized the themes of increasing complexity, integration and progress. It also incorporated in multiple ways the concerns of Political Economy. That noted, there was still an empirical and often Empiricist approach to the Philosophy of Science underlying these trends. But Political Economy in both the early and late 19th century became increasingly separated from Evolutionary Social Theory.

Any account of the history of evolutionary theory, whether it treats of biological or social evolution, must address the impact of Darwin. In my discussion of Darwin, I pointed to his strong connection to the inductive and Empiricist bent of 19th-century philosophy of science, though again, this can just as easily, and perhaps more fruitfully, be viewed through the lens of Critical Common Sensism. The other influence on Darwin was 19th-century Evolutionary Social Theory as well as Political Economy. While Darwin was a creature of his era and his work reflects the biases of his era, what went into his writing is not the same as what came out. Darwin's arguments were used, abused, misused and often misinterpreted to support a wide range of social agendas. Whether we are speaking of Social Darwinism or Reform Darwinism, neither had actually that much to do with Darwin and still drew more heavily on Lamarck. In the late 19th and early 20th centuries, Political Economy faced two paths: continue its close association with Evolutionary Social Theory or separate from it. Mainstream Political Economy increasingly went down the latter. Yet others in the era, whom we have come to consider today as Anthropologists, Sociologists and Economists took the former path. This path was similarly tied to an empirical understanding of social processes which I have argued was strongly influenced by the Pragmatism of Pierce and Dewey, which is notably a form of Critical Common Sensism.

Yet in the 20th century not only did the mainstream of Political Economy become separated from Evolutionary Social Theory, but to varying degrees, this was the norm throughout the social sciences. This trend is one of the most puzzling in the history of the social sciences and it is a story without a clear villain. Yet as I emphasized in Chapter 4, there were identifiable factors at work. One of these was a narrowing of the meaning of science as well as a kind of hyper empiricism in Anthropology. But the opposite also held: an emphasis on overly abstract, formal theory reinforced the emphasis on static structural and equilibrium analysis. Another factor was disciplinary specialization. Yet another was the rejection of biological explanations for human behavior, brought on in reaction to the speculative and at times reactionary and racist implications of some 19th-century Evolutionary Social Theorists. Similarly, anti-communism was a significant factor. If there is any thread that unites these seemingly disparate trends, it is the emphasis of high modernism on technocratic, allegedly non-ideological solutions to the problems of industrial society. This trend was the most prominent in the discipline of Economics but was only distantly related to the vision of science espoused by the logical positivists and Karl Popper. It is common to blame much of this on physics envy by social scientists, and physics envy was certainly prominent and played a role. But in economics, the real problem was envy of formal mathematics.

Yet the same period was marked by persistence and ultimately renewal of Evolutionary Social Theory across the social science disciplines. Here again, the common unifying themes are clear. One is the emphasis on concrete, empirical understanding of social processes and their interconnections. Much of the Evolutionary Social Theory of this era either implicitly or explicitly looked to Pragmatism, and especially to Dewey's Pragmatism for Philosophical guidance. In all cases, Evolutionary Social Theory was explicitly linked to a broad conception of Political Economy. Marxism also played a significant role in the persistence and revival of Evolutionary Social Theory. But it was not a dogmatic application of Marxist concepts but an open, flexible and empirical application of Marxism. Some of the academic Marxists of the era were critical of the Soviet Union, while others were not.

In the late 20th and 21st centuries, the initial revival gained steam and Evolutionary Social Theory has in varying degrees become respectable again. Even amongst theorists who do not necessarily call themselves evolutionists, there is a clear focus on the problem of change over time. Here again, I have noted the multiplicity of factors at work. Clearly, changes in the Philosophy of Science, starting with the quasi-evolutionary understandings of scientific progress embedded in the neo-positivist contributions of Kuhn, Lakatos and Laudan helped to create space for pluralism. Critical Realism and Critical Common Sensism however have provided a stronger foundation on which to build. In addressing these two approaches, I have taken the path of Critical Common Sensism and will not repeat those arguments herein. And of course, the increased prestige of evolutionary biology has provided a basis for social scientists to look to biology as both type science and a source of analogies. How much conscious application of Philosophy of Science contributes to theorizing in the social sciences in general is unclear. It can certainly help us to clarify what it is we want to accomplish and provide guidance on how to go about it. Yet Philosophy of Science has not for the most part directed paths of research in any area of science, but the concrete, empirical focus of these different paths, coupled with the willingness to traverse across disciplinary boundaries has clearly been a large part of the story. The future of Evolutionary Social Theory will consequently, most likely be one that emphasizes both empirical detail as well as abstract theoretical analysis.

Index

Note: Page numbers followed by "n" denote endnotes.

For Product Safety Concerns and Information please contact our EU
representative GPSR@taylorandfrancis.com
Taylor & Francis Verlag GmbH, Kaufingerstraße 24, 80331 München, Germany

www.ingramcontent.com/pod-product-compliance
Lightning Source LLC
Chambersburg PA
CBHW071353220926
51613CB00009B/190
9780367772925